What they're saying about . . .

Ecstasy: The MDMA Story

"It is possible Bruce Eisner's book will play a role in dispelling misconceptions about MDMA. The book is a splendid summary of the drug's history, usage and effects.
—Stanley Krippner, Ph.D.,
author of *Healing States, Dream Working, Personal Mythology*

"Bruce Eisner has spent time in both the world of academic psychology and as a journalist covering the psychedelic scene. He has written a masterly book about an important new mind-changer which is both scholarly and readable. I enthusiastically recommend it!"
—Timothy Leary, Ph.D.,
performing philosopher

"The first compendium of the pertinent MDMA data, Eisner's book is helpful, wise and balanced."
—Peter Stafford,
author of *Encyclopedia of Psychedelic Substances*

"This book presents the significant findings concerning MDMA, or 'Ecstasy' . . . The very large numbers of people who now self-experimenting with this drug should benefit from the wealth of information—including the fact that longer-term effects on the brain are still unknown . . .
"It is absolutely certain that a new world is dawning in which alterations of brain function and states of consciousness will be accepted and of great value . . . A substance such as MDMA—reminiscent as it is of Homer's Nepenthe—will banish many of the now 'normal woes' of everyday life."
—R.E.L. Masters, Ph.D.,
co-author of *Varieties of Psychedelic Experience*
and *Mind Games*

ECSTASY

The MDMA Story

by Bruce Eisner

Foreword by Stanley Krippner, PhD
Introduction by Peter Stafford
Bibliography by Alexander Shulgin, PhD

Published by Ronin Publishing, Inc
P.O.Box 1035 Berkeley, CA 94701

Published by: Ronin Publishing, Inc.
Post Office Box 1035 Berkeley, CA 94701

Ecstasy: The MDMA Story
ISBN: 0-914171-25-9

Printed in the United States of America
First printing 1989

9 8 7 6 5 4 3 2 1

Project Editors: Sebastian Orfali and Beverly Potter
Cover Art: Ray Garst and Ron Carskaddon
Manuscript Readers: Aiden Kelley, Alexander Shulgin, Lester Grinspoon, Timothy Leary, Ralph Metzner, Claudio Naranjo
Copy Editor: Peter Stafford
Typography: Peter Stafford, Sebastian Orfali
Chemical Drawings: Christopher and Kim Workdelay
Half-tones: Norman Mayell

U.S. Library of Congress Cataloging in Publication Data
Bruce Eisner
        Ecstasy.
        1. Psychology. 2. Hallucinogenic drugs.
3. Psychopharmacology. I. Title.

Dedication

To David B

Acknowlegements

To Peter Stafford, who typeset this book three times and read it at least 17 times, Alexander Shulgin, who offered generous help and guidance. Kim and Christopher Workdelay for chemical drawings and comment. Sebastian Orfali, who patiently guided me through the steps from manuscript to volume, Claudio Naranjo, to whose Gurdjieff I attempt to play Ouspensky, Irene Ehrlich, for support and encouragement; and to the many therapists, anonymous pamphlet writers and other brave explorers who first ventured into the territories I have mapped.

The author has made every effort to trace the ownership of all copyright and quoted material presented. In the event of any question arising as to the use of a selection, he offers his appologies for any errors or omissions and will make the necessary corrections in future printings.

Thanks are due to the following:

Ralph Metzner, *Through the Gateway of the Heart,* (© 1985, Four Trees Press)

Timothy Leary, Ph.D. "Ecstatic Electricity", *New York Talk,* 1985

Claudio Naranjo, M.D., *The Healing Journey* (© 1973)

Joe Klien, "The New Drug They Call Ecstasy: Is It Too Much to Swallow?" (© 1988) New America Publishing, Inc. Reprinted with the permission of *New York* Magazine

Alexander T. Shulgin, Ph.D., "Twenty Years On My Ever-Changing Quest" in *Psychedelic Reflections,* (© 1983)

George Greer, M.D. and Requa Tolbert, N.S., "MDMA: A New Psychotropic Compound and its Effects in Humans" (© 1986)

George Greer, M.D. "Using MDMA in Psychotherapy/Big Sur, California, March 10-15, 1985 (© 1986)

"Getting High on Ecstasy," (©*Newsweek,* April 15, 1985)

Peter Stafford, *Psychedelics Encyclopedia* (© 1983)

Contents

List of Illustrations

Foreword

by Stanley Krippner, Ph.D.

In 1984, the U.S. Drug Enforcement Administration initiated a process that ended in the classification of MDMA as a Schedule I drug, equivalent to narcotics and regarded as having no medical use. Since that time, a number of physicians, researchers, and psychotherapists have fought this classification through legal means, insisting that MDMA can make unique and valuable psychotherapeutic contributions. Although the outcome is still unsettled, it is obvious that the proponents of MDMA are fighting an uphill battle.

Even though the psychotherapeutic use of prescription mood-changing and behavior-modifying drugs permeates American society, and even though the sale of these drugs is a multi-million dollar business, there has been virtually no support for MDMA by either psychiatric organizations or by pharmaceutical companies. I would propose several reasons for this state of affairs.

In the first place, MDMA is not only capable of changing one's mood and modifying one's behavior; it can alter one's way of thinking as well. American psychiatry has found it easier to use mood-changing and behavior-modifying drugs than to utilize mind-altering substances. A client's mood usually can be calmed or stimulated through medication, and a client's behavior can be modified in fairly direct ways. Psychiatrists are pleased when a client's mood swings can be stabilized and when a client's erratic behavior can be brought under control. They admit that some individuals will show paradoxical reactions to medication, but will insist in the predictability of drugs' general outcomes.

On the other hand, most psychiatrists find it difficult to justify using substances that can produce novel ways of conceiving reality, and unusual ways of being in the world. They will use drugs that inhibit hallucinations, block disordered thought patterns, or halt repetitive verbalizations. But such mind-altering drugs as MDMA, LSD, and psilocybin have the reputation of evoking unconventional thought; as a result, it is justifiable to dismiss them as more trouble than they are worth.

Secondly, MDMA can intensify clients' thoughts and feelings regarding their therapist. Transference phenomena can magnify during an MDMA session and a client's relationship with his or her therapist can intensify profoundly. The ordinary problems of transference, counter-transference, and projection produce so many complications in psychotherapy that few practitioners would want to risk augmenting this predicament.

Third, the use of MDMA violates the structure of psychoanalytically-oriented psychotherapy which is geared toward a 50-minute hour, not the three- or four-hour session that the proper use of MDMA demands. These lengthy sessions are often justified with the claim that psychotherapy is accelerated as a result of MDMA. But psychiatrists usually are suspicious of any modality that claims to expedite psychotherapy in the absence of a slow unraveling of a client's defenses. Various humanistic and transpersonal approaches to psychotherapy could make allowance for the demands of MDMA, but neither orientation has permeated the highest levels of the psychiatric establishment and their influence in legal and governmental circles is negligible.

Opposition to MDMA in psychotherapy is not limited to psychiatrists. Most of those psychologists who practice behavior modification are wary of MDMA not only because of the time factor but because it admits to the possibility of quick "insights" and "breakthroughs," not the step-by-step learning and relearning that characterizes most behavioral approaches. In addition, when a psychotherapist is trained to use MDMA, part of one's apprenticeship involves taking the drug oneself. This first-hand experience is not needed before a psychologist uses behavioral techniques or before a psychiatrist employs stimulant or depressant drugs, or the other medications that are frequently employed in psychiatry. In fact, the ecstatic effects of MDMA are looked upon as "pathological" or "dysfunctional" by many psychotherapists. If someone suggests that they try MDMA themselves, they might retort that this would be tantamount to ingesting poison to learn about toxic psychoses.

Finally, psychotherapists who use MDMA often have abandoned the medical model that permeates most of contemporary psychiatry. The goal of these divergent therapists is sometimes described as facilitating the development of "fully-functioning human beings" and in going "beyond adjustment" in the enhancement of "human capacities" and the "human potential." These terms are suspect to a psychiatrist trained to look at his or her clients from the model of disease, or a psychologist whose education has emphasized faulty learning as the cause of a client's maladaptive behavior.

As a result of these factors, very few psychotherapists have been interested in the therapeutic use of MDMA. As a result, pharmaceutical companies have seen no profit margin in its development, and have lacked the motivation to finance investigations into the drug's effectiveness. It is possible that Bruce Eisner's book will play a role in dispelling misconceptions about MDMA. The book is a splendid summary of the drug's history, usage, and effects. There is little likelihood that MDMA will become a major psychotherapeutic tool in the near future. However, the readers of this book may conclude that it deserves a chance to demonstrate its worth in the hands of those therapists whose sensitivity, training, and expertise have enabled them to use it to alleviate the distress of those clients who come to them seeking to be relieved from their suffering.

Introduction

In your hands you hold the first book that treats the issues raised by MDMA (aka "Adam," "Ecstasy," "XTC") in a comprehensive way. MDMA is, of course, the empathy-enhancing compound that came to immense public attention in the '80s, and then rode the crest of a fifth major wave washing psychedelia over a small, significant part of humanity.

Every mind-affecting molecule has effects unique to itself. The properties of MDMA were appropriate in these circumstances because it introduced the mass use of, and access to, a non-threatening empathy-generating mechanism. Bruce Eisner's account places an associated intellectual fermentation in wide-ranging context, based upon first-hand acquaintance and diligent study.

* * *

The *first* of the preceeding waves of psychedelic enthusiasm extends all the way from prehistoric times up until the end of the 19th century, during which members of *all* societies (except for Eskimos, most of whom had no direct plant access, and also, possibly, some Polynesians) stumbled upon and ritualized use of selective vegetative matter ... that enlarged the scope of the mind in ways that appeared both healing and inspirational.

A *second* large psychedelic wave rolled in around the start of the 20th century, once German pharmacologists isolated and then reproduced mescaline—the first synthetic of a mind-changing sort.

A *third* psychedelic wave was kicked off by Albert Hofmann's discovery of LSD's psychoactivity in 1943—a catalyzing event of such magnitude that by the late 1960s immersion in psychedelia got noticed by 'most everyone.

After that immense inundation, the 1970s saw an ebbing—which only petered out as mushrooms (containing psilocybin and psilocin) encouraged another flush of enthusiasm for psychedelia. This fourth incursion spread due to these mushrooms' gentleness, "naturalness," wide distribution and a leap in home production (so that those serious didn't have to travel to Mexico, as many people had supposed, but could actually grow a major psychedelic in the basement).

Such a quick rundown on a psychedelic past brings us to the present subject—MDMA's role in ushering in a fifth wave of fascination with these mind-changers. Located along with several hundred molecules that could be placed in a "psychedelic" category, this one stands out as unusually benign—a substance that offers users the possibility of a contrived "heart-opening," and that also, as one therapist describes it, makes clients "unbelievably honest!"

* * *

As with fundamental innovations, arrival of a critical mass of people having interest in and access to MDMA framed many old questions in a new context. It also raised matters that had not come to the fore. Here I will attempt to group just over a dozen such central questions, and indicate pages in this book where Eisner lays out relevant historical/anecdotal evidence well-documented by the end of the '80s. For starters, let's take up four prompting concerns:

1. What are the principal characteristics of MDMA experience?
2. How "natural" is MDMA?
3. Is it "psychedelic"?
4. How about "consistency" of the experience, and its overall "reliability"?

1. MDMA's chief characteristics. MDMA "strengthens" the ego, however you define that, as does an amphetamine, but not in a cold, strong-aimed way. It softens defensiveness and gently removed obstacles to communication, so one speaks directly from the heart. Often to their surprise, users find they say what they really feel, without fear of being hurt by that honesty.

MDMA also removes walls of isolation between individuals so that even strangers speak to each other in familiar, intimate ways. Insight and affinity-enhancing qualities evoked momentarily can be applied either to relationships and/or other matters of personal concern. These changes are subtle, but are recognized as significant by a majority of experiencers.

The de-stressing aspect is experienced mentally as well as physically; in certain instances, this can be dramatic. For most people, MDMA produces the sense of relaxation felt after several days of vacation. While the experience itself lasts only about four-six hours, an "afterglow" may linger for a few days, a week, a month, or possibly up to a whole lifetime. (See pp. 1-4, 6, 10, 33-34, 38-39, 42, 46-47, 51, 58, 70-71, 75)

2. Natural substances led the way. MDMA is a "semi-synthetic," a molecule similar to those found in nutmeg, mace, crocus and dill, as well as the over-the-counter cold remedy Sudafed. So far we don't know of this molecule's existence in the realms of fauna and flora, but it is evident that most brains contain regions quite sensitive to it. Nutmeg and some of the others have histories as mind-alterants, but the experiences they catalyze have usually been accompanied by rather unpleasant physical effects.

Nutmeg, for instance, is sometimes described as a psychedelic of "last resort," since it has been used by prisoners and sailors when no other mind-changer has been available. Chemical manipulation—in this case, the N-methylation of an amine addition—heightens desirable aspects sought from the natural substances, while reducing such physical side-effects as dryness of mouth and aching joints.

Of course, in a wider sense, everything that exists—even things produced in a laboratory—is "natural," arguably "non-artificial." (See pp. 138-142, 139-143)

3. Is MDMA a "psychedelic"? This special category of psychoactive substances—introduced to us by mescaline, LSD and psilocybin mushrooms—affects thinking and feeling in half a dozen major ways. One of these, the visual, is very prominent in the classic literature, and has been emphasized by the media—although most users don't think of it as the essence of the experience. In the case of MDMA, effects manifested in the visual sphere are minimal except when large amounts are taken. Thus, the MDMA experience is most often thought of as distinct from that usually accessed by "psychedelics."

Yet ways of interacting with the environment and other people are noticeably similar to many of those experienced after mediation of earlier "psychedelics." In MDMA is represented another pole of the psychedelic realm, where affinity and focusing are heightened in a gentler but still powerful way.

With classic psychedelics, transformations frequently are both extreme and, for the most part, internalized, somewhat like that terrible, wonderful night during which Ebenezer Scrooge was visited by Ghosts of the Past, Present and Future, and awoke so grateful to be alive that afterwards he was a shockingly transformed individual. MDMA seems to offer a benign route to many similar consequences as are produced by the more well-known "psychedelic" catalysts. (See pp. 3-4)

4. A high "reliability." Even without prompting as to effects, at least 90% of those who try MDMA experience consequences—a "heart-opening," and a lessening of stress and defensiveness—that cause this compound to be of great fascination to many. This remarkable inclusiveness can, as multiple experience shows, be raised further by slight, as well as easy, environmental manipulation.

A very small group of first-time MDMA users—considerably fewer than occurs with other psychedelics—still feel somewhat ill at ease when given this "drug" ("sacrament," "medicine," whatever you want to call it), perceiving only the drawbacks often associated with amphetamines or cocaine, such as chill, jaw clenching or an amorphous general physical discomfort. (See pp. 76, 96)

5. Is MDMA dangerous?
6. What about brain damage?
7. How about possibilities of addiction and/or abuse?

5. Dangers. Range between an effective dose and an overdose is much smaller in regard to MDMA than with most other "psychedelics." Thus, care taken in measurement of dosage is an important consideration. Eisner correctly emphasizes that no one should ever take more than a quarter-gram (250 mg.) at a time. (It should also be pointed out that although larger amounts have been used for various reasons, no death attributable to MDMA ingestion has thus far been credibly documented.)

Effects in physical respects are generally mild. The main one observable is that MDMA causes a slight rise in blood pressure (for up to about an hour and a half). Little else is of any serious consequence for those in reasonable health.

Nonetheless, in interests of safety, no one should take this substance if suffering from heart disease, high blood pressure, or epilepsy, or if taking MAO inhibitors, or if pregnant. (See pp. 1, 9-10, 19-25, 113-114, 118-119, 124, 156-158)

6. Brain studies. Reports in *Science* magazine and *The Journal of the American Medical Association* have raised the spooky fear that MDMA causes neurotoxicity. As might be expected, airing of this possibility— as hedged and remote as has been suggested in original presentations— was highly trumpeted in the press.

The studies, however, have been based on immense amounts of MDMA given repeatedly to laboratory animals, and have been accompanied by the qualification that the results may not apply to ordinary human usage. Over the last two years, more careful studies indicate, preliminarily, that there seems no such risk at the human dose level, and that no negative behavioral or functional effects are as yet associated with MDMA.

Extensive animal testing as well as examination of human spinal fluid of MDMA users is currently taking place. These results to date are summarized (for the first time) in Appendix II of this book. (See pp. 19-21 and Appendix II)

7. What about addiction, or other potentials for abuse? MDMA is difficult to overuse because effects diminish rapidly if taken repeatedly over any short space of time. Under such circumstances, the resulting experience also tends to enhance undesirable qualities that often accompany abuse of amphetamines or cocaine. Thus, the route of using excessive MDMA appeals to very few.

Desirable MDMA experiences just simply cannot be achieved repeatedly without spacing out use. An interval of four days is minimally necessary to do this—which, apparently, involves integration of the previous experience(s). For those with an abusive personality, MDMA would not thus likely be a "drug of choice." Its characteristics so used are quite unrewarding. (See pp. 15, 18-19, 22, 26, 121)

8. What is good MDMA "set" and "setting"?
9. Is MDMA synergistic with other substances and practices?
10. How can desirable qualities be enhanced, and encouraged to linger?

8. Optimal conditions. MDMA is best taken in a comfortable, familiar setting, free of distractions and interruptions, in the presence of a trusted friend or friends—or, as still frequently happens, in a relaxed therapeutic situation.

Since this compound encourages an extraordinary honesty with little defensiveness, a session should not be casual—and those at hand should not include persons who possibly would take advantage of exposed vulnerabilities sometime later on. Attention beforehand should especially be paid to how intentions and heightened sensitivities might affect a partner or some other significant loved ones.

Music to be played during this "contrived" interval, if chosen at all, should be instrumental, "uplifting," choral or one's own personal favorites. In general, "heavy metal," "heavy rock" and "heavy" classical music are best avoided, as these are dissonant with the mood that MDMA typically evokes.

MDMA is best taken on an empty stomach, since food tends to reduce its effects. Eating during the experience might also be kept to a minimum for the same reason, and because some have suggested that a possible "anesthization" could maybe lead to choking. Most users won't be inclined to eat anyway, although they might desire fruit juices and a small amount of simple foods. Plenty of water should be at hand to counter possible dehydration.

As for recalling thoughts and interactions that might be of value later, a recorder or various writing instruments could be provided for in advance (and tested that they are operational). (See pp. 96-99, 102, 104-108, 110-112)

9. Synergies. MDMA is synergetic with most psychedelics. Effects are diminished, however, by considerable amounts of alcohol or marijuana. It may be dangerous taken together with cocaine. A glass of wine or a few tokes of grass, on the other hand, may help when "coming down," to take the "edge" off—especially for those sensitive to amphetamine-like compounds.

When used with other psychedelics, MDMA is frequently taken first and in a lessened dosage, so as to optimize a good mindset. Because the sum is considerably greater than individual parts when things interact synergistically, dosages for each compound should be less than when used normally.

Much experience shows that MDMA also intensifies almost any exploration of spiritual disciplines/techniques, such as meditation and yoga. Again, when used with a partner, trust usually has to be established, given that MDMA frequently points up fundamental disagreements that may before have been covered over superficially. (See pp. 122-126)

10. Strengthening effects. To get the most possible out of this experience, delay normal routines to the extent reasonably possible—hopefully leaving the following day sufficiently free so as to allow a mulling over of new considerations that arise. Here is given a chance to put one's life more in order, best done as gracefully, delicately and thoughtfully as possible.

Supplements of potassium, magnesium and zinc, plus tyrosine (an amino acid), a high protein meal and a good night's sleep, are also often recommended after a session. (See pp. 89, 100-101)

11. What questions does MDMA raise for society?
12. What does it tell us about "stress" and "grace"?
13. Finally, what are left as unanswered questions?

11. Societal concerns. The "mini-vacations" provided by MDMA illuminate pressures that we all may well have learned to ignore in order to get on and "muddle through" our ordinary lives. They also show that we are operating under deprivations not nearly as evident to us in "an ordinary" state of mind—such as a fair amount of lack of compassion and empathy for others.

Integration of MDMA-prodded insights into our daily lives has to come step-by-step, and is not likely to be as easy as might have been envisioned during the experience itself. As a psychiatrist, Rick Ingrasci, whom you'll hear from later, expressed this, "MDMA is like getting a glimpse of the picture on the box of the jigsaw puzzle of life. You still have to put the pieces together." (See pp. 26, 59, 67, 126-133)

12. Acceptance of this "gratuitous grace." The chance to give in via MDMA to one's "underlying mysticism," sense of wonder, and feelings of love for a fellow human and/or one's "fate" is frequently overwhelming—so much so that some users may try to deny the validity of the evoked experience . . . when later back in their usual states of mind and their everyday routines. It may seem "unfair," for an instance, that such a level of exultation could have been achieved via mind molecules without the exertions and deprivations that accompany traditional methods for "enlightenment." This attitude may arise especially among those imbued with the "Protestant ethic," and/or various religious notions of an essential sinful condition predestined for humans.

Alternative views opened up by MDMA can thus be troublesome to the individual user, as well as society. It appears now, at the end of the '80s, that an eventual integration will come about only after a considerable amount of conflict. To express a factor in this briefly, the idea of a "free lunch" is not all that easily accepted—even when it comes as first-hand experience. (See pp. 59, 66-67, 90, 93)

13. Unanswered questions. At present, it is not known why MDMA is "an access code" to largely unused or undeveloped aspects of personality that many people would like to experience with greater regularity. How does it reduce mental, emotional and physical stress? When does it open the user's heart? (See pp. 135, 145)

* * *

Discussion above and evidence to be presented ahead, if these have any validity at all, indicate that scheduling MDMA into the most banned drug category of all may well have been one of the most criminal acts of our recent U.S. government. A fairly immense amount of money—not, though, billions!—was spent taking depositions from highly credentialled witnesses in a charade, as it turned out, in which evidence presented was then entirely ignored. With a signature, the administrator of the DEA was empowered to, and did, sweep aside what bulked up to ten volumes of testimony and a 90-page decision from its own judge based on a hundred solid "findings."

This is unfortunate, given abundant evidence in this book alone as to how beneficial this MDMA substance can be for both its user and for society as a whole. While it is true that such evidence is "merely" first-hand, and largely not presented with "scientific rigor," it should at least be remarked that much more can be substantiated for the transformative qualities of MDMA than for that of psychoanalysis. Reasons for this have been summarized by Debby Harlow, a San Francisco MDMA researcher: "It is virtually impossible to prove the efficacy of any form of psychotherapy or personal growth method (with or without chemical adjuncts) since the benefits accrued are largely subjective. We simply don't have standardized measures for human happiness, personal growth and interpersonal fulfillment."

* * *

Examples from MDMA research already have illuminated areas in which whole population segments of suffering humanity could be helped. Use of MDMA for alleviation of the stresses produced by incidents of rape, and for that experienced among war veterans, recalls for me one of the most charged sentences to come from Freud: "For psychoanalysis to change neurotic suffering to ordinary human misery is no small event."

Progress clearly available from MDMA is now curbed by our government and cannot even be researched. Think about that!

The same can be said for aid that MDMA has to offer psychotherapy. No other tool to date offers such an increase in 1) rapport, and 2) access to relevant personal data, and yet for reasons Krippner describes in his foreword to this book, this priceless advance has been thrown away. Testimony provided by Eisner shows what has been lost.

Driving this marvelous tool to underground usage guarantees an increasingly perverse edge to the delicate but robust potentials it once had. Adulteration, contamination, surreptitious use and dosing, subjecting users to more haphazard conditions—in the future millions of trips will carry added weight after the criminalizing of this profoundly human experience. Explorations will, nonetheless, continue . . . due to MDMA's inherent worth.

As a final point, effects so far have been such that what MDMA does, and is famous for, now carries on by itself. This extraordinary compound has raised such questions and possibilities as to shift a significant amount of contemporary thinking. That will continue, even if MDMA were banished from the face of the earth tomorrow.

—Peter Stafford

Ecstasy, *by Maxfield Parish.*

Preface: Ecstatic Easter

Gretchen invited me by letter to meet her in La Jolla, a fashionable beach community north of San Diego, California.

She would be visiting her son there in early April 1978, flying in from Woodstock, New York, where she had run a boutique.

I had met Gretchen the year before in Santa Cruz. At age 66, her personal history would make a fascinating autobiography. Included would be this gray-haired Jewish Austrian's escape from Nazi Germany, her marriage to a wealthy businessman, and her socialite years as well as her interest in Eastern philosophy that led her to seek out an acquaintance with Alan Watts. From there, her life-road led to setting up lectures for Timothy Leary during the heyday of psychedelia in the mid-'Sixties.

I spent the night in the small house which her son had rented for this visit. We spent the evening talking about a series of interviews she was doing. She also talked about a new drug her son had taken, called MDMA, which was similar to a drug I had tried, MDA.

Indeed, in ten years prior to my La Jolla visit, I had taken a variety of psychedelic substances. My roots were in the 'Sixties counterculture. At this time, I was enrolled at the University of California, Santa Cruz, where I later completed a B. A. in Psychology.

"What is the drug like?" I asked Gretchen. "Is it just like MDA?"

"I'm not sure exactly what it's like, but my son told me that it is somewhat different than MDA. It lasts for a shorter time, it's legal, and it's supposed to help people communicate in a unique way."

"I'd like to try it, " I volunteered enthusiastically.

"Well, my son is bringing some in the morning. I'll ask him to bring you some, too."

We awoke about 8 a.m. on Easter Sunday. Gretchen switched on a radio program by one of her recent interviewees, Gabriel Wisdom. The "Joyful Wisdom Hour" was a program local to the San Diego area, consisting of an upbeat combination of futurist news and New Age gossip by host Wisdom, as well as music and interviews. My introduction into a new environment, renewing my acquaintance with Gretchen, and the optimistic tone of the program provided an upbeat mindset for the experience I was to have. Gretchen's son—a handsome, young man in his early thirties, a recent Ph.D. in Cognitive Psychology from U.C., San Diego, currently involved with artificial intelligence and computer research—arrived at Gretchen's apartment. He briefed me a bit further about the effects of MDMA. He told us that he would not take it himself, but would instead be a guide for us during the experience. We took the small white capsules and set off by car for San Diego's Pico Park. It was a sunny, blue-skied spring day.

La Jolla is a tourist town, full of specialty shops and restaurants and people on vacation. We arrived at the park and plunged into the woodsy expanse by foot. After about five minutes of walking, I began to feel the effects of the MDMA. The first sensation was breathless awe. It was as if I were seeing the world for the first time, crisp and clear and new. This feeling reminded me of my initial experience with LSD. But this time there were no visual changes. Everything appeared as it did before, but different somehow—more intense, fresh, novel.

Gretchen also began showing the effects of the MDMA. We began to talk excitedly as her beaming son led us to the botanical gardens. As we examined exotic flora marked by signs with Latin names, we kept up a lively conversation covering a wide range of topics and people. The tone was consistently optimistic.

Our next stop on the park tour was at the Space Museum. We strolled past exhibits of space capsules past and present (this was pre-Space Shuttle 1978). The space jewelry in the gift shop caught our attention. Especially alluring were the necklaces and earrings with holograms (our first look at this sort of high-tech adornment).

From the museum, we walked close to the far end of the park, with what both of us agreed was an unusual amount of energy. We then sat on a grassy hill overlooking a playground.

Families of U.S. Marines sat on picnic benches around the play area, as their children frolicked in the sun.

Gretchen, who enjoys small children, sat smiling and contemplating the scene beneath us. Normally, I abhor military people, especially Marines, because of my background in the anti-Vietnam War movement. But the crew-cut, khaki-clad Marines and their families seemed transformed in this MDMA-inspired state. They were no longer stereotypes, but human beings, men and women and children sharing a quiet

Easter Sunday in the park. With my normally judgmental outlook suspended, I felt nothing but love and compassion for everyone I saw—including Marines.

With this insight came a peacefulness, a meditative calm. No anticipation of future events, no regrets from the past marred the experience of the moment.

As we walked back to the car, the peacefulness continued, as it would for the remainder of the day. We talked excitedly about our adventure, and the wonders of this new mind-altering substance.

In the ten years since the experience that Sunday in the park, I have continued to use MDMA periodically. None of the subsequent experiences quite duplicated the wonderment of the first. However, the nature and direction of the experiences began to shift into new avenues of insight.

These concerned powerful new connections and communication with friends and lovers. The focus of my life seemed to turn, as the result of my experiences, away from concern with transcendental spirituality and toward interpersonal relationships and the wonders of day-to-day life. The ability to communicate in a direct manner with people that I encountered during my sessions stayed with me.

Also during this decade, I have witnessed many people, in groups or one-on-one, take their first dose of MDMA and open up. The experiences I observed have given me a new appreciation of the good side of human nature. People have sent me short papers or pamphlets, reports of sessions, or guides to the use of Adam, Ecstasy or some other colorful alias for MDMA. I have integrated this material into the book you are about to read.

I have attempted here to weave all this data, along with personal exploration and participation with others, into the first comprehensive overview of MDMA. In it, you will find the history, the psychology, the chemistry, the biology, the methods of use, and the possible future of this interesting new substance and its descendants.

Chapter I. Introducing Adam

You discover a secret doorway into a room in your house that you did not previously know existed. It is a room in which both your inner experience and your relations with others seem magically transformed. You feel really good about yourself and your life. At the same time, everyone who comes into this room seems more lovable. You find your thoughts flowing, turning into words that previously were blocked by fear and inhibition.

After several hours, you return to your familiar abode, feeling tired but different, more open. And your memory of your mystical passage may help you in the days and weeks ahead to make all the other rooms of your house more enjoyable.

This metaphorical door exists in the form of a new and experimental mind-changing compound. It goes by many names, "Ecstasy (XTC)," "Adam," "Presence," "Clarity," "Zen," and "M," but the initials of its chemical name are MDMA (or the also correct MDM).

Early History

Although it has come to public attention only recently, MDMA is not a newly synthesized compound. It was originally developed in 1914, the first year of W.W.I. in Germany. It was patented by Merck Pharmaceutical Company, then for the most part forgotten for the next forty years.

In 1953, the Army Chemical Center (supporting research at Michigan) gave MDMA to guinea pigs, rats, mice, monkeys, and dogs, in order to find out how toxic it might be. It was found to be less so than its chemical cousin, MDA, with which it is often compared. (The history of MDA is much fuller than that of MDMA, and will be covered in Chapter V).

It wasn't until 1976 that the first report was published which indicated the psychoactivity of MDMA in humans. The journal article was by Alexander Shulgin and a collaborator, D.E. Nichols. We will come across Shulgin's name several times in this book, especially when discussing the future of mind-changing drugs. He is a research biochemist, whose revelatory experience with mescaline sulphate in the mid-'Sixties put him on an "ever-changing quest of curiosity," developing and personally exploring a wide range of psychoactive substances. Nichols, who is now at the Department of Medical Chemistry of Purdue University, has also contributed much to this field, and we will also encounter his name throughout this book.

Shulgin and Nichols conclude:

> Within the effective dosage range, 75-150 mg orally, the effects are first noted very quickly, usually within a half-hour following administration. With most subjects, the plateau of effects is reported to occur in a half-hour to one hour. The intoxication symptoms are largely dissipated in an additional 2 hours except for a mild residual sympathiomimetic stimulation which can persist for several additional hours. There are few physical indicators of intoxication and psychological sequelae are virtually non-existent. Qualitatively, the drug appears to evoke an easily controlled altered state of consciousness with emotional and sensual overtones.

Yet even before the publication of the Shulgin/Nichols report, the diffusion of MDMA into society had begun. Some reports of early underground batches of MDMA start as early as 1970. Among those who noted the compound's promise, there was fear that MDMA might become a "street drug" as LSD had, and be quickly banned. LSD had been mainly a research tool of psychotherapists for the first twenty years after its psychoactive effects had been discovered. When publicized by the Harvard Psychedelic Research group, it became the "sacrament" of the Hippies and the recreational drug of the Youth Culture. The use of this powerful mind-changing agent by several million inadequately prepared users, often taking improperly made LSD, led to some well-publicized "bad trips." For this reason, as well as others we will discuss later in the chapter, possession of LSD was made a felony.

Learning from these earlier mistakes, those who experimented with MDMA, many of them psychotherapists, attempted to control the dissemination of information about the drug as well as the substance itself. They hoped that enough informal research could be done before it became public to keep it from suffering a fate like that of LSD and mescaline.

Differences Between MDMA and Major Psychedelics

Aside from this attempt at secrecy, another factor—the differences between MDMA and its predecessors—helped keep things quiet. MDMA is a member of a new generation of psychoactive substances which are, in many respects, different from major psychedelics. Indeed, some refuse to consider it a psychedelic drug at all. They would rather use descriptors like "feeling enhancer" or "empathogen." The latter term, coined by Ralph Metzner, is explored more fully in Chapter II.

How does MDMA differ from LSD, mescaline, or its close chemical relative, MDA, for that matter? Perhaps the most important distinction between MDMA and the others is that MDMA is more specific in its effects.

Stanislav Grof, M.D., former National Institute of Mental Health (NIMH) LSD researcher and author of three books reporting the results of his experiments, has classified LSD as a "non-specific amplifier of brain functions." By this, he means that LSD tends to enhance almost every aspect of mental experience, from amplifying and distorting any or all of the senses and the revelation of the contents of the unconscious mind. The LSD taker is bombarded with more of almost everything, positive as well as negative. This is, for the most part, also true for the other major psychedelic drugs.

MDMA does not produce many of the effects attributed to these major psychedelic drugs. It is not hallucinogenic in normal doses, and it does not disrupt "ego-integrity," a term psychologists use to describe our ability to function in the world. Coordination is not lost during the MDMA experience, and there are no disorganizing effects on thought processes.

Instead, MDMA focuses selectively on a few of the many mental functions that LSD may affect, including emotional ecstasy, capacity for empathy, serenity, self-awareness, and "noetic" feelings. The last, noetic feelings, are the experience of seeing the world in a fresh way, as if for the first time—as a child sees it.

The LSD experience is sometimes referred to by psychologists as involving "depersonalization." That is, the experience of existing as a separate personality or "ego" is disrupted by LSD. MDMA does not normally produce depersonalization. Instead, the effects are ego-strengthening.

MDA is closer in its effects to those of the major psychedelics (LSD, psilocybin, mescaline). It has some depersonalizing qualities as well as mild hallucinogenic effects. The latter are much less pronounced than with LSD. At the same time, it promotes emphathetic communication and interpersonal exploration in the same manner as MDMA, although, again, not to the same degree. MDA appears to be a less selective, more globally active representative of the family of phenethylamines of which it is a member, whereas MDMA is a more specific enhancer of empathetic awareness. In fact, MDMA might be considered the prototype of a new class of psychoactive compounds, the "empathogens," as we will discover in the next chapter.

As a result of these differences between MDMA and its predecessors, the experiences catalyzed by MDMA are nearly always positive. The set (expectations of the user) and the setting (the environment in which the drug is taken) have much less influence on the outcome of the MDMA experience than is true for LSD. The depersonalizing, hallucinatory experience of LSD requires much more preparation and structuring than MDMA does to produce a favorable outcome. And even with the most careful planning and environment, the dramatic consciousness changes produced by LSD can be frightening or even shattering for some people.

When large numbers of people on bad LSD trips appeared at hospital emergency rooms during the 'Sixties, the phenomenon attracted the attention of the government and the media. But only eight people in the entire country sought treatment in hospital emergency rooms after using MDMA during the four years from 1977 (when the drug first appeared on the street) to 1981, according to the government's Drug Abuse Warning Network (DAWN). More are admitted for alcohol-related problems in any two hours of a single day than in those four years. Between 1981 and 1985, not a single admission to any of the DAWN-monitored hospital emergency rooms was reported.

Dissemination of MDMA into Society

The benign nature of the MDMA experience, along with the purposeful efforts of those who used it to keep things quiet, contributed to the low profile that MDMA exhibited from its introduction in 1977 until 1984.

During that time, MDMA spread through underground channels which included psychotherapists, psychiatrists, long-time psychedelic drug explorers, yuppies, and a remarkable assortment of individualists of all kinds. The main uses of MDMA were as a facilitator for interpersonal exploration and communication between lovers and friends, and, among the professionals, as a tool for psychotherapy. For these purposes, MDMA turned out to be quite reliable. By this time, it was

Alexander T. Shulgin, Ph.D., first reported on the effects of MDMA.

called "Adam" or "Ecstasy" by many of those who used it.

Ralph Metzner, Ph.D., who named this class of compound "empathogens," has noted in the unpublished "The Nature of the MDMA Experience & Its Role in Healing, Psychotherapy & Spiritual Practice":

> Perhaps the most interesting code name for MDMA, that seems to have originated with a group of therapists on the West Coast, is the term "Adam," by which is meant not Adam as man, but rather Adam-and-Eve as androgynous ancestor.
>
> The figure of Adam is a highly important symbolic figure in Gnostic and Hermetic writings, and C.G. Jung wrote extensively about it. He represents "primordial man," the "original being," the "man of Earth," the condition of primal innocence and unity with all life, as described in the Bible's account of the Garden of Eden. Feelings of being returned to a natural state of innocence, before guilt, shame and unworthiness arose, are common in these Adamic ecstasies; and so are feelings of connectedness and bonding with fellow human beings, animals and all the forms and energies of the natural world.

The other popular name for MDMA, "Ecstasy," was chosen for obvious reasons. The man who first named it "Ecstasy" told me that he chose the name "because it would sell better than calling it 'Empathy.' 'Empathy' would be more appropriate, but how many people know what it means?" In mid-1984, the calm waters of MDMA use began to feel some ripples, forerunners of the waves of the storm that was to follow. Hardly a word had been written about Adam until Bill Mandel's flippant piece, "The Yuppie Psychedelic," appeared in the June 10, 1984, edition of the *San Francisco Chronicle*:

> Shades of Timothy Leary! A defrocked Harvard professor appeared on the Marin County intelligentsia circuit a few months ago preaching the wonders of a new psychedelic drug.
>
> Called "Adam," it has been turning up recently in rather unlikely circles. Adam is spreading faster than a secret restaurant tip among educated professionals in their 30's and 40's, non-kooky baby boomers who experimented with psychedelics 15 years ago and then forsook them for careers and family.
>
> Could this be the last hurrah of the '60's, a final nostalgic

harkening to a golden age when "bald spots" were on ski slopes, not one's scalp? Back then, Leary and Richard Alpert (who later became Ram Dass) left psychology professorships at Harvard to become guides on the LSD Magical Mystery Tour.

No, Adam is very definitely of the '80's. According to people who've taken it, this new psychedelic isn't supposed to teach you anything or take you anywhere. It was designed simply to stimulate the pleasure centers of the cerebral cortex . . .

Many who used Adam were relieved to find that its chemical name was incorrectly given in this slick mix of fact and fallacy, a combination which was to typify much of the media coverage that was to follow. Mandel says, "The name 'Adam' is probably derived from the chemical name, methyloxy-methylene-dioxy-amphetamine (MMDA)." MMDA is one of Adam's close chemical cousins, and had been scheduled by the Comprehensive Controlled Substance Act of 1970—which contains lists of drugs prohibited by the federal government—along with MDA. By specifying the wrong name in the article, attention to MDMA was averted.

But this respite was to be short-lived. The next month, the World Health Organization asked of its member governments about the use of more than twenty known psychoactive substances of the chemical class called phenethylamines. MDMA was on the list. Checking records of drug seizures, WHO identified MDMA as the only drug on the list found a significant number of times.

After a year of collecting data and planning in collaboration with the Food and Drug Administration, the Drug Enforcement Administration (DEA) published a notice in the July 27, 1984, edition of the *Federal Register*, that it intended to include MDMA in the Comprehensive Substances Act as a Schedule I drug, equivalent to a narcotic and deemed to be without medical use.

The DEA could not have anticipated what happened next. A group of self-described "physicians, researchers, therapists, and lawyers" was established under the name of a Florida-based nonprofit corporation formed earlier by proponents of Buckminster Fuller, Earth Metabolic Design Laboratory. Concurrently four individuals, Professor Thomas B. Roberts, Ph.D., George Greer, M.D., Professor Lester Grinspoon, M.D., and Professor James Bakalar, retained a Washington D.C. attorney, Richard Cotton. Cotton, on Sept. 10, 1984, sent a letter to Francis

Mullen, Administrator of the DEA, requesting that a hearing be held to determine whether MDMA should be scheduled, and if so, what schedule it should be placed in.

The initial hearing was held on February 1, 1985, in a room on the twelfth floor of the Washington, D.C., Drug Enforcement Administration offices. Presiding was administrative law justice Francis Young. Also present were two DEA attorneys, Richard Cotton, and a pharmaceutical company attorney not interested in MDMA, but interested in a procedural question discussed in the *Federal Register* with regard to the hearings about whether a drug could be placed in a category other than Schedule I of the Controlled Substance Act if there was no currently accepted medical use.

In the hearing, it was decided that three future hearings would be held, one in Washington, D.C., another in Kansas City, Missouri, and the third in Los Angeles. These hearings would try to address five questions decided by general agreement of the contending parties: (1) Is there accepted medical use of MDMA? (2) Is there lack of accepted safety for MDMA when used under medical supervision? (3) What is the relative abuse potential of MDMA? (4) If there is no accepted medical use of MDMA, can it be placed in a category other than Schedule I? (5) If MDMA can be placed somewhere other than Schedule I, where should it be scheduled, if at all?

Judge Young commented that the decision process could take up to a year. Those who were interested in using the drug therapeutically hoped that during this period, much more research could be done with human subjects to prove the efficacy of MDMA for psychotherapy. But events of the next several months placed a dark cloud over these expectations.

California Conference

Esalen Institute, perched on cliffs above the surging Pacific Ocean, is eleven miles south of the small town of Big Sur, California. The site of hot mineral springs, it was once the residence of the Esselen Indians, who considered its waters to have remarkable healing properties. Since its founding in the mid-'Sixties, Esalen has been a vortex for new ideas and methods involving humanistic psychotherapies and consciousness sciences.

Esalen has also been the base of operations for Stanislav Grof, M.D., who has conducted research on LSD for nearly thirty years, both in his native Czechoslovakia and with funding from the National Institute of Mental Health in Bethesda, Maryland. Grof, and Esalen co-founder Dick

Price, both interested in the promise of MDMA, opened up Esalen as a grounds for a conference of researchers in the field.

Co-sponsored by Earth Metabolic Design Foundation, the conference was held from March 10-15, 1985. It was reported on by George Greer, M.D., in the Spring 1985 issue of *Advances: Journal for the Institute for the Advancement of Health.* Some of this report is excerpted:

> Among the 35 participants at the meeting were 5 veteran researchers on psychoactive drugs (Francesco DiLeo, M.D., Stanislav Grof, M.D., Robert Lynch, M.D., Claudio Naranjo, M.D., and Richard Yensen, Ph.D.) and 4 psychiatrists who use MDMA in their clinical practice. On the fourth day of the meeting, George Greer, one of the psychiatrists, directed a session in which 13 participants took MDMA; each person was monitored separately by a physician or psychiatrist. Among the professionals present, the combined clinical experience in using MDMA during the past several years totaled over a thousand sessions . . .
>
> Psychiatrists Joseph Downing, M.D., and Philip Wolfson, M.D., presented results of an unpublished, recently completed toxicity study of 21 human subjects, all of whom had taken MDMA in the past. Other than a brief and moderate rise in pulse and blood pressure, the researchers found no significant abnormalities before ingestion or up to 24 hours afterward . . .
>
> The reports on the benefits of MDMA, although anecdotal, were uniformly positive. In the discussion of MDMA's effects, the clinicians using it felt it possessed a unique action that enhanced communication, especially in couples in therapy. The drug reduced defensiveness and fear of emotional injury, thereby facilitating more direct expression of feelings . . .
>
> Reports of MDMA's facilitation of individual psychotherapy were also favorable. Many subjects experienced the classic retrieval of lost traumatic memories, followed by the relief of emotional symptoms. Victims of child abuse and sexual attack experienced the most dramatic benefits. Wolfson also reported having multiple MDMA sessions with psychotic individuals and their natal families, leading to improvements in the patient's functioning and ego integration . . .

None of those that took MDMA had any complications; some found the session emotionally intense. The two days remaining in the conference allowed for follow-up discussion and analysis. The people who took MDMA regarded the experience positively and felt the drug encouraged self-insight . . .

The group favored assigning MDMA to a lower Schedule, reserved for drugs with moderate-to-low abuse potential, thus allowing for prosecution for illicit trafficking and the continuation of ongoing studies of MDMA's therapeutic potential. In support of this position, it was pointed out that the Drug Abuse Warning Network—a federally funded national clearinghouse of information—had listed only 8 emergency-room visits as a result of MDMA and that since the drug's appearance in the 1970's, no deaths in conjunction with MDMA use had been established. The participants agreed that although MDMA was not a proven therapeutic agent, its supervised experimental use with full informed consent was medically acceptable and safe.

MDMA Goes Public

Newsweek, in the April 15, 1985, issue, printed in its Life/Style section an article titled, "Getting High on 'Ecstasy'." It began:

This is the drug that LSD was supposed to be, coming 20 years too late to change the world. It is called MDMA—or "Ecstasy"—and users say it has the incredible power to make people trust one another, to banish jealousy and to break down barriers that separate lover from lover, parent from child, therapist from patient. Yet unlike LSD, it does not also break down one's ability to distinguish between reality and fantasy, so that it appears free of many of that drug's unfortunate side effects. A New York writer who tried it compares it to "a year of therapy in two hours." A Benedictine monk from Big Sur, Brother Steindl-Rast, says "a monk spends his whole life cultivating the same awakened attitude it gives you." Of course, not everyone is taking it for the insights it provides. It has become popular over the last two years on college campuses, where it is considered an aphrodisiac. Drug-abuse clinics have begun seeing kids who take a dozen or more doses a day to achieve an amphetamine-like high. Apparently the nation is on the verge either of a tremendous breakthough or a lot more kids too strung out to come in from the rain.

The next major media exposure for the suddenly publicized drug was on network television's "Phil Donahue" show, which turned out to be a rollicking free-for-all taped before a vocal New York audience.

The show began with Donahue poking fun at MDMA by first suggesting that the Iranians might dump it in the water supply. Then, as Ayatollah Khomeini lands at the Washington Airport, we welcome him with open arms—rendered open and loving by the new drug.

As Donahue sampled audience opinion, the immediate reaction was that they didn't like the idea of a new drug. Donahue then gave an appeal for the information to be heard, since much of the false information given in the drug scare of the late 'Sixties had resulted in kids being told that heroin was the same as marijuana.

On the panel was Rick Ingrasci, M.D., who used MDMA in his Massachusetts medical practice; Mel Riddle of Straight, Inc., a drug abuse center; Gene Haslip, Deputy Director of the DEA; and Charles Schuster of the Drug Abuse Research Center, University of Chicago.

Ingrasci said that he did not consider the drug a panacea, and was not advocating that people take it all the time. He was simply suggesting that it be used in therapeutic circumstances to help people work through difficult emotional problems and improve their quality of life.

Mel Riddle spoke next, with a strongly anti-drug line, suggesting that many kids who come to him have used the drug, and some were completely messed up after just one dose.

Gene Haslip was introduced by Donahue with a lecture on the problems that the hard-line policy of the Reagan administration toward drugs has created. Haslip replied with a statement that he wanted to get MDMA off the street and made a Schedule I drug.

Charles Schuster of the Drug Abuse Research Center, University of Chicago, took what at first seemed a moderate position, suggesting that the drug be held out of Schedule I until research was done with it, as is done with other drugs which are being tested for possible medical use.

However, this was followed by a rather sensational statement. Schuster announced that he and two other researchers from the Drug Abuse Research Center had found that MDA, the "parent compound" for MDMA, caused brain damage in rats, and therefore might also in humans (oddly, the research paper they published in *Science* stated their position in much more conservative language, as we will see later in this chapter).

However, the tone of the program was changed by the articulate testimony of several patients of Rick Ingrasci, who spoke from the audience. The first case history was from a woman whose marital problems were helped by an MDMA session in the context of psychotherapy (this case is detailed in Chapter III). The second to talk, Diane Watson, a cancer patient, spoke emotionally about how MDMA had helped her deal with the diagnosis that she had terminal cancer and only six months to live. MDMA, she said, was a catalyst to help her deal with the anger and the pain of her terminal disease. She stated, "MDMA is not an ecstasy drug. It allows you to see the world more clearly and to heal yourself. You realize that you don't need negative emotions, old emotions any more, and you can let them go."

There were many testimonials from the audience, pro and con. Advocates and "anties" were given time to make brief statements. Clearly, the statements by those helped by MDMA therapy made a deep impression on the studio audience, but still there were many who remained skeptical of the advent of another new drug.

The floodgates had now opened, and a deluge of media copy and videotape spilled forth. An article appeared in the May issue of *Psychology Today*, by Jack Shafer, a reporter writing a book about the increase in synthetic drugs appearing in the drug underground. His previous magazine publication, in the March 1985 issue of *Science '85*, "Designer Drugs," portrayed the dangers of synthetic heroin substitutes such as alpha-methyl fentanyl, also known as China White. In this article, "MDMA: Psychedelic Drug Faces Regulation," Shafer attempted to present both sides of the controversy of another designer drug, the much safer MDMA.

On the lighter side, Doonesbury's Uncle Duke hosted a conference entitled "Ecstasy: Whither the Future" at Baby Doc College. The comic events were depicted by Gary Trudeau:

Doonesbury takes off on MDMA. (DOONESBURY Copyright 1985 G. B. Trudeau. Reprinted with Permission of Universal Press Syndicate. All rights reserved)

Ron Siegel, Ph.D., a pharmacologist who researches psychoactive drugs at the UCLA School of Medicine under grants from the National Institute of Drug Abuse (NIDA), emerged as the major representative of the DEA's attack upon the safety and usefulness of Adam. He was featured in *Psychology Today* as well as in subsequent articles in *Time*, *Life*, and *New York*.

Rick Doblin, a 31-year-old co-founder of Earth Metabolic Design Laboratories, became the major pro-MDMA figure in the media coverage, although he was subjected to heavy criticism by his more conservative colleagues in the organization because of differences in strategies of action.

Doblin first tried MDMA in 1985 and quickly became an activist for the substance. Wrote Joe Klien of *New York* Magazine:

> Even before the Federal Government entered the picture, Rick Doblin sensed that MDMA would become a political issue. "Compassion has political implications. Empathy has polical implications," he says. Doblin decided to contact various government agencies, to show good faith by *telling* them all about MDMA and asking guidance. He contacted Nancy Reagan's anti-drug group, the National Federation of Parents for Drug Free Youth. He contacted the Food and Drug Administration and the National Institute on Drug Abuse and the United Nations. He proposed cooperation. He proposed joint research into MDMA. He proposed to the United Nations that MDMA be used in a project called "Shaping a Global Spirituality While Living in the Nuclear Age."

Currently, Doblin is beginning graduate work at Harvard and working on a proposal to set up a pharmaceutical company—Orphan Pharmaceuticals, Inc. This pharmaceutical company would conduct animal tests, human tests, and clinical trials in an effort to establish the therapeutic efficacy of MDMA.

During the beginning of 1985, another development that would affect the fate of MDMA also occurred. A laboratory in Texas, which first began operating in 1983, started producing unprecedentedly high amounts of MDMA. Ron Siegel, in the *Psychology Today* article, estimated that 30,000 doses of MDMA were being made each month. This laboratory was said to be producing a kilogram—8,000 doses—per day or 240,000 doses per month. These were made into tablets and sold in brown bottles labeled "Sassyfras."

"Sassyfras" brand MDMA was being sold, according to the DEA, at parties in which "pyramid sales" were organized. Participants paid $20 for a sample tablet and were recruited to find other sellers. This prompted Senator Lloyd Bentsen, a Democrat from Texas, to write to John C. Lawn, "Acting Administrator of the DEA," asking for an emergency ban on MDMA.

Indeed, Congress had given the DEA the power to place any drug in Schedule I for one year, because of the deaths and crippling disease attributed to the synthetic heroin nicknamed China White.

On May 31, 1985, a news conference was held in Washington by the DEA. John C. Lawn, in an Associated Press dispatch published in the June 1 *New York Times*, states, "All the evidence the DEA has received shows that MDMA abuse has become a nationwide problem and it poses a serious health threat. This emergency action is a stopgap measure to curb MDMA abuse until the administrative process can be completed." The story goes on to bluntly state, "Officials of the drug agency said their intention was to replace the emergency ban on MDMA with a permanent ban within one year."

The Problem with the DEA's Handling of the Drug Problem

The actions that the DEA took in this matter are typical of its past patterns of action on other newly popular drugs. This "hardball" approach to drugs—smear publicity, severe penalties, kick-down-doors enforcement—has not eradicated problems with drugs in the U.S. Indeed, all it has created is public confusion about drugs and a huge black market.

There is no question that there is a serious drug problem in America. The most widely abused drugs are not even thought of as drugs at all. The addictive drug known as nicotine, sold legally in cigarettes, is clearly the most commonly abused drug. Next in popularity is one of the most dangerous and certainly the most lethal of all drugs sold, alcohol—found in liquor, beers, and wines. This drug is legal and sold even in grocery stores.

If you don't like any of the list of government-approved mind-alterants, you might choose one of the banned alternatives. But then you risk the wrath of the Drug Enforcement Administration. The DEA is the latest in an alphabet-soup series of agencies, beginning with the Federal Bureau of Narcotics, that have attempted to enforce the nation's drug laws. These drug laws cover an increasingly long list of drugs, and their penalties become relentlessly more severe.

Of course, the reason that alcohol is now legal is that the 18th Amendment to the Constitution, which instituted Prohibition in this country, did not work. In fact, there are few laws against any drug at any time in history that have worked. Edward M. Brecher and the editors of *Consumer Reports* in 1972 published *Licit and Illicit Drugs*, an excellent account depicting the consequences of instituting such repressive legislation.

Particularly fascinating is the section on heroin and the opiate drugs. The account begins with the situation with respect to morphine and the opiates that existed in the nineteenth century. At that time, these Schedule I narcotics were available over the counter. Because the opiates are highly addictive, many people who tried them got hooked on the preparations then available.

Although the opiates and heroin are addictive, they are not damaging physically. They are in no way as destructive physically as alcohol, for example, which has been demonstrated to cause brain and liver damage. They are psychologically dangerous, however, in that they put people into a dull stupor.

More severe problems with heroin and the opiates arose after the Harrison Narcotic Act was passed in 1914 and began to be enforced. This action created a black market in heroin. Because of the government sanctions, prices of heroin on this black market are a thousand times as high as the drug costs from a pharmacy. The high cost forces those addicted to heroin to steal or prostitute themselves in order to pay for their drugs. Heroin's price also brings huge profits into the hands of criminal syndicates.

In addition, much of the black-market heroin is cut (diluted) with other materials, some of which are toxic. Occasionally, dangerous synthetic drugs are substituted for heroin; these can cause severe physical impairment or even be lethal. Yet heroin users, once addicted, have a poor prognosis for recovery.

The case of heroin demonstrates the consequences to be expected when a drug is made illegal.

First, the price of the drug goes up, and its distribution is taken out of the hands of experts and put into the hands of criminals.

Second, it criminalizes a group of people who use a particular substance. For heroin, penalties can range up to life in prison.

Third, making a drug illegal usually leads to adulteration of the substance or its being replaced by another compound.

Another account in *Licit and Illicit Drugs* illustrates the mishandling of drug use and misuse in this country—the case of LSD. Prior to 1963, LSD was a little-known but promising tool for psychotherapy.

In 1963, there was a media blitz publicizing the ouster of Timothy Leary and Richard Alpert from Harvard University because of their experimentation with psychedelic substances. LSD became, almost overnight, a household word, and a subculture of users arose.

Because of the increase in use, and because it became associated with the counterculture which included hippies and anti-Vietnam war activists, a polarization of the country on the question of LSD use developed.

In 1966, sensational media stories accentuated this division. One concerned a 5-year-old baby in Brooklyn who accidentally swallowed an LSD sugar cube. She had her stomach pumped and recovered quickly, with no lasting psychological harm. The other was about a murderer who claimed that he had killed while on LSD. Subsequently, it was revealed that the man was a paranoid schizophrenic. But initial headlines—"LSD MURDER" and "BABY HOSPITALIZED ON LSD"— are what stick in public memory, and these two sensationalized stories were catalysts for the institution of felony penalties for the possession, sale, and manufacture of LSD.

Subsequently, the media became increasingly hostile to LSD use. In 1967, TV and newspapers were filled with reports that LSD broke chromosomes. It was speculated that deformities in children, similar to the Thalidomide scandal of 1962, would be the result of LSD use. But subsequent investigations found no abnormalities in the offsprings of LSD users. Many of those who refrained for a while from using LSD returned to it, becoming skeptical of any negative media stories regarding drugs.

Some researchers felt and still believe that the promise of LSD and other proscribed psychedelic drugs such as mescaline and psilocybin was not allowed sufficient exploration by researchers. *Psychedelics Reconsidered* by Lester Grinspoon and James Bakalar presents the case for the reopening of research with these potentially useful substances.

All of the media attention to LSD and its hazards had two effects. First, it increased usage dramatically. From a small number of relatively sophisticated and dedicated users, LSD use spread until it became a recreational drug in high schools and colleges and even among Vietnam soldiers.

It has been repeatedly demonstrated that almost any publicity about a psychoactive drug, negative or positive, will stimulate use of that substance. Expectations about an LSD experience strongly influence the nature of the experience. The drug makes a person suggestible, and prior beliefs about its effects govern the course of the experience. Prior to 1962, there were very few negative experiences reported by those who experienced LSD.

But with the polarization of attitudes toward the drug, those with an interest in seeing LSD banned played up every negative experience. Soon, the number of bad trips and even LSD suicides rose sharply.

As with heroin, making LSD a black market drug led to impurely manufactured and adulterated LSD. This also produced more negative reactions among underground users.

So the result of the incredible publicity about LSD was (1) to increase use, (2) to provoke the proverbial "LSD bummer," (3) to criminalize idealistic middle-class youth, and (4) to discourage research into promising new modes of psychotherapy.

The DEA was set up to police drug use in America. It receives its funding in relation to the severity and scope of the drug problem. Because it is involved in enforcement of drug laws, the DEA's members tend to view any drug use (other than alcohol, cigarettes, and coffee) in a negative way. The DEA also has strong economic interest in having widely used drugs made illegal. The more drug criminals there are to hunt and arrest, the more funding the DEA receives, and the larger the organization becomes. Giving the DEA the power to decide which drugs to criminalize could lead to a constantly expanding police organization always needing more tax monies.

DEA Tackles MDMA

Many of the problems of criminalizing drugs are apparent in the handling of MDMA. Also, many of the biases of the DEA have been revealed in the way it proceeded in having the drug placed in Schedule I.

During the hearings to decide whether MDMA should be made a Schedule I drug, it may have become apparent to the DEA that its case was falling apart. It was difficult to show a high potential for abuse of MDMA. It was possible to show that the drug was used, however, with exhibits of amateur fact sheets, some of which I have quoted from in this book. Many of these pamphlets are testimonials to MDMA's efficacy.

But those who testified for the Earth Metabolic Design Foundation universally affirmed that there were no people whose lives had been harmed by MDMA. Because of the rapid rise in tolerance caused by repeated use, and the buildup of unpleasant side effects, most people learn quickly that MDMA can only be used occasionally. Taking too much is just not rewarding.

For the same reasons, it can be said that MDMA is not an addictive drug. It is true that some people like to repeat the experience. But it is generally found that the less often MDMA is taken, the more meaningful the experience is. The tendency is to take it less frequently after the first two or three exposures. Also, there was little evidence that MDMA was dangerous psychologically. The data from DAWN emergency rooms cited earlier demonstrate that there are few "bad trips" on MDMA. Richard Seymour, of the Haight-Ashbury Free Clinic, reports that most of those who do have a bad time and come into his clinic are provided with a supportive environment and reorient themselves as soon as the drug is metabolized. Being nonaddictive and relatively free of negative psychological phenomena, even in unsupervised situations, MDMA looks like a remarkably safe drug, even safer than the most commonly used recreational drugs, illegal marijuana and legal alcohol.

As MDMA became popular and publicized, it was clear that the DEA was dedicated to banning the substance. In an article, "Federal Authorities Want to Ban Ecstasy," printed in the *San Francisco Examiner*, May 19, 1985, by staff writer John Flinn, this was clear: " 'We're going to ban Ecstasy within the next several months', DEA assistant administrator Gene Haslip vowed. 'By next fall, Ecstasy will be as rigidly controlled as heroin. It's extremely dangerous.' "

Then, when the DEA ban was announced on May 31, the major reason given for the evoking of the DEA's emergency powers was a study done at the University of Chicago and submitted for publication in *Science*. The study revealed that the drug *MDA* has been shown to cause brain damage in rats.

When this report was examined more closely, however, it became clear that many aspects of the report made its application to the use of MDMA by humans highly questionable.

The drug used in the study was MDA, which is chemically distinct from MDMA. While they are both empathogens with somewhat similar mental effects, they are molecularly different, and probably affect the brain in different ways.

Testimony of two hearing witnesses, medical chemist David Nichols and June Riedlinger, pharmacist, presented good evidence for the chemical distinction between the two substances. According to Nichols, there is no cross-tolerance between MDMA and MDA. If you take MDMA until it no longer has an effect, you can then take MDA and it

will still have an effect, and vice versa. This points to separate sites of
action in the brain.

Both Riedlinger and Nichols point out that MDA and MDMA have
opposite isomer activity in their effect on the brain. Actually MDA,
according to Nichols, can be thought of as two separate psychoactive
drugs, with each of the stereoisomers having quite different psychological effects. MDMA has only one active (s) isomer, the opposite of the
more active MDA isomer. The DEA's own report points out that there
is evidence that MDA and MDMA have different pathways of action
within the nervous system. (These chemical aspects will be explained
more fully in the Appendix.)

Alexander Shulgin, Nichols' colleague, commented that MDA resembles MDMA, but it also resembles the over-the-counter allergy
remedy Sudafed (pseudoephedrine hydrochloride). Should we place this
commonly-used patent medicine on Schedule I along with MDMA?

Several other clear objections to the Chicago study are found in the
following excerpt from the research report itself:

> Our study raises the question of whether MDA produces
> 5HT neurotoxicity in humans. Given differ-
> ences in species, dose, frequency and route of admin-
> istration, as well as differences in the way in which rats and
> humans metabolize amphetamine, it would be premature
> to extrapolate our findings to humans. It should also be
> noted that the doses of MDA required to produce 5HT
> neurotoxicity in the rat (5-10 mg/kg) are roughly three to
> five times higher than those required to produce hallucin-
> ogenic effects (approximately 1.5 to 3 mg/kg). *Hence, doses
> of MDA generally ingested by humans may not be sufficiently
> high to induce 5HT neurotoxity unless humans prove to be more
> sensitive than rats to the toxic effects of MDA.*

The "differences in species, dose, frequency, and route of administration" refer to the procedures followed in the experiment, in which
the drug was (1) given to rats rather than humans, (2) given in the much
larger doses, as noted in the subsequent sentence, (3) given every twelve
hours for two days, and (4) given intravenously
(injected in the vein) rather than taken orally, the usual route of
administration in humans. Taking a drug orally results in smaller
amounts of the drug reaching the brain than if taken by i.v. injection.

In August 1985, Intox Laboratory performed a further study in which
a group of rats were given an escalating series of rather stiff doses of

MDMA. They were started off at 25 milligrams per kilogram of body weight, and the amount was increased by 25 mg./kg. each day thereafter. The average psychoactive dose taken by humans is about 2 milligrams per kilogram.

Eventually, all the animals died when the dosages reached between 150 mg./kg. and 300 mg./kg. This is about 150 times the normal human dose. When the rats were examined, there was no evidence of histological brain damage. Although the second study does not use the same techniques as the first, it must raise doubts about the evidence provided by the former study. Subsequent animal and human studies examining the toxicity question are discussed in Appendix II .

Ron Siegel's Anti-MDMA Crusade

In addition to the questionable issue of brain damage, much of the DEA's other negative evidence rests on the study of recreational users done by Ronald Siegel of the UCLA School of Medicine. Siegel has had a high profile in many media reports about MDMA. In an article in *New York*—"The New Drug They Call Ecstasy: Is it Too Much to Swallow?," by Joe Klien—some excerpts from Siegel's statements suggest the nature of Siegel's attack on MDMA.

> "My reaction is 'Here we go again'," says Dr. Ronald Siegel of the UCLA School of Medicine. "Every few years you get one of these miracle drugs that's going to save the world and make everyone feel good. My favorite was PCP. Remember what they used to call that? The *Peace* Pill. At low doses, people were reporting serene, tranquil, peaceful experiences. Then it hit the street and the name changed—it became angel dust—and dosages increased and it was cut with God knows what, and you began to get all the reports of bizarre, violent behavior. So now we have Ecstasy. If you take it, you might become a self-actualized empathetic, caring person, or you might become a nauseated person, or you might have a severe psychotic reaction. Among street users, we're seeing all of the above." . . .
>
> The effects of the drug, he says, seem very similar to those of mescaline. "They're from the same pharmacological family," he says. "You know, the molecular twists and turns that the chemists are playing with—MDA, MMDA, MDMA—raise nice, interesting academic questions, but

out on the street, the experience is the same: hallucinations, disorientation, psychotic episodes."

It is possible that because of the milder, more subtle effects of MDMA, inexperienced users are doubling and tripling the dose. It's also probable that after the recent media coverage, enterprising drug dealers are calling everything from speed to powdered sugar Ecstasy. "We're getting people who claimed to have taken this drug who are disoriented for days on end," says Siegel. "We've had people locked in fetal positions for as long as 72 hours. We had a psychotherapist that took it, disappeared, and turned up a week later directing traffic."

Siegel, in his statements, compares MDMA with two hallucinogenic drugs. PCP, which has a deservedly bad reputation, is nothing like MDMA, in either its chemical structure or its psychological effects. By linking the two, the negative reputation of PCP is pinned on MDMA. The reader is led to think, "Another PCP, huh? Let's get this stuff off the street."

Siegel also alleges that MDMA and mescaline are almost identical in their effects, and that the chemical differences are superfluous. Yet this is certainly not the case. As we explored in the preceding, MDMA is not a hallucinogen as mescaline is—even in double or triple the normal doses. If it is taken in double or triple doses, it produces unpleasant overstimulation; so high doses are normally avoided by users.

Then there are the repeated allegations by Siegel that MDMA can lead to psychotic reactions, and that sometimes these psychotic symptoms do not go away. As we discussed earlier in this chapter, the record of MDMA is one of remarkable safety. The percentage of severely negative reactions is very low. The cases that Siegel mentioned of prolonged reactions must even be rarer. Siegel is probably mentioning every horror story he has heard about the drug.

When hundreds of thousands of people take a psychoactive drug, there are bound to be a few psychotics or prepsychotics who take it, and some of these will be triggered into psychoses by it. With MDMA, unlike LSD or mescaline, the actual number of these reactions has been shown to be quite low. Ronald Siegel is employing a rhetorical trick. By mentioning every extreme case, he makes the casual reader think that MDMA produces psychotics by the score, and that they could end up crazy if they should experiment with the compound.

When Siegel mentions that "cut" and adulterated MDMA is going to be distributed, in doses that are too large, he should recognize that this is the common effect of putting any drug into the black market by enacting stiff legislation. This occurred with heroin and LSD, and since the July 1, 1985, criminalization of MDMA, the same stories of adulteration and substitution and cutting are being heard about MDMA. Until then, almost all of what was represented as MDMA actually was the real substance.

The result of making MDMA a Schedule I drug has been that experimentation with MDMA has been effectively stopped, and that people with an interest in taking it have been turned into potential felons. If it had been placed in Schedule III instead, then medical

Ronald Siegal, Ph.D., witness for the DEA.

experimentation could have continued, and only street use would have been criminalized, although not to the same extent as with Schedule I. Schedule I drugs require research protocols which are prohibitive to researchers without huge grants.

One last example of Siegel's distortions comes in an *Omni* article called "Chemical Ecstasies":

> One dealer gives written "flight instructions," promising that while XTC [Ecstasy, or MDMA] is "kissing in your veins" during the hour-long voyage, you'll experience happiness, security, peace, and freedom. That should end all wars, but secret U.S. Army tests in the 'Fifties found that it also ended the lives of experimental animals. Low doses reduce toxity, but leave subjects with clenched jaws, wiggly eyes, and high blood pressure . . .

Tom Riedlinger comments on the above in an article in the *Journal of Psychoactive Drugs*:

> Trivialization and deliberate distortions are obvious in the foregoing. Siegel is a specialist in psychopharmacology. He therefore knows perfectly well that *all* substances are toxic to humans at some dosage level. Drug experiments with animals typically include a test where dosages are increased incrementally until death occurs, in order to establish where the toxic threshold lies. Siegel chooses not to point this out, preferring instead to convey the impression that MDMA is toxic at low doses—which for humans, at least, is not true. He does acknowledge his duplicity implicitly, however, when he writes that "low [read: therapeutic] doses reduce [avoid the dangers of] toxicity." The side effects he mentions are acknowledged to occur in many patients and in different combinations, but virtually always are no more than mere vexations—acceptable risks.

More Publicity

The kind of media coverage that MDMA got for several months after its criminalization was somewhat reminiscent of the hysteria and hyperbole of the anti-LSD crusade of 1966-69.

Perhaps an extreme example of this is a column by Shari Roan printed in the July 2, 1985, issue of the Dallas *Sun Sentinel.* The column, titled "Designer Drug Dangers," is here excerpted:

> A drug lauded by a small group of psychologists as a consciousness-raising aid became an illegal substance as of Monday. But federal Drug Enforcement Agency officials and drug abuse counselors fear they haven't seen the end of the controversy surrounding "Ecstasy."
>
> After years of therapeutic use among a small group of psychologists, Ecstasy (MDMA) recently has become popular among some college students and gays. The hallucinogenic drug has less severe effects than LSD, and some therapists say it reduces anxiety and promotes empathy in patients.
>
> DEA officials, however, say the drug is a dangerous and scientifically untested substance. The DEA called for an emergency ban on Ecstasy after University of Chicago researchers found the drug works by destroying large numbers of vital brain cells and may speed up the aging process in a manner similar to the muscle degeneration produced by Parkinson's disease. The DEA also reported 31 deaths from the drug, mostly in the San Francisco Bay area, with 26 of those deaths occurring after Aug. 1, 1984.

When I read the above newspaper clipping sent by a friend, I immediately called up Alexander and Ann Shulgin to ask them why I had not heard about all of this. Ann Shulgin answered the phone. When I read her the report, she replied, "They mixed everything up. All of those statistics and the Parkinson's disease portion is about MPTP, an unexpected by-product of MPPP."

Immediately it dawned on me that this reporter, in her fervor to get out the anti-dope news, had taken information from two sources and intertwined them in a curious fashion. A strange twist, because the law that was used to ban MDMA resulted from the scandal around synthetic heroin.

The last piece published in a national magazine during the media blitz was in the August 1985 issue of *Life* magazine. The article was generally a balanced view of the controversy. However, you would not know this by the title and accompanying bold headlines on the first page of the story. The title was "The Trouble with Ecstasy." Underneath the title, in bold black letters, is, "THE DRUG IS SEDUCTIVE, CONTROVERSIAL, DANGEROUS—AND NOW ILLEGAL." It's clear what message the casual reader would get from this sensationalistic treatment of MDMA.

Conclusions of the Hearings

The three hearings on MDMA, in Los Angeles, Kansas City, and Washington, D.C., produced ten volumes of testimony from DEA witnesses and from professionals who wished the drug to be placed on a lower and less restrictive schedule so that further research would not be curtailed.

Some highlights of this testimony included two staff members of the Haight-Ashbury Free Medical Clinic facing each other from both sides of the issue, and agreeing that they had seen little abuse of MDMA in their practice. Depositions included statements by Alexander Shulgin and David Nichols distinguishing MDMA from MDA.

Ron Siegel, who had failed to show up at the Los Angeles hearings, did later testify on behalf of the DEA in Washington D.C. He based his statements on a study of "street users." In a positive vein, Siegel stated that he did not find compulsive use patterns developing for MDMA and thought that it did not have a high potential for abuse.

Some other aspects of Siegel's testimony repeated the questionable assertions in the media. He declared MDMA a "hallucinogen" not much different from mescaline. He also told his favorite horror story about the Chicago psychologist who took MDMA once and ended up directing traffic on a busy boulevard.

In the same courtroom, one of the government's chief witnesses, John Docherty, former chief of the Psychosocial Treatment Branch of NIMH, told the court that he supported further MDMA research and that "MDMA is at the confluence of two great trends in psychiatry: psychotherapy and pharmacology," because it had been shown to enhance rapport between therapists and their clients. Studies have demonstrated that rapport is one of the few factors reliably significant in psychiatry.

On May 22, 1986, the DEA's Administrative Law Judge Francis Young in a two-part, 90-page decision recommended that the compound be placed in Schedule III. "The administrative law judge finds and concludes," he wrote, "that prior to its being proscribed effective July 1, 1985, MDMA did have a 'currently accepted medical use in treatment in the United States.' It is not presently being used in treatment because it has been proscribed." The judge itemized 100 "findings" from the testimony that had been received. On the question of abuse, he declared that "The evidence of record does not establish that, in the context of §812, MDMA has a 'high potential' for abuse."

The DEA issued several objections to the judge's decision, including a charge that he was "biased." Richard Cotton issued a sharp rejoinder. "The DEA staff has reacted with knee-jerk hostility to what are serious and real medical issues. Moreover, their position that the evidence in this record warrants a finding that MDMA has a 'high' potential for abuse is—frankly—preposterous . . . The evidence doesn't exist . . . Nevertheless, the DEA staff is determined to place MDMA in Schedule I, come hell or high water, and it isn't going to let the facts, law, or even common courtesy to the Administrative Law Judge stand in its way . . ."

One of the litigants, Lester Grinspoon, decided to appeal the DEA administrator's decision to the First District of Appeals. Richard Cotton agreed to continue as attorney on the case.

Recent Events

Thus, by mid-1986 MDMA was a Schedule I drug and no longer hot media copy. While its use continued underground and legal battles raged, the first books on the subject were published, and a major conference held.

Through the Gateway of the Heart by Sophia Adamson, a collection of first-hand experiences about 44 individual and ten group experiences, was published about this time. Some of my favorites of these experiences are excerpted in Chapter IV.

The Haight-Ashbury Free Clinic sponsored the first major conference open to the public focusing on this newly popular feeling-enhancer called "MDMA: A Multidisciplinary Conference," which presented most of the important figures in the MDMA scenario. Held May 18 and 19, 1986, in Oakland, California. The conference was well attended and especially by a large percentage of individuals in the helping professions.

Perhaps the highlight of the conference was Dr. Rick Ingrasci's passionate appeal to continue his therapeutic work with MDMA. Chemists Shulgin and Nichols were there to present chemical and pharmacological aspects. James Bakalar, George Greer, and Joseph Downing, three litigants in the MDMA scheduling challenge, gave accounts of their work. Ron Siegel tried to show he wasn't a bad guy by playing up the favorable aspects of his research. From the same side of the question, Frank Sapienza, a DEA spokesman, presented that agency's point of view. A sexual panel at the end, which was surprisingly dull despite the lively topic, concluded that MDMA was a "hug" drug rather than an aphrodisiac.

THROUGH
THE GATEWAY
OF THE HEART

Accounts of Experiences with MDMA
and other Empathogenic Substances

Compiled and Edited by
Sophia Adamson

Through the Gateway of the Heart *is an excellent book of vivid first-hand MDMA experiences.*

June Riedlinger, D.Pharm., testified at the MDMA hearings.

JOURNAL OF PSYCHOACTIVE DRUGS

A Multidisciplinary Forum

MDMA: PROCEEDINGS OF THE CONFERENCE

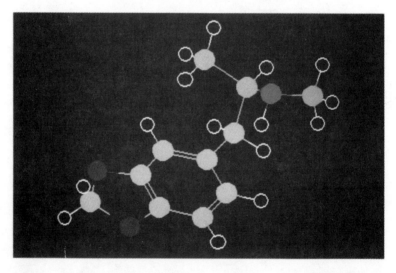

VOLUME 18   OCTOBER-DECEMBER 1986
NUMBER 4 $20.00

THEME EDITORS:
RICHARD B. SEYMOUR
DONALD R. WESSON, M. D.
DAVID E. SMITH, M. D.

EDITED BY:
E. LEIF ZERKIN
JEFFREY H. NOVEY

"Proceedings" of the MDMA Conference in May, 1986 was published in Vol. 18, No. 6 of the Journal of Psychoactive Drugs.

A monograph entitled *MDMA* by Richard Seymour of the Haight-Ashbury clinic was given to all attendees. It provided the first, albeit brief, overview of the topic in book form (available from Haight-Ashbury Publications, 409 Clayton St., San Francisco, CA 94117, $17). Papers from the conference were collected into a special edition of the *Journal of Psychoactive Drugs* (October-December, 1986). There were articles by many of the presenters at the conference which contributed greatly to the volume of published academic information about MDMA.

With the exception of an occasional local newspaper feature or small magazine story, MDMA would now almost seem to have never existed. There was no evidence of a massive groundswell of use or abuse. Few people were arrested for it or appeared in hospitals suffering from its effects.

The DEA promised researchers that it would facilitate research for those qualified after scheduling, but researchers instead found that it was virtually impossible to get a research protocol approved; scientific studies became impossible.

Then, in September 1987, the First District Court of Appeals issued a decision. It ordered the DEA to vacate the ruling placing MDMA in Schedule I on a permanent basis.

The First Circuit Court ruled that the DEA did not lawfully follow the correct criteria for deciding whether or not MDMA met the standard for "currently accepted medical use in treatment in the United States" and for "accepted safety for use . . . under medical supervision."

With the ball back in its court, the DEA was only required to reconsider the matter administratively. The DEA decided quickly that they had been right all along and placed MDMA back again in Schedule I, effective March 23, 1988.

It appears now that this ruling will stand for a long time. Those who have fought so long against the disproportionate power and financial resources of a DEA seemingly adament in its desire to keep MDMA a scheduled drug may now give up. There is still legal recourse but every legal victory the researchers have seen has been negated by the fiat of the DEA Administrator.

And just as I am completing this saga, I am surprised to discover a story titled, "Ecstasy: Poll Says 40% at Stanford Have Tried It" on the first page of my morning newspaper, the *San Jose Mercury News*. Also today, a story with the same theme in the *San Francisco Chronicle* by Science Editor David Perlman reports:

More than a third of all Stanford University undergraduates may have used the illegal drug called Ecstasy
according to a student poll that was reported yesterday.

In a letter in the current issue of the *New England Journal
of Medicine,* Dr. Stephen Peroutka, a Stanford neurologist,
reported that 39 percent of 369 students interviewed in a
random sample said they had used the drug at least once.

Some said they had taken it 25 or more times, but four to
five times was the average use, the poll showed.

The survey [was] conducted anonymously under Peroutka's supervision by two undergraduates who stationed
themselves on Stanford's "White Plaza" to conduct their
interviews.

One last bit of recent media attention, "Tune In, Turn On, Go to the
Office Late on Monday," appeared first in *Rolling Stone* and was recently
reprinted in P.J. O'Rourke's humorous collection, *Republican Party
Reptile.* O'Rourke tries to describe the mental effects of MDMA:

If you think of your mind as an animal act (as good a
metaphor as any, since bugger-all is known about how
psychoactive drugs work in the brain), Ecstasy gets right in
the cage and bangs the anxiety bear on the head with a lead
pipe. It has the big cats up on their footstools making like
stuffed carnival prizes. And it brings on the adorable fox
terriers in party hats who walk on their hind legs, ride on
ponies, and jump through the hoops for four hours.

And so, hopefully with a smile, ends my story of the discovery and
history of the key to the door to that other room I pictured in the
beginning of this chapter. In the following chapters we will explore the
dimensions of our "alternative state of consciousness" room as well as
the use and possible future of this new key to ecstasy.

Chapter II.
What is an Empathogen?

"To empathize is to see with the eyes of another, to hear with the ears of another, and to feel with the heart of another."
—an anonymous English author, quoted by Alfred Adler

Enhanced communication and the exploration of interpersonal relationships are two of the most talked-about effects when MDMA comes up in conversation among users. Indeed, it is this quality that must distinguish MDMA and its chemical relatives from all other drugs. True, amphetamines and cocaine push people to talk a lot, but oftentimes meaning gets lost in the chatter. Also, these stimulants orient the individual toward self-absorption. Talking becomes a means for self-gratification rather than a means of communication.

The unique quality which the MDMA family possesses can be summed up in one word: empathy. In fact, Ralph Metzner, Ph.D., Dean of the California Institute of Integral Studies, proposed this new name for a group of substances in an address at a 1983 Conference at the University of California, Santa Barbara, on "Psychedelics and Spirituality."

> Another group of drugs are the phenethylamines, of which MDA is an example. Instead of calling these "psychedelic drugs," I'd like to suggest the name "empathogenic." Empathogenic means "empathy generating." Everyone I've mentioned this name to thinks it is a good one. These drugs don't produce visions as LSD does. They don't produce multileveled thinking or objectivity toward your mind as LSD and the psychedelics do. They generate a profound state of empathy for self and other in the most general and profound terms. A state of empathy where the

feeling is that the self, the other, and the world is basically good, is all right. This state can be referred to as the ground of being, the core of our being, a still point of our being.

Then individuals using these substances in therapy can look at their own problems from the standpoint of stillness and empathy. They are able to do changework on themselves very rapidly, compared to ordinary therapy.

In this chapter, we will explore the interpersonal nature of the MDMA experience. This dimension can be characterized as "empathetic," but will also touch on other aspects of the interpersonal encounter, including those of a sensual or sexual nature. The next chapter will discuss the intrapersonal facet of MDMA sessions, perhaps best represented by chemist David Nichols' term "entactogen."

What is Empathy?

The modern use of the word "empathy" began in 1897, when the German psychologist Theodore Lipps published a description of a process of aesthetic appreciation. Lipps used the term "Einfuhlung" to designate losing self-awareness on the part of an observer, as that individual views a painting or a piece of sculpture. Further, it denotes the tendency of the subject to fuse with the object that absorbs his attention. Edward B. Tichner, a psychologist at Cornell University, then introduced "empathy" as the English equivalent for the original German.

According to Katz, who wrote a book on the subject, "When we experience empathy, we feel as if we were experiencing someone else's feelings as our own. We see, we feel, we respond, and we understand as if we were, in fact, the other person."

Empathy means projecting our imagination outside of ourselves and into another human being. The experiencing of someone else's lifespace might be either physical, imaginary, or perhaps both.

At this juncture, you might be asking, "Empathy. So what? What is the value of taking a substance that can help you go beyond yourself and understand how others think and feel?"

Empathy is both enjoyable and a useful experience for healthy people to have. And for those emotionally troubled, it can be invaluable as therapy. In the direction of growth and self-actualization, the experience of empathic contact offers the strengthening, deepening, or revitalization of existing relationships as well as helping in the formation of new ones. In terms of therapy, empathy promises to teach people to be kind to each other, to love one another rather than hurting.

When the emotionally troubled can get out of their selfish way of seeing the world and stand, for a moment, in someone else's shoes, they begin to realize that others have feelings and senses and hurt, just like they do. This may go a long way to deter them from violence. In a world of too little love and too much violence, any tool accentuating the former and reducing the latter is worth looking into.

Empathy also helps in healing close relationships. MDMA has been used in family therapy and marital counseling to get meaningful dialogue going within these relationship systems. MDMA sessions enhance intimacy and allow for direct, loving, and honest verbal communication of what is real and meaningful between participants.

Using Empathy in Couples Therapy

The following is an account of the work of Rick Ingrasci, M.D., a Massachusetts physician from an article by Joe Klien in *New York* magazine:

> The first time Bob Littlehale took MDMA under Dr. Rick Ingrasci's supervision, he experienced an epiphany. "I realized I loved my wife. It was an enormous feeling, it just filled my chest," says Littlehale, a prominent Massachusetts physician. "I had to pick up the phone and call her. She was at work. It didn't matter. That feeling has stayed with me, too. This stuff won't let you forget."
>
> "He sounded totally joyful," Marie Littlehale recalls. "He didn't sound spaced or dull or buzzed. It was pretty embarrassing."
>
> Though they have taken the drug together since Bob's epiphany, the Littlehales are quick to point out that MDMA hasn't saved their marriage; after 24 years of sporadic warfare, it may not be salvageable. "But it *has* made us a lot more aware of the issues at stake," Marie says: "It's really helped us along in the process of figuring out what we want to do."
>
> "It's not a panacea," says Ingrasci. "It won't save an unhappy marriage. But I've found it to be incredibly useful."
>
> Before he learned about MDMA from friends, Ingrasci had built a sucessful practice based upon holistic principles, emphasizing the connection between mental and physical health. He was especially well known for his work with people who suffered from serious illnesses. In fact, Marie

Littlehale first visited Ingrasci because she believed she was in the early stages of multiple sclerosis. The Littlehales spent about a year in therapy, individually and as a couple, before Ingrasci suggested MDMA as a possibility.

"I took the drug before I ever gave it to a patient," Ingrasci says, "and experienced an enormous sense of well being. I don't recommend it for everyone. Usually, I'll simply suggest that mind-altering drugs are one of several possible therapeutic strategies. If the patient decides that's what he or she wants, I'll set a two-hour appointment for them and tell them to come an hour early to take the drug."

Ingrasci gets his MDMA from a local chemist. He administers it either in capsules or as a powder mixed in fruit juice.

Rick Ingrasci, M.D., a Boston therapist who used MDMA in couples-therapy.

"About half the people have a mild physical reaction—tightened jaw, nausea, some anxiety—that passes pretty quickly," he says. "Usually people just begin to talk, but sometimes I have to take a more active role. With couples especially, sometimes they'll just want to sit here hugging or rocking back and forth, and I'll have to say, 'Listen, folks, let's get down to the business at hand.' "

Drug-Induced Empathy?

A question that may arise here is: *How can a drug, a chemical substance we ingest, produce a human experience like empathy?*

Drugs don't produce experiences; experiences occur in people. MDMA changes the electrochemical balance of the brain in ways that we still do not understand. By changing the chemical nature of the brain, it is as if a neurological switch were flipped, providing the MDMA user with access to an alternative state of consciousness. As the individual "opens up" in this new state, normal defense patterns are temporarily suspended. In this changed mental posture, empathy and some other characteristic experiences are more likely to occur.

This whole area of "drug affects experience" touches on a complex philosophical and psychological issue: the relationship between the brain and the mind. Without attempting to answer this classic enigma, we can see that what empathogenic compounds do is trigger the experience of empathy within the body/mind (whether body and mind are the same thing or just interrelated).

Experimental Empathy

Empathy and its effects were a major theme in the report on the first formal study of MDMA with humans carried out by George Greer, M.D., and Requa Tolbert, R.N. George Greer is a psychiatrist and Requa Tolbert is a psychiatric nurse. They are married and living in New Mexico, and they used MDMA in his psychotherapy practice until it was criminalized. New Mexico and California are two states that permit a physician to use drugs in their treatment of patients, and allow them to manufacture the drugs themselves with peer review and informed consent.

In order to investigate the effects and usefulness of MDMA, Greer and Tolbert initiated a pilot study of MDMA. They used none of his private-practice patients in the study, instead recruiting a group of 29 subjects by word of mouth. The group was screened to exclude serious psychiatric problems and contraindicated medical problems, such as heart disease or hypertension. They reported on this pilot investigation in the *Journal of Psychoactive Drugs,* Oct.-Dec. 1986:

> Every subject experienced some benefit from MDMA during his or her session. 27 felt closer and more intimate with anyone present. (The other 2 had solo sessions.) All 21 subjects who had sessions in couples or groups experienced more closeness and/or enhanced communication. And 2 found it easier to receive compliments or criticism . . .

> It is our general conclusion that the single best use of MDMA is to facilitate more direct communication between people involved in a significant emotional relationship.

> Not only is communication enhanced during the session but afterward as well. Once a therapeutically motivated person has experienced the lack of true risk involved in direct and open communication, it can be practiced without the assistance of MDMA. This ability can not only help resolve existing conflicts but also prevent future ones from occurring due to unexpressed fears or misunderstandings.

> Regardless of the mechanism, most subjects expressed a greater ease in relating to their partners, friends and coworkers . . .

Norman Zinberg, associated with the Harvard Medical School, did a study of MDA as an investigation "in the phenomenology of consciousness change." His results were published in the January-March 1976 issue of the *Journal of Psychedelic Drugs.*

In his study, Zinberg conducted several MDA sessions. He observed, "It was the repeated insistence on empathic awareness of what others were thinking that fascinated me."

Zinberg attempted to find out more about the nature of these empathic sensations by speaking separately to individuals having such experiences. He reports:

> Not only was such a subject able to describe what others felt, e.g. "A is thinking of sex with B" or "I think C is lost in childhood memories or relationship fantasies with D," but they were also able to say something about the cues that led to these conclusions—the way somebody was now dripping with sand, the way the lines formed around a person's mouth, or the way somebody looked over there and then looked away. These cues were ones that I had not noticed until they pointed them out to me. However, the intermediate steps of how the cues led to the final, empathic

awareness could not be articulated. I would then drift over to the person we had been talking about, and asked what s/he had been thinking. 80% of the time my original respondent was correct down to quite fine details.

It was remarkable, and it gave me some sense of why some psychedelic users of my acquaintance had become interested in ESP. I asked particularly if this empathy was based on unusual closeness to a particular individual and usually was told, "No." In fact, it seemed to operate as effectively with people who were not close friends.

Although Zinberg's study was done with MDA, it is relevant in our discussion. I pointed out earlier that MDMA is a more pure empathogen than MDA; if MDA displays empathic effects, certainly MDMA would. I will use data from MDA studies thoughout this book. It should be understood that the two substances do not have identical effects. They are, however, in the same family. Information gathered from any of the members of this family are true, to a certain extent, about all of them.

Opening Up

The initial phase of the MDMA experience occurs about half an hour after ingestion. This period leasts from 15 to 25 minutes. It is at this time that the sensation of "opening up" is felt most intensively. Claudio Naranjo, M.D., author of *The Healing Journey* and an early collaborator in Shulgin's research, called this period of the session, "a brief, fleeting moment of sanity." During this "peak," unexpressed feelings or emotions flow freely between participants in the session. B. Van Alstyne, in "Some Personal Observations on the 'Adam' Experience," states:

> The major effect we have noticed is definitely RELA-TIONAL [author's caps] in nature. That is, the XTC tends to dissolve the barriers people normally interpose between themselves and others, and thereby allows the true feelings present at the heart level to manifest themselves. This is immediately felt when the drug first comes on. Upon looking at your partner's eyes, you will no doubt find that you are seeing her or him in a way that you have never experienced before, or perhaps only rarely or partially. There is a sense of incredible beauty and perfection in your perception of the other person, and a feeling of absolutely unconditional love. Social factors which may have con-

ditioned your love for that person, such as considerations about the person's opinions, goals, habits and particularly FEARS about the state of the relationship or its eventualities, are felt in a completely different light, if at all. Communication becomes effortless, even when worries or differing feelings are expressed. There is the certainty that the other individual is perfect and infinitely beautiful just as he or she is, even when the differences expressed have been issues in the relationship up to the present. IT SEEMS possible ONLY TO BE IN A TRUTHSPACE [note: relating truthfully] during the XTC experience and the truth experienced is the truth that grows out of unconditional love.

Unconditional love refers to the sort of love which places no expectations on the beloved. It comes from a total acceptance of the individual just as they are. It can be seen as an interpersonal reflection of the feeling of the "all rightness of the universe"—seeing just the basic fact of being alive as sufficient for happiness, with all of life's troubles and cares—experienced on MDMA intrapersonally. This experience of unconditional love is similar to the unconditional positive regard that Carl Rogers recommends that therapists have toward their clients.

In fact, MDMA has been consistently heralded by therapists as facilitating an open relationship between therapist and client, in which material that might normally be withheld can be expressed. This makes it useful, for example, in a diagnostic interview early in therapy. Therapists call this sort of approach "breaking down the walls" between therapist and client or "good transference."

A possible use for good transference would be in hypnotherapy. For deep hypnotic trance, it is essential that there be trust established between hypnotist and subject. MDMA may facilitate conditions of trust. This has been corroborated by anecdotal information from hypnotherapists I know, who have attempted trancework using MDMA. They have found that MDMA facilitates induction of trance and results in deeper trances.

Another concept relevant to the special kind of relating we are talking about is what theologian Martin Buber called the "I-Thou" relationship. Buber contrasted the "I-Thou" with the "I-It" relationship. The former is authentic contact between two people in which each respects the other's basic humanness. The "I-It" relationships are interactions which reduce each of the partners to lifeless objects. In the vernacular of the time, it is the difference between "fucking" (I-It) and "making love" (I-Thou).

The MDMA experience often has this same quality of enhanced authenticity. Interaction between partners turns away from superficial issues and toward a deeper "soul" connection, away from "I-It" and toward "I-Thou." David Robinette, a hypnotherapist from Santa Cruz, California, comments on MDMA's effects on relationship formation.

> The therapeutic value of "ecstasy" (MDMA) may lie in its capacity to act upon the heart center, expanding the feeling/sensory/emotional body into higher, more subtle realms. It also acts upon the perceptual center in the forebrain, metaphorically called the "third eye," amplifying perceptions of the finer permutations of human interactions.
>
> This can allow for a deeper bonding process to take place in relationships where for some reason the natural bonding process has been prevented from occurring. Bonding is the capacity to connect meaningfully on a deeper feeling level to one's self or another in a relationship of trust. The bonding capacity is ordinarily developed at birth. It is the secure, trusting relationship with the mother that allows for mature pair bonding late in life. Where that capacity has been co-opted by a system that does not regard the infant as a fully developed human being nor sees the necessity of early infancy and childhood bonding, MDMA holds promise of allowing a healing to take place on those primary feeling levels.

A useful model of what occurs during the MDMA experience can be found in the psychology of Wilhelm Reich. Reich, a student of Sigmund Freud, developed a theory centered on the body and movements of biological energy within the body. In a normal, healthy individual (a rare bird in our society), the energy moves throughout the body in pulsations. In this state of free-flowing energy, which Reich labeled "orgastic potency," a person is capable of expressing emotions and of full sexual orgasm.

However, for most of us, the traumas involved in growing up in our society, with its restriction on sexual expression, leads to blockages of bioenergy in the body, which Reich called "character armor." This muscular armoring occurs in certain parts of the body. These regions of armoring include the pelvis, the chest, and the face. Orgasm is restricted to the genital region and does not extend throughout the body, as in a healthy person. Reich departed from Freud's verbal couch therapy by actually attempting to manipulate the body in order to break down the armoring. It appears that MDMA might also accomplish the same goal. Alfred Scopp, Ph.D., a clinical psychologist, observed, "MDMA is analgesic. The effect of MDMA is to relax the muscular armoring. This results in the bringing to the surface of associated psychological trauma, defense or mental pain, which is then easily released."

To speculate a bit, perhaps the bubble-bursting phenomenon noted above is the process by which repressed negative emotional exeriences from the past can be brought to the surface. On an interpersonal level, this results in direct expressions of previously repressed feelings and a way of behaving which is freed from habitual patterns.

Sexuality

The following is from an article, "Psychiatrists Defend New Street Drug for Therapy" by Miles Corwin in the *Los Angeles Times*, Monday, May 27, 1985.

> [MDMA] is known as "the love drug" on college campuses where it is considered to be an aphrodisiac, but users who were interviewed said it precipitates emotional, not sexual feelings.
> "You can't sleaze with it," said student Jeff Manning, who has taken the drug several times for the "experience." "Your true emotions come out and nobody's going to do something they don't want to do."

The question of whether MDMA is an aphrodisiac is perhaps one of the most fascinating and complex aspects of its interpersonal effects. This is because MDMA both intensifies and changes the nature of lovemaking.

The answer to the aphrodisiac question hinges upon what definition is used for the term "aphrodisiac." James Gawin, in the *Journal of Psychedelic Drugs*, July-Oct. 1978, points to a disparity between the classical definition of aphrodisiac, used in scientific studies, which emphasizes the enhancement of sexual drive or libido, and a broader notion of aphrodisiac, which includes the substance's effect on subjective pleasure experienced in sexual activity, without considering its effects on libido.

When the classical definition of aphrodisiac is used, then no such substance has thus far been developed or discovered. Gawin suggests "expanding the definition of aphrodisiacs to include an effect of a pharmacological substance on the subjective pleasure of sexual experience, independent of any effect at all on what is commonly considered libido or sexual drive."

Once this new meaning for aphrodisiac is accepted, then many psychoactive substances can be examined as such aphrodisiacs. Gawin goes on to describe MDMA's chemical relative, MDA:

> Perhaps the most significant potential for sexual benefit through the use of pharmacologic substances rests with MDA (3, 4-methylenedioxyamphetamine). MDA has gained some underground notoriety as a sexual stimulant of sorts and has also been proposed as an adjunct to psychotherapy . . . It seems to unite some of the sexual enhancement and increased pleasure derived from stimulants with the ability to enhance affect, facilitate self-insight and enhance interpersonal empathy in a manner common to the hallucinogens but without the perceptual alterations, depersonalizations or disturbances in thought which often prevent the hallucinogens from being useful therapeutically or as consistent aphrodisiacs . . . Several authors . . . have noted that MDA brings feelings of deep interpersonal needs and of effects described as "love" to the surface. In all, it appears that the "enhancing stimulant" and "emotional components" of the drug actions may merge in sexual situations to produce an "affective" aphrodisiac.

Several individuals have looked at the relationship between MDA or MDMA and sexuality. Zinberg, in another observation from his previously mentioned MDA study, notes:

> Sexual relationships were possible, especially as the drug waned, but during the height of the high, people described a greater interest in general, diffused sensualism than in specific sexuality, such as intercourse or masturbation.
>
> (Although two subjects told me that when they had taken the drug alone, and only then, did they become sexually preoccupied and masturbate frequently.) This sensualism showed itself in a wish to touch others or to feel the sand, grass, water, flowers or the like. Again, the desire to touch or pleasure in touching was specifically pansexual, and often not connected to everyday closeness.

Another early explorer of the effects of this group of mind-changers is Andrew Weil. Weil, reporting on the effects of MDA in the *Journal of Psychedelic Drugs:*

> Participants may feel very loving toward one another, but the feelings are not explicitly sexual because MDA tends to decrease the desire for orgasm. For many people the experience of enjoying physical contact and feeling love for others in the absence of a specific hunger for sex is unique and welcome.

A third view of the sexual experience, this time specifically about MDMA, is offered by B. Van Alstyne in his unpublished "Some Personal Observations on the 'Adam' Experience":

> Probably the most striking and beautiful experience for us, as well as for many others who have utilized Adam as a relational tool, was the way in which our sexuality integrated into this heart-consciousness. Adam is NOT an "aphrodisiac" in that it has no direct stimulative effect on the sexual channels. In fact, I noticed that my ability—and, more significantly, my desire—to build up a charge of ORGASMIC [author's caps] energy in the usual manner was noticeably inhibited. What does occur, however, is a complete dissolution of any artificial barriers to the expressions of LOVE. So when it FEELS appropriate to express love sexually, there are no BARRIERS TO DOING THIS. (During and after our first trip, we scarcely got out of bed for two days.)
>
> But the QUALITY of the lovemaking experience is what is so completely transformative. There is the feeling of being CONSCIOUS about the fact that you are here, now, making love with your bodies. We found a wonderful and magical naturalness about using our bodies in this way, and especially about using our senses to appreciate our bodies and what we were doing with them. I discovered a completely uninhibited fascination with touching my partner's body intentionally, slowly, consciously, using all my senses wide-open, watching our bodies intently with rapt fascination and wonderment. Again, the incredible ORDINARINESS of it all was quite amazing to me . . .
>
> We both had the feeling that the only factors affecting whether people would become sexually interactive during the Adam experience were 1) their own level of sexual

orientedness with people in general, and 2) the perceived
appropriateness ON A HEART LEVEL (rather than a socio-
cultural level) of being sexual with a given other or others.
More simply, we don't see that there would likely be a lot of
internalized stress or struggle going on as part of this
experience; if two or more people involved in an Adam trip
felt a desire to be sexual with each other as an expression of
their immediate feelings of love and connectedness, they

Andrew Weil, M.D., author of The Natural Mind.

would probably do so quite spontaneously and naturally. The point is that the experience of Adam deletes both COMPULSION and INHIBITION, whichever is present, with regard to sexuality.

In an article published in the October 1985 *Journal of Psychoactive Drugs*—the first survey of MDMA's effects on human sexuality, "MDMA and Human Sexual Function"—John Buffum, Pharm.D., and Charles Moser, Ph.D., summarized their findings.

> It appears that MDMA does not increase sexual excitation or sexual desire in a majority of individuals. For both males and females, MDMA enhances the sensual aspects of sex. This may be due to the increased feelings of emotional closeness.
>
> Almost half of the males and a third of the females indicated that they felt more receptive to being sexual while under the influence of MDMA, but this effect was not paralleled by an increased interest in initiating sexual activity in either the men or the women. While a majority indicated that they would use MDMA as a sexual enhancer, most of the subjects who had used MDMA during sex reported increased emotional closeness. It is curious that a drug, which can increase emotional closeness, enhance receptivity to being sexual and would be chosen as a sexual enhancer, does not increase the desire to initiate sex.
>
> The subjects who were surveyed found that MDMA makes orgasm more difficult to achieve, especially for males. Erectile ability was decreased in almost half the males. No other sexual effects occurred in a majority of subjects.

The preceding observations allow us to generalize about MDMA, its close relative MDA, and their relationship to sexuality, as follows:

Both substances can be classified as aphrodisiacs under Gawin's definition of the term. These empathogens seem to encourage physical contact, yet make that contact less specifically sexual. The need to achieve orgasm is decreased, but the pleasurable feelings associated with body contact are increased. This diminished drive toward orgasm has some interesting correlates. Reich's example of the individual who has reached orgastic potency is one of these. The orgastically potent are not locked into mechanical fixation on their genitals during sexuality. Perhaps, then, experiences on empathogens might provide a model for orgastic potency.

An Oriental parallel to this is to be found in the tantric yoga of the Hindus and the Buddhists. In tantric yoga, the sex partners attempt to lie quietly in sexual union without movement for long periods of time. They are advised to avoid orgasm, instead focusing on the energy exchanged between them. There is an attempt made to turn the sexual act into a sacred ritual. Here, again, the substances we are examining provide an experiential model.

Another common theme found in accounts looking at MDMA and sexuality stress that it demands authenticity in love-making unlike cocaine, alcohol, and Quaaludes which have a reputation as seduction drugs. Some promiscuous gays in the New York bar scene who use cocaine in one-night sexual pickups found MDMA to be an unsatisfactory substitute. Sleazy, selfish motives become transparent under its influence. Because MDMA encourages expression of deep feelings, it is difficult to put up a phony front during the experience.

Is the Experience "Real"?

Taking MDMA so dramatically affects interpersonal behavior that there is a constant question asked of the experience: "Were the expressions of love, caring, and sex real, or was it just the drug?"

This resembles the question posed in the oft-told parable by the Chinese sage Chuang Tsu. Chuang Tsu once had a dream about becoming a butterfly and flying through meadows filled with flowers. He awoke from the dream, and asked, "Am I a man who dreamed he was a butterfly, or a butterfly who is now dreaming he is a man?"

It is this sort of question that compels me to use the term "alternative state of consciousness" rather than "altered state of consciousness." Our ordinary reality or the reality we agree upon by consensus is seen as just one possibility among a wide range of alternatives.

The MDMA experience, in this context, is an alternative state of consciousness in which normal patterns of defensiveness are either changed or vanish entirely. Defenses have evolved for a reason, but can become rigid and dysfunctional. Certainly, to be open and loving is not always appropriate for every situation we find ourselves in.

But the fact that defenses exist in our ordinary consciousness does not make them part of any "real" reality, and another state of consciousness, in which they don't exist, therefore a "false" reality. We could evaluate states of consciousness according to some other standard, such as: "Which state is functional to the individual?" or "Which state is esthetically pleasing?" Certainly a nondefensive, loving state would be judged useful or beautiful by many in such a context.

Of course, compatibility of partners in the MDMA state does *not always* mean that they will continue to get along well in day-to-day life. Timothy Leary, Harvard professor turned LSD guru turned computer software author, tells this story of his own courtship, and issues a warning:

> Barbara and I proceeded to a French restaurant where we consumed a delicious dinner and a bottle of Maison Pierre Grolau. Felt pretty mellow as I remember it. Then Barbara, whose goal in life is to get higher and closer, looked at me with that "let's do it, baby" twinkle in her eye. What could I do? The greatest successes in my life have come from saying

Timothy Leary, Ph.D., didn't want to wait six weeks to marry . . .

"Yes" to Barbara's invitations. We each dropped one pill. I waved to the waiter and made a signing motion. The drug hits me before the waiter returns with the check. ZAP! Barbara looks at me and laughs. "You're so lucky," she sighs. "It always hits you first."

I'm sitting there feeling better than I've ever felt in my life (and I've had some good times). "Look," I say, "you're gonna have to pay the check and take a spoon and ladle me into the cab." Barbara shoots me an envious look. We look in each other's eyes and smile. This is it. We both understand everything. All the defenses, protections and emotional habits are suspended. We realize joyfully how perfect we are

Barbara Leary.

designed to be. Apparently the only thing to do is caress each other.

Well, the experience went on and on. We started to come down after three hours and took another hit. Lots of funny things happened. We chatted away like new-born Buddhas just down from Heaven.

The next day we flew back to Hollywood. Three days later we were married. I should state here that some people have termed X-T-C the "Instant Marriage Syndrome." Lots of people who didn't know each other too well have shared the experience, activated the love-empathy circuits, and rushed off the next day to get married. In some cases, after rose-colored smoke clears, the couple realize that although they did, for a while, share the highest region of love, the practical aspects of their life were not in sync. You might say it's a cosmic summer romance. In fact, it got so bad in Boulder, Colorado that bumper stickers and T-shirts were printed saying, "Don't Get Married for Six Weeks After X-T-C!"

Although Leary advises caution, his marriage with Barbara has lasted ten years, and is still going strong.

Chapter III.
The Uses of an Entactogen

When MDMA initiates begin to describe their experience, the most common themes mentioned are interpersonal. Words and phrases that will probably be sprinkled through an account of the first journey into the world of MDMA include "communication," "love," "opened up," "contact," "deep connection," "empathy," and other terms that indicate that the individual was able to relate better with others.

Yet there is another dimension of the MDMA experience—the world within, the intrapersonal. In fact, still another term for MDMA was coin d by David Nichols, of the Department of Medicinal Chemistry of Purdue University. He calls MDMA an "entactogen," which is a composite of Latin roots that means "allowing for a touching within." This facet of MDMA as entactogen—affecting a transformation of the inner *psyche*—has uses in therapy and problem solving, meditation, self-actualization, and creativity; and will be the focus of this chapter.

Having made the distinction between the *inter*personal and *intra*-personal modes of experience, we should note that the two aspects are intimately linked. When a person feels better about others, he or she also feels better about herself or himself. Feeling better about ourselves is the inward side, and feeling better about others the outward side, of the same experience.

I noted this relationship in the last chapter when discussing what could be called a feeling of "the all-rightness of the universe." There was a concomitant experience in the interpersonal domain—"unconditional love." Here "all-rightness of the universe" and "unconditional love" are like mirror images of each other.

Each reflects the other in its own world. What exactly is this feeling named "all-rightness of the universe"? Well, normally people experience a certain amount of anxiety during day-to-day existence. Worries about various areas of life—money, sex, illness, death, etc.—cloud our ordinary consciousness. We are wrenched from enjoying the present moment by nostalgia and regret about the past, as well as uncertainty about and fear of the future.

Now imagine that the clouds lift and that blue sky breaks out, spreading until it fills the entire half-hemisphere surrounding us. The blue sky is the mind unfettered by problems. Just being alive now seems all that is necessary to be happy. All of those other conditions that were placed on happiness before—a new car, a prettier nose, a job promotion, sex with all those beautiful women/handsome men—disappear. They would be wonderful, but, as Alan Watts once said, "This is it!"

In Claudio Naranjo's *The Healing Journey*, which we will discuss much more fully later in this chapter, another member of the family of drugs of which MDMA is a part, MMDA, also exhibits this "all-rightness of the universe" feeling.

Naranjo states:

> The perception of things and people is not altered or even enhanced, usually, but negative reactions that permeate our everyday lives beyond our conscious knowledge are held in abeyance and replaced by unconditional acceptance.
>
> This is much like Nietzsche's *amour fati,* love of fate, love of one's particular circumstances. The immediate reality seems to be welcomed in such MMDA-induced states without pain or attachment; joy does not seem to depend on the given situation, but on existence itself, and in such a state of mind everything is equally lovable . . .

Much the same affect Naranjo attributes to MMDA can also be said of its close relative, MDMA.

Paradoxical Effects

In his address at the Santa Barbara conference mentioned in the last chapter, Ralph Metzner compares this intrapersonal experience on MDMA to "the ground of being, the core of our being, a still point of being."

During many Ecstasy sessions, there comes a moment of calm, of complete stillness, which some meditators have compared to the headspace achieved during the practice of meditation. Because MDMA is a modification of amphetamine, it is this stillness which drug researchers pointed to when they suggested the class of drugs represented by MDMA and MDA as having a "paradoxical effect." When someone takes an ordinary amphetamine such as dexedrine or methedrine, they most usually become agitated, restless and driven. Yet this class of amphetamine derivatives—oddly, paradoxically—brings a peaceful, relaxed, calm state upon the mind and the body.

Effects on the Individual

In the last chapter, some of George Greer's and Requa Tolbert's pilot-study results relevant to the interpersonal effects of MDMA were reviewed. The following are some excerpts of the study which discuss the main intrapersonal effects observed. The first are "some benefits" reported:

David Nichols, Ph.D., defined a new class of psychoactive compounds—the "entactogens."

All 29 subjects reported positive changes in their attitudes or feelings. Sixteen felt warmer, fresher, more alive, euphoric, or loving feelings. Ten mentioned greater self-confidence or self-acceptance, and ten felt their defenses were lowered. Two of these and five others reported undergoing a therapeutic emotional process. Five participants said they had a transcendent experience. Five noticed having fewer negative thoughts or feelings. Three felt more self-aware or self-grounded, and two reported feeling blessed or at peace.

Twenty-two subjects reported some cognitive benefit: an expanded mental perspective, insight into personal patterns or problems, improved self-examination or "intrapsychic communication" skills, or "issue resolution." Five subjects used a low dose (50 mg) to facilitate their creative writing abilities—four in a group session and one alone. All found it quite useful. Five subjects reported clear cognition or enhanced presence of mind. ("Subjective Reports of the Effects of MDMA in a Clinical Setting," Greer, Tolbert, *Journal of Psychoactive Drugs*, Oct.-Dec. 1986.)

Every subject but one in Greer's study had some purpose or goal, other than curiosity and most had multiple reasons for taking the drug. Greer reports:

Sixteen of these [participants with goals] felt their purpose was completely realized, Four reported significant progress made toward all their goals, and seven felt that

George Greer, M.D., and Requa Tolbert, R.N., the MDMA therapy team that authored the first clinical study.

some of their goals were realized while others were not . . .

Eighteen (18) subjects described positive changes in their mood or emotional state, lasting from several hours to several weeks, and averaging about one week. Fourteen (14) reported having more good feelings. Five of these specifically mentioned euphoria or improved mood, and four mentioned an increase in energy. Eleven (11) reported feeling more relaxed, calm, detached, serene, and/or less anxious or agitated . . .

Twenty-three (23) subjects reported positive changes in attitude lasting from a week to a follow-up time of two years. Again, the average duration was roughly a week . . .

Sixteen (16) subjects reported belief changes that persisted after sessions, but rarely did two report the same specific change. All changes resulted in a more positive belief about themselves, individually or in their relation to others or to the world in general.

Implications of Early Research with Related Compounds

As these benefits and positive changes suggest, MDMA has important uses in psychotherapy. Before going on to examine the results of the Greer study with respect to its therapeutic implications and descriptions of specific cases, let us consider why the MDMA experience is useful therapeutically. Not much has been published examining this question. Only one book to date has addressed the therapeutic uses of Ecstasy—published in 1974, *The Healing Journey* by Claudio Naranjo, M.D.

I feel quite lucky to have had Claudio Naranjo as teacher of a class that I attended in Humanistic Psychology, when I was an undergraduate at the University of California, Santa Cruz, where Narajo was a visiting professor in the Spring of 1978.

Naranjo is a Chilian psychiatrist with a Ph.D. in mathematics and a background as a concert pianist. *The Healing Journey* is about Naranjo's use of four drugs—MDA, MMDA, harmaline and ibogaine—in his psychiatric practice. He calls the first two "feeling enhancers" and the latter two "fantasy enhancers."

Although the book was completed in 1970, the work within it was carried out between 1965 and 1966 in Santiago, Chile, which is also where the MDA chapter was written and the book on the four drugs conceived. At the time, Naranjo was a research psychiatrist at the pioneering Centro de Estudios de Anthropologia Medica at the medical school of the University of Chile.

MDA, MMDA and MDMA are all members of the same chemical family. Perhaps one of the most fascinating facets of what we have learned from studying these substances is that although there is a strong family resemblance in their main effect, each also differs in a clearly distinguishable fashion; so an individual who has had several experiences with each can tell them apart. In the Appendix to this book, "The MDMA Family Tree," we will find that this variation has been named the "structure-activity relationship" and described in a paper by Alexander Shulgin published in *Nature*. In it, he shows how differences in mental effects can be predicted by varying the actual chemical structure of the molecule. This relationship will also have implications when we explore the future of these compounds in understanding and controlling the human nervous system.

Naranjo wrote that the family of "phenylisopropolamines, [i.e.] MDA and MMDA, is characterized mainly by its effects of feeling enhancement, sharpening of attention, increased fluency in associations and communication."

From there, Naranjo goes about distingushing between the two drug relatives.

MDA, according to the Chilian psychiatrist, is a "Drug of Analysis." By this, he means that its therapeutic effect is brought about by exploration of past events, similar to psychoanalysis, which emphasizes the effect of early childhood events upon the individual. Naranjo says of MDA, "regression occurs so frequently and spontaneously that it can be considered a typical effect of the substance, and a primal source of its therapeutic value."

In contrast, "MMDA and the Eternal Now" is the chapter title given the other feeling enhancer. He says of the peak experience sometimes elicited by this substance:

> It is possible to speak of both individuality and dissolution, but these are blended into a characteristic new totality. Dissolution is here expressed in an openness to experience, a willingness to hold no preference; individuality, on the other hand, is implied in the absence of depersonalization phenomena, and in the fact that the subject is concerned with the everyday world of persons, objects and relationships.

The MMDA peak experience is typically one in which

the moment that is being lived becomes intensely gratifying in all its circumstantial reality, yet the dominant feeling is not one of euphoria but of calm and serenity.

Naranjo's therapy with MMDA appears to utilize two principles. First, he takes advantage of the mood of serenity and detachment brought on by the drug to explore his patient's problems. He states, "As different as spiritual detachment and healthy psychological functioning may be, I believe that the latter may gradually develop in the presence of the former, making the therapeutic implication of such a peak experience an indirect one. One of the ways in which a mood of serenity may result in further change is that it increases the possibility of insight, much as an analgesic can permit surgical exploration of a wound."

A second principle, used in MMDA therapy, is the hope that the new modes of experience achieved on MMDA will carry over into the patient's life in the days after the actual end of the session. Naranjo suggests:

> The state of mind reached under the facilitation of MMDA is not something that simply lasts for a given time and then is lost, but one that may be *learned*. Once a person has used his mind in that way, he has easier access to the same way of functioning. And in this learning, whereby a desirable attitude can be "remembered" not only intellectually but *functionally* (as the movements of writing and walking are remembered when we do them) after it has been adopted once, lies, I believe, one of the major justifications for the edification of an artificial peak experience. This could be likened to the guiding hand which holds that of a child to show him how to draw a letter, or those of the practitioner in M. Alexander's system, showing a person how to stand or sit so that he can feel the "taste" of rightness, or, in the conception of Mexican shamans using *peyotl*, the guiding hand of God. Once in possession of such discrimination or knowledge, it is up to the individual to remember it and put it into practice.

In each of Naranjo's two chapters, case histories and session reports of patients are discussed to demonstrate the relations between drug action and therapeutic effect. In the use of MDA, Naranjo employs a psychoanalytical approach to the therapy, with its emphasis on remembering and working through of childhood traumas. With

MMDA, he uses the more existential Gestalt therapy, which emphasizes a centering in the present moment. In both chapters, some remarkable breakthroughs in neurotic conditions are described.

How does MDMA compare with these other family members? First, Adam is shorter-acting than the other two. MDA lasts for 8-12 hours and MMDA somewhat shorter, but MDMA lasts only 3-4 hours. Like MMDA, MDMA is a drug that brings the user into the "here-and-now." But it also can act like MDA, to bring forth repressed experience from childhood. MDMA resembles MDA in its stimulation of speech. In fact, it is more of a stimulant than MDA and increases verbal fluency much more. In addition, the peak experience that occurs on MDMA is sometimes euphoric, thus differing from the "serenity and calm" of MMDA.

When Alexander Shulgin performed his 1976 research on the effects of MDMA on humans, Claudio Naranjo was the research psychologist on Shulgin's research team. This was described in *New York* magazine:

> "The effect (of MDMA) was much different from MDA," recalls Dr. Claudio Naranjo, who worked closely with Shulgin. "MDMA was not hallucinogenic. It seemed, too, less toxic than MDA. When administered in small doses, there were few, if any, side effects; a slight tightening of the jaw, some nausea, and those would pass in the first half-hour. And the psychological effect—it was completely different from any other drug. It was like a brief, fleeting moment of sanity."

Another unique aspect of MDMA is its emotional dimension. It is often described as "heart-opening." As I mentioned earlier, MDMA is the most purely empathogenic of this family of substances.

MDMA can induce an experience of the "eternal here-and-now" as MMDA does, and can also help in the uncovering of repressed experience from the past. Thus, MDMA-assisted therapy can combine elements of both techniques.

For example, a woman who was raped is under the constant duress of the memory of the act. She is given MDMA and suddenly feels wonderful, freed from the negative condition she has been in. This can be used by the therapist in two ways. First, the therapist might talk to the woman about the circumstances surrounding the rape while she is in a trouble-free frame of mind. This would allow her to work through the painful memories without repressing them.

In addition, the woman is given, during her glimpse of an alternative state of consciousness, a chance to see what life is like without fear. This experience of pain-free existence can be remembered by the woman in her post-session life and employed to free herself from the trauma.

Uses in Psychotherapy

The following is a real-life account of a trauma victim's psychotherapy, published on the front page of the *Los Angeles Times*, in an article by *Times* staff writer, Miles Corwin:

> San Francisco—Kathy Tamm was walking to her car following a meditation class in Menlo Park when she was abducted, taken to a wooded area, tied up, beaten and then tortured for several hours. For six months after the incident she underwent intensive therapy, but she showed little progress.
>
> She had terrible nighmares. She was terrified to leave the house. Every unexpected noise, every shadow assulted her senses and brought back visions of the attack.
>
> Tamm, 39, a San Francisco marriage and family counselor, said she was "suicidal, at the end of my rope." As a last resort, Tamm and her psychiatrist (Dr. Joseph Downing) decided to treat her with MDMA, an experimental drug that some psychiatrists had found effective with traumatized patients.
>
> "I've taken it several times, and each time I felt a little less fearful," Tamm said. "The drug helped me regain some measure of serenity and peace of mind and enabled me to begin living a normal life again.
>
> "For the first time, I was able to face the experience, go back and piece together what had happened. By facing it, instead of always burying it, I was able to sort of slowly discharge a lot of horror."

In addition to traumatic conditions such as rape, MDMA has been employed for its psychotherapeutic value in a number of other applications. These include substance abuse (addiction to cocaine, alcohol, etc.), phobias, psychosomatic disorders, neurotic disorders such as minor depression and anxiety, and terminal illnesses. The use of MDMA with terminal illness is illustrated in a case study presented by Requa Tolbert, R.N., and George Greer, M.D., in an unpublished paper in 1985, "The Clinical Use of MDMA":

John was a married man in his early seventies, father to an adult son and daughter. A retired geophysicist and gentleman farmer, he had always been a successful man, in charge of his own life. At the time of his sessions he had been told that he was among the longest-lived survivors to date with multiple myeloma: a mestatic cancerous condition of the bone marrow, which was diagnosed in 1975. He underwent group therapy for two years (predating his cancer diagnosis) to help with depression over family problems. On being diagnosed with cancer, he began therapy in a group format, where he learned deep relaxation, mediation, and visualization to combat his cancer and assist in pain control. He did, in fact, learn to achieve states where his pain was as reduced as it was with narcotics, but still endured much pain.

At the time of our first meeting, his main complaint was "movement pain" from four collapsing vertebrae, secondary to the cancer. Over the past months, the pain had increased, decreasing his physical and sexual activity, ability to go fishing, or to fly his plane. He was also troubled by the depression which usually followed the numerous fractures of his spine which necessitated confinement to bed. The goal of his session with MDMA, which he wished to take with his wife, was to cope with his pain in a better way and to receive help in adjusting to his current life changes.

During his first session, he and his wife remained in separate rooms with eyeshades and headphones on for five hours. John would hum along with the classical music being played. Shortly after his extra dose of 50 mg. of MDMA, he announced ecstatically that he was free of pain, and began singing aloud with the music and repeatedly proclaiming his love for his wife and family. He spent several hours in his rapturous state. Afterwards he said this was the first time he had really been pain-free in the four years since the current relapse of his myeloma had begun. He described his beautiful experience of being inside his vertebrae, straightening out the nerves, and "gluing" fractured splinters back together.

In a letter two weeks after his session, he stated that his pain had returned, but that his ability to hypnotically "re-anchor" his pain-free experience greatly assisted him in reducing the pain by himself. John had four MDMA sessions spaced over the course of nine months: each time he achieved relief from his physical pain, and had greater success in controlling painful episodes in the interm by returning himself to an approximation of the MDMA state. He noted in particular that the feelings of cosmic love, and especially forgiveness of himself and others, would usually precede the relief of physical pain. He describes an episode from his second session:

> "As I was finishing the meditation, time ceased to exist, my ego fell away, and I became one with the cosmos. I then started my visualization of my body's immune system fighting my cancer, of the chemo-[therapy] joining with my immune system to kill the cancer cells in my vertebrae and of positive forces coming from the cosmos to fight my cancer. Gradually I went deeper in to where the feelings of love, peace and joy were overwhelming. Although I had heard the new age music before, many details of the music became clear and more beautiful."

The results of the pilot study "Subjective Reports of the Effects of MDMA in a Clinical Setting" by George Greer and Requa Tolbert, which I have mentioned previously, had some interesting implications for the therapeutic use of MDMA.

There were nine participants in the study who had disorders that are listed in *The Diagnostic and Statistical Manual (DSM III)* of the American Psychiatric Association. This book is a list of psychological problems classified into labeled categories with groups of symptoms for each designated disorder.

Greer and Tolbert report:

> All nine subjects with [DSM III] diagnoses reported significant relief from their problems. Two subjects reported full and lasting remissions: subject No. 17 with dysthymic disorder (followup after nine months) and subject No. 23 with a postabortion simple phobia of sexuality and possible pregancy. All three participants with atypical or mixed personality disorders (Nos. 5, 9, and 13), and the four other subjects with depressive disorders (adjustment disorders with depressed mood in Nos. 6 and 22, dysthymic

[depressive] disorder in No. 17, and atypical depression in
No. 16) reported improvement.

There were some other benefits reported in Greer's and Tolbert's study
with respect to therapy. One was a tendency among participants for
relief of low self-esteem and toward greater self-acceptance. Another
use indicated by the Greer and Tolbert study is in the area of substance
abuse. Half of the participants in this study reported decrease in the use
of mind- or mood-altering substances after their session. One
noteworthy aspect of this drop in substance use is that it took place
without any specific intervention on the part of the researchers.

Thus far, we have discussed treatment of less severe mental
disorders. But what about the major psychotic problems such as
schizophrenia or major depressive episode? Nothing like formal
scientific study has been done, but the experiences of two psychiatrists
with these type of patients, given in testimony during the MDMA
Scheduling Hearings, gives promise that this new psychiatric tool might
have usefulness in these disorders.

The first case is reported by San Francisco psychiatrist Joseph
Downing, M.D.

> F.R., forty-year-old highly successful entrepreneur, was
> referred by his business consultant, a distinguished older
> woman attached to a pre-eminent consulting firm. F.R. had
> several depressive symptoms, a moderately severe stress
> syndrome, and the recurrent and obsessive thought that he
> would do away with himself at age 43 as had his father, also
> a depressive. He had seen three psychiatrists over a period of
> six years for these symptoms, finding the antidepressive
> medication prescribed ineffectual, and offensive in its side-
> effects. Psychotherapy had no effect. "I played good boy and
> bullshitted my way through with them, like I do everybody
> else."
>
> He presented himself as moderately anxious, empty,
> resenting the general opinion that he "had life made."
> Comprehensive examination showed a moderate stress
> syndrome with hormonal depletion but generally excellent
> physical condition. He had taken MDMA previously.
> Although these experiences had not uncovered any of his
> past, he specified that he wished to use MDMA as part of
> his therapy. Knowing its general usefulness in depressive
> states, I agreed.

We arranged a day-long session, which produced a flood of repressed material that emerged into consciousness; he and his sister were very badly battered and traumatized for many years by their father who was repeatedly jailed, placed in psychiatric hospitals, then returned home until he repeated his psychotic behavior. The tragic cycle ended only when the father ended his life with carbon monoxide when the boy was seven. I have rarely heard more vicious details from persons who have survived physically intact and sane.

Joseph Downing, M.D., used MDMA in his therapy practice.

The man is still in treatment, making good progress with the prospect of having a normal emotional life in a few years. I can say, and I firmly believe, that this absolutely central historical material would never have emerged without the use of MDMA in a proper setting, with a therapist he trusted, and with the effect of MDMA, he was able to acknowledge this previously repressed history of abuse.

Philip E. Wolfson, M.D., is another psychiatrist who testified at the MDMA Scheduling Hearings. Currently he is on the staff of Sequoia Hospital in Redwood City, and is awaiting a faculty appointment at the University of California-San Francisco School of Medicine, where he teaches in the Psychiatric Aspects of Medicine Program. For years he has worked with individuals and families experiencing psychotic crises. The following are remarks about a man diagnosed by his previous psychiatrist as "schizophrenic":

> I wish to report . . . the case of a 27-year old male whom I would describe as a "flagrant" borderline individual with long bouts of psychoses beginning in his 25th year. He was hospitalized at that time with symptoms of frank delusions, hallucinations, extreme paranoia, negativism, homophobia, and a fixed persecutory set of delusions centered on an entity called the "force." Of a well-to-do family, this individual was sent to some of the better institutions in this country in the family's quest for help. This man remained largely refractory (did not respond) to lithium, which was given to control manic elements, and to neuroleptics (major tranquilizers).
>
> I first saw him a year prior to this report under intensive family and individual-treatment circumstances on an out-patient basis in San Francisco. His family took up residence in the city in order to work with me. He was extremely elusive, negative, lacking in insight, and extremely suspicious and guarded. He refused to use medication immediately after discharge from the hospital in Texas where he had been confined after having demonstrated his psychosis to the local police there. The parents had brought him by air to San Francisco and we began our work.
>
> The work was successful in allowing him to continue his travels with an increased degree of safety and a reduction in

paranoia. He refused to stay put and intimacy issues [prevented] a positive transference for any length of time or a positive interaction that would allow for reduction of symptoms based on increased trust. A period of re-parenting with the mother's cooperation was partially successful in re-establishing a connection that needed to be bolstered. However, he could not move from a regressed state to a more integrated ego state.

I followed his activities at a distance in consultation with the parents as he used up his money and used up his options. Hospitalizations occurred along the road. Calls from doctors would arrive shortly after he left his protective umbrella. Eventually he ended up with his brother in Denver, quickly wore out his welcome by outlandish activities, and ended up voluntarily admitting himself to a

Phillip E. Wolfson, M.D., used MDMA to treat psychotics.

state hospital after having committed some bizarre acts following their initial refusal to take him in. After several weeks of hospitalization, with his consent and his parents consent, he and they came to California and therapy was resumed, this time with the aid of MDMA.

The first session was profound in the change in this individual's sense of self. Connections of an affectional nature were made with his parents and myself and the openings of trust experience began. For the first time in two years, he experienced a glimpse of a positive self-image and loving feelings that did not panic him. The afterglow of this session lasted several days with intensity, but recognition of that positive self-image has lasted permanently. A second session ten days later consolidated his sense of difference, increased his ability to cope with the delusions that he continued to experience, and enabled him to view himself as potentially redeemable from the "ape" image that he carried of himself.

We are now in the third stage of psychotherapy, there having been a hiatus of six weeks between this last experience and the start of this new work. A considerable distance needs to be traveled. Longstanding characterological issues are in the way. Manic energy and a depressive core remain apparent. Nonetheless there is a greater sense of independence, and an ability to tolerate some degree of aloneness and perceptual-cognitive changes that allow for a new experience of the world. Much remains to be done and MDMA is a vital ally in this work. This man continues on other medications which are suspended for brief periods of time when doing work with MDMA.

Dr. Robert Masters, a psychotherapist who is also a pioneering researcher with mind-altering drugs, points to the effectiveness of MDMA in the treatment of severe depression. As he has observed it, the tendency of MDMA to eliminate negative ideations and emotions extents to even near-suicidally depressed patients. The breaking up of emotional and ideational patterns—also muscular ones—provides the "crack in the iceberg" which then allows the syndrome to dissipate—sometimes altogether and even permanently after just a single session. When only temporary relief is a result, then a second or third session with the drug might be warranted.

As with most other clinical applications, a good deal more evidence is needed to allow anyone to state that this approach is always without hazards. However, limited experience suggests, Masters says, that there may be no better therapy available when the depression is extreme to the point of causing great suffering or even endangering a patient's life.

One last possible use of MDMA that has been suggested, but, as far as I know, not tried as yet, is with autistic children. Two different authorities have independently suggested this: June Reidlinger, in the previously mentioned article in the *Journal of Psychoactive Drugs*, as well as Morris A. Lipton, Ph.D., M.D., Professor of Biochemistry and Director of the Biological Sciences Research Center of the University of North Carolina at Chapel Hill. The latter testified at the MDMA Scheduling Hearings:

> Childhood autism is an essentially untreatable condition in which the child is unable to relate to significant people in his environment. MDMA might be tried with such children, partly because this distresssing illness is otherwise untreatable and partially because the reported effects of enhancing communication among adults might be helpful in autism.

The Quest for Self-Actualization

Although the treatment of mental problems is a most important use for MDMA, Maslow and other humanistic psychologists assert that the lack of pressing mental problems is not all there is to being healthy. There is another dimension to mental health—toward increasing wellness and self-actualization. This is a use of MDMA for the rest of us.

The employment of MDMA for this purpose is not just recreational. The pursuit of self-discovery or of a spiritual path is a valid option for many who attempt to go beyond the shallow consumerism and pop veneer of modern life. These individuals are generally sound, healthy people who have an interest in becoming more creative, more loving, more effective. For these people, there is a questing after answers to the basic life questions—where did we come from, why are we here, where are we going?

Since the beginnings of our species, many human cultures around the globe have used sacred plants for healing and for spiritual insight. Shamans were the specialists of their tribe, given the role of using and administering these indigenous psychoactive substances. The goal in using these plants is to allow for transformation of consciousness, a transcendance of ordinary ways of viewing reality.

When we depart from ordinary consciousness, we find that each of us has our own hell and our own heaven within. Alternative states of consciousness can be difficult, fearful, painful places as well as pleasurable, beautiful, ecstatic regions to experience. In the Preface to *The Healing Journey*, Claudio Naranjo asserts that both realms of consciousness can be useful—"The Healing Power of Agony and Ecstasy." Naranjo favors a balanced approach, which views both types of experiences as "material" which can be used to benefit the individual if handled the proper way and viewed in the appropriate context.

With MDMA, experiences are mostly pleasant, especially for healthy people who would use the substance for self-actualization.

Abraham Maslow, who came up with the concept of self-actualizing people, also suggested that these people evolve through the achievement of what he called "peak experiences." These life episodes provide glimpses of our possible selves toward which we can grow. The experiential model that the term "peak-experience" comes from is the mountain climber who strives to reach the crest of the mountain. As the mountaineer arrives at the top after days of sweat and cold and precarious footwork, he or she looks around, takes a breath, and has—a "peak experience."

Other kinds of experiences like this include the alternative state of consciousness achieved by a long-distance runner in top form, the transcendent sexual orgasm that shatters the barriers between partners, the "aha" feeling we sometimes get when everything seems to be in harmony and working perfectly, and many other times in life when we reach an optimum place of awareness and functioning.

These peak experiences are viewed by those who have them as self-validating and self-justifying. They carry their own intrinsic value and are an appropriate end in themselves. But in addition, they have after-effects which can be therapeutic for the sick (as we saw above), as well as help the healthy toward self-actualization. Maslow, in his *Toward a Psychology of Being*, published in 1962, says of these after-effects of peak experiences:

> 1. Peak experiences may and do have some therapeutic effects in the strict sense of removing symptoms. I have at least two reports—one from a psychologist, one from an anthropologist—of mystic or oceanic experiences so profound as to remove certain neurotic symptoms forever after
> . . .
>
> 2. They can change the person's view of himself in a healthy direction.

3. They can change his view of other people and his relations to them in many ways.

4. They can change more or less permanently his view of the world, or of aspects or parts of it.

5. They can release him for greater creativity, spontaneity, expressiveness, idiosyncracy.

6. He remembers the experience as a very important and desirable happening and seeks to repeat it.

7. The person is more apt to feel that life in general is worthwhile, even if it is usually drab, pedestrian, painful or ungratifying, since beauty, excitement, honesty, play, goodness, truth and meaningfulness have been demonstrated to exist.

The ultimate aim of these peak experiences, according to Maslow, is to become a self-actualized person. Self actualization, as Maslow explains it in his last book, *The Further Reaches of Human Nature*, "means experiencing fully, vividly, selflessly, with full concentration and total absorption ... At this moment, the person is wholly and fully human." Maslow goes on to explain that self-actualization is an ongoing process and that it demands using one's intelligence. It means working to do well at what you want to do, always striving for excellence.

Self-actualized people, according to these theories, have more peak experiences than others. And each peak experience is a transient glimpse of what it is like to be self-actualized.

As we found earlier in this chapter, different sorts of peak experiences are common to specific sorts of empathogens. MDA has its characteristic one and MDMA has another. Empathogens, as a class, have a characteristic peak experience unique to empathogens. Claudio Naranjo, in a personal correspondence, characterized this peak as "earthly paradise in comparison to the heavenly paradise of LSD and hallucinogens of that category."

Each of these different peak experiences is a distinct insight into self and reality. Perhaps when we have mapped out peak experiences of different substances in a methodical way, we will find the particular usefulness of each to therapeutic work or self actualization.

These substances can be thought of, in the context of a quest for self-actualization, as part of a particular path toward growth. Certainly, the drug by itself is not the entire path. Any chemical can only enhance what we already bring to it, the framework that we use it within. Chapter V, "A Guide to the Use of MDMA," will elaborate how our life history and orientation, expectations, session goals, personality, the people we associate with, and our environment all help shape the course of an MDMA session. To stress this point, the experience occurs inside of human beings, and the psychoactive subtance is merely the catalyst for that experience.

How does MDMA act as such a catalyst for self-actualization? By giving us a taste of peak experience, a little model of what self-actualization is like, it gives us something to work toward. Just as an artist might see a painting in one visionary glimpse and then dedicate himself to expressing it in oils, those who experience an MDMA-induced peak experience may work toward self-actualization in their life.

A particularly good example of this is meditation. Earlier in this chapter, I mentioned that in many MDMA sessions, there comes a period when a profound calm washes over the body and the mind, which is perceived as a vivid stillness.

Many meditators spend years before they attain this level of experiencing. An article by Mark Corwin, *Times* Staff writer, in the May 27, 1985, *Los Angeles Times*, states,

> Brother David Steindl-Rast, a Benedictine monk from the Immaculate Heart Hermitage in Big Sur, tried the drug at a conference on the medical uses of MDMA. Steindl-Rast, who was a psychologist before he entered the monastery, said the drug facilitates the search for the "awakened attitude" all monks seek.
>
> "It's like climbing all day in the fog and then suddenly, briefly seeing the mountain peak for the first time," he said. "There are no shortcuts to the awakened attitude, and it takes daily work and effort. But the drug gives you a vision, a glimpse of what you are seeking."

Ralph Metzner and Sophia Adamson, in their unpublished essay, "The Nature and Role of the MDMA Experience," remark,

> One meditation teacher has suggested that the Adam experience facilitates the dissolving of barriers between body, mind and spirit—the same separation within the individual that can be observed in society . . .
>
> Mind and body can be coordinated: mind including feelings has a positive empathic attitude toward the body, which in turn feels accepted and protected. Thus, instinctual awareness as well as mental, emotional and sensory awareness can all function together, rather than one being the focus at the expense of the other. Similarly, Spirit or Self is

no longer felt as a remote abstract concept "above" somewhere, but rather one senses the presence of spirit infusing the structures of the body and images and attitudes of the mind.

Awareness is expanded to include all parts of the body, all aspects of the mind and the higher reaches of Spirit. This permits a kind of re-connecting, a re-membering of the totality of our experience, an access to forgotten truths.

A group consisting of two married couples living together have written an account of a series of MDMA experiences that they shared collectively and as separate couples between July 1984 and January 1985. The following is their evaluation of the value of these sessions in terms of working through psychological issues encountered on their road to self-actualization:

When we began co-living, we had approximately five two-hour group sessions, plus many individual sessions, with a therapist we consider extremely competent. She is a California-licensed MFCC. We have this baseline for comparing non-MDMA therapy and our MDMA experience.

One outstanding distinction is that MDMA has always moved us *immediately* to a psychological clarity and depth unprecedented in our everyday life. We immediately know with total clarity exactly what we want, what we need, and what we are ready and willing to release. We only wish non-MDMA therapy were of such power. Another difference is that we have integrated radical changes following every MDMA trip. In therapy, we felt positive changes, but progress was incomparably slower, less dramatic and often more superficial or subject to backsliding. With MDMA, each event occurs at a depth level far beyond the level at which we previously perceived the "issue," and thus issues dissolve and disappear as we are ready for that. Without MDMA, this occurs only ponderously, and depends on whether the dialogue, bioenergetics or other forms of therapy is "suited" in terms of depth . . . MDMA seems to operate without requiring that a therapist assess issues and whether others have a greater need to work with a therapist, or have issues MDMA cannot reach . . . We have stressed our intentionality and preparation. Those we have talked with who have used MDMA (about 12 people including ourselves) all have evinced intentionality and some preparation; none sees MDMA as a "recreational" drug. Three are practicing therapists and nine are not.

We are not addressing treatment of psychotic or equivalent conditions. We find MDMA an invaluable aid in going from good mental health toward our full emotional, mental and spiritual potential. MDMA is the most appropriate and powerful tool we have found for the purpose of becoming more fully human and spriritual, as sought by transpersonal and humanistic psychology.

Creativity Enhancement

When writers, artists, or inventors talk about the creative source of their invention, often they describe a sudden inspiration or vision or dream; yet this creative process is as difficult to explain for the artist as spiritual experience is for the mystic.

There are myriad examples of this. Some report having pondered a problem for months, and suddenly finding the solution while asleep during a dream, or in a creative flash while doing something completely apart from trying to solve the problem. The placement of the elements in the periodic table of elements by Dimitri Mendeleev, for example, came to him during a dream.

What is common to many of these stories of creative inspiration is that, in some way, the consciousness of the individual was altered from her or his ordinary waking state when the problem was solved. Willis Harman, James Fadiman, Robert Mogar, Myron Stolaroff, and others at the Institute for Psychedelic Research at San Francisco State College gave low doses of mescaline or LSD to 22 volunteers. These were professionals who were faced with technical problems that they were unable to solve. At the time the report was written in November 1965, six of these individuals had found concrete benefits from their experiences in their work. The report gives intriguing accounts of chemically induced inspiration. Oddly, this was the last research project completed before LSD was criminalized in 1966.

Again, as in the reports of creative experience *au naturale*, there was an altered state of consciousness in which the creative act took place. It may be that these states gave the individual greater access to the unconscious, which presumably spins away solving problems we pose to it without our paying any conscious attention. Then suddenly it disgorges the solution into consciousness.

It is often mentioned by people who take major psychedelics and

MDMA that experiences on MDMA are much easier to remember, probably because the state of consciousness accessed on Adam is not as different from our ordinary awareness as the state entered into via LSD or its relatives. Thus, creative experiences while on MDMA would be easier to remember and, perhaps, to use in our ordinary waking world. One possible drawback for MDMA in relation to creativity would be that it does not usually produce visual hallucinations. Visionary artists who use the vivid and colorful excursions into the realm of psychedelia probably would not find similar benefit with MDMA.

However, the experience of the creative writer should be different. You will remember that MDMA usually stimulates verbosity. If this increased fluidity of word production could be applied to the task of writing, then MDMA might prove to be a useful tool for the enhancement of creativity.

This writer (while MDMA was still legal) has used MDMA for this purpose with good results and has heard favorable reports from other writers as well. Greer and Tolbert were the first people to test MDMA on writing creativity somewhat formally.

Five of the subjects in the Greer pilot study used low dosages, around 50 mgs., to facilitate their creative writing abilities. Four took MDMA in a group setting, and one alone.

Greer and Tolbert report, "As mentioned previously, five subjects had low-dose (50 mg) sessions specifically for the purpose of facilitating their creative writing. All reported being satisfied with the results."

Of course, this report leaves us wondering what, indeed, the results were. Still, it is an indication that creativity enhancement might be yet another use for MDMA. Certainly, we can hope that future studies (if these are permitted) will examine this question in a more structured manner.

Especially useful would be a study which used some kind of product, an essay on an assigned topic, for example, that could be used to evaluate the results.

The Inward Journey

So it can be seen that gregarious, extroverted, empathogenic Adam has an inward side. Just as the tendency of MDMA to enhance interpersonal contact can be used, so can the introspective dimension of the experience. Although it is convenient to divide the experience, it must be emphasized that the experience with MDMA is a holistic event. Therapeutic effects reported are based on both internal and external change.

Chapter IV. Some Experiences

I swallowed, hoping to God the source was reliable; that this really was it and not some new amalgamation of PCP or even LSD . . .

Some time later I looked at my watch. Forty minutes had passed. I looked at my friend. Was she any different? Could I see into her soul as had been promised? Was I feeling great empathy and love?

No, in fact we were having an argument. Tired of the park, she wanted us to go home, while I preferred to stay there with the hilltop view of London. My heart was beating a little faster, but I put it down to anxiety.

Another twenty minutes passed. Still nothing. Perhaps the drug was just too subtle for me. Disappointed, I gave in to her wish to go home. We started down the hill. But by the time we reached the bottom I'd forgotten how to be angry. We were having a new conversation, examining our goals in life. What had we done so far? Had we *really* followed those vows of adolescence? Did either of us know what it was like to be close to another human being? For the first time in years I confessed my childhood yearnings to become a marine; she told me she'd wanted to marry Woody Allen. Defences were dropping at a rate it normally took people months to achieve. Suddenly I knew I could trust her with my closest secrets . . . strange because not half an hour before I wouldn't have cared if I never saw her again in my life. I told her this and we both laughed . . .

—Peter Nasmyth, *The Face* (1986)

Question: What are your impressions of MDM?

Well, first I was amazed. The first time I took it was the first time I had actually been able to experience a real sense of hope for all the bad situations going on everywhere. I had always had "We need peace . . .," etc., but I never thought it was actually a possibility. The first time I took it, I thought, "Oh, my God, this might just be the little tool that we need." I think it's so good that a lot of people will probably take it and it will probably have a really major effect upon things in the next five years or so.

It suspends—it takes away all the silly things that we do to ourselves, and lets us act freely and love ourselves. And when we do that, we love everyone else and everything.

Another interesting thing about it—for a long time I thought you really had to take it intelligently and have a big briefing beforehand and think real hard about it, you know? Then I came into contact with a bunch of people who had just taken it with no knowledge whatsoever of any of the philosophical things. And I asked them about it, and they told me the same intellectual things about it as I would have said to them. They figured it out for themselves, which I thought was pretty interesting. I mean, they talked about easier communication.

I don't know—it's a pretty wonderful thing. It's a thing that lets people be their best.

The thing that it helped me with most is self-esteem. Because while I was on it, I would notice things that I would usually do—and I just wasn't doing them. Then, afterwards, I just thought, "Why do that anymore?" It really improved me quite a bit. It made me more extroverted I think.

I think generally it's just going to make people a little bit nicer to each other. It makes people want to be nicer to each other.

Another fascinating thing—the best thing about it is that it's completely accessible later. I mean, you can remember everything, and in that sense it makes it a very good tool for learning. You take it, and you can get better using it, become a better person.

As for other people I've seen using it, I've seen some pretty amazing things! Two years ago, I knew a guy named Bill—and he was like the most down guy. I mean, he's extremely funny—had a great sense of humor—but he's just very cynical and very down all the time. Didn't enjoy anything. And I saw him like two years later—about three months after he had taken MDM for the first time—and he was just completely changed. He was all smiles and cheerful, it was really amazing. This was where I went back to college, and everyone said, "Have you seen Bill? Have you seen Bill? Go see Bill, and you'll just freak out!"

Everyone I've talked to about it, I've gotten a lot of positive feedback. People just tell all these amazing stories about it.

Parents—I know a few people who have taken it with their parents and who have felt incredible about it. My friend Andrea. Her situation with her parents—I guess they're like New York kind of socialites. Her father is a curator, and there has always been a lot of pressure on her. And she just didn't like her parents at all. I mean, just basically there was no communication going on. But she talked them into taking it with her. I was there and it was pretty amazing.

At first they started off talking about things that they had done to each other that weren't good. And then pretty soon—I don't know, I think it was her dad that said it. He just said, "Well, wait a minute. We all know that those things happened, but now we're completely conscious of it so let's just go from here." And since then, it's been a lot better. She's become good friends with her parents—that's what she told me.

The reason why they took it was that there were a bunch of us—friends of hers—and we took it there, in her house. They were home, but they didn't know. And then the next day, they were asking her, "Why was everyone acting so nice? And why was everyone giving people hugs? Why was this going on?" And so she told them. And I guess they were impressed enough by watching us the night before that they decided to do it too, which was pretty wild. That is a pretty difficult point, to convince your parents to take it.

As for difficulties, the only thing I would warn against really is making a bunch of decisions for yourself while you're on it. I think you need to take it, and then experience for yourself what happens, and then think about it afterwards. Because I know one person who took it, and then made a whole bunch of ultimatums based upon how they were feeling, and then when they came down they felt really bad because they didn't really carry through with them. So I think the thing to do is to come down and integrate the whole thing later.

The first day she was just really sort of sad because she couldn't be as great as she thought she could—something like that. But then the second or the third day after that, things started coming back, and it ended up she was quite a bit happier than she had been before. She was pretty sad for awhile.

I've never really seen a failure story, nor people who've felt disappointed. Well, actually, I know two guys who took it thinking that it was a hallucinogen—and so they were disappointed at first, but then after a few minutes they decided they liked it better than that anyway. I haven't really seen anything negative.

With LSD, it provides a really good set to begin a trip with. It takes away paranoia and all that sort of thing.

The times I take it, about the first thing I think is, "Wow, that was pretty important—I'm going to think about that for a long time." I think a lot of people have that—which is good because it keeps it where it has a really low abuse potential. Because the first reaction isn't to take it more and to take it again. But to wait, and to think. It seems like the longer you wait in between, the more incredible it is and the more you learn. That's something of my attitude toward it.

I generally use about 150 milligrams—just one dose. I don't know, taking a whole lot just doesn't appeal to me.

That first experience was an enormous release. That hope was actually possible. The war is over, and I can actually feel like a tiny part of what it would feel like if it was over. It was pretty incredible, this feeling.

Actually, when I first took it, I thought, "Oh, my God, this drug is so incredible!" But since then, having taken it a few more times, I've seen that it's actually the people you are with that makes it incredible. I mean, I pretty much always have a good time, but the depth of the experience depends on who you are with.

It can be really amazing with just one or two or various small groups of people—just really good friends. But the first time I took it was at a fairly large party with a lot of people I didn't know. And I guess that's why the focus was so much on self-esteem, because the whole night I spent just walking around talking to people and meeting them on a really core level, without being any of our superficial selves. Just the real core me. And that was just an incredible feeling—to feel free enough to just do that, without playing games. And to this day, like some of those people—I don't know where they work or what they do, but I feel that I know what they're all about. The heart, or whatever.

If you can get a large group of people who are all into group experience, and sit around in a circle or something, and tell stories or hold hands—well, we had this sort of wild theory that there's some kind of pool of love, and humans are a conduit, and our job is to get it down here to the physical world. So we had one session with that kind of idea in mind. Like the idea was to get as much of the love from out there down here to the real physical world as we could. There were like twenty people with all that same focus. And everybody got much higher than they would have, just because of the group and everybody thinking about the same thing. It doesn't really change the person, it's just really the people and if they act the way they live.

Another thing that's good about MDM is that it's not so wild—or it allows people to access mystical areas within themselves because it's not so scary as the major psychedelics like LSD. I think that's why more people will take it—because it's a lot more accessible than normal, and it helps people overcome their fear of exploring the mysticism within themselves.

—Peter, from Wesleyan University,
quoted in Peter Stafford's *Potentialities of MDM*

All the following accounts appear in *Through the Gateway of the Heart*, compiled by Sophia Adamson and available through Four Trees Publications, Box 31220, San Francisco, CA 94131 for $14.50 plus $1.00 for postage and handling.

Affirming Who I Am, Where I am Going

37-year-old female, graduate student, systems designer

Set: self-exploratory, meditative

Setting: at home, with therapist/guide

Catalyst: 150 mg. plus 50 mg. MDMA

Whatever I can say now only dimly reflects my meeting with myself under Adam's influence. These phrases and ideas from the transcript remind me of some of the highlights:

> There's an opening that wasn't there before . . .

> It's clear that everything I'm about, and everybody is about, is just loving God, and how to do that . . .

> Guide: Does this remind you of your previous psychedelic experience?

> Answer: This is quite different. Much more important. Much more personal, much more relevant. Much easier to carry back and to apply. I've got so much love and

compassion that attaches itself to anything in the vicinity and tries to make it seem appropriate. That's when I forget that what I'm all about is loving God—then I try to put too much into any relationship.

There are still levels of integration to do around sexuality ... There's a real confusion of some kind ... a real split ... Now I'm listening to my inner voice—usually I tend to avoid it . . . Sex can be a way to get closer to God, but I haven't been choosing in such a fashion that it's going to be ... It's been very helpful to be celibate because I can see so much more clearly and easily where my sexual energy goes, where my attractions are.

What is the source of my arthritis? Blocked energies. I need to get in touch with what I want, and let the knowledge lubricate my joints; no more stoppage of anger or love. Let it *all* flow through!

Guide: So love lubricates the joints!

Material about a sexual molestation incident—first reported during a hypnosis session several weeks ago—has had much more meaning for me since I heard the tape of the Adam session. In it I sounded like I was seven years old. The impact comes from the deep recognition of how many ways the event molded my responses to the world around me, in part because of the distrust of my parents that was focused by the incident. Reliving this incident helped to free up my energy and emotions in a number of ways; it feels like this process will be ongoing for some time to come. The understanding and resolving of this incident is not only helpful to me personally; it can be a vehicle for my reaching out to others with similar experiences.

In general, my journey with Adam affirmed who I am, what I am doing, where I am going. The affirmation was experienced through an opening of my heart rather than as a deepening of intellectual understanding, although some of that has also occurred.

The Adam, the set, the setting, and the invaluable input and support of the therapist/guide created a sense of receptivity, wonder, love, and joy. In this set and setting, with empathy for all aspects of life, learning took place whose content was easily and deeply received. My desire to access such learning is great, in part because recalling these lessons elicits the highly desirable state of consciousness in which the learning occurred. The content itself also seems to take on a certain desirability, making it more readily available than much that I have learned under more traditional circumstances. Just writing about the state now, almost a week later, still brings back the sense of wonder, love, and joy that I felt at the time.

My mind tends to scurry about, trying to give form to some of the issues that were raised on the trip, but which still seem incomplete. These include a deeper understanding of my confusion about/dissatisfaction with past relationships, sexual matters, use of alcohol, and future plans for my internship, dissertation, and profession. Despite the attention that these topics get, I am for the most part holding them lightly; I have a clear sense that my journey with Adam is far from over; much is being considered and reflected upon below the surface of my conscious awareness. To the extent that I have addressed these concerns I am very well satisfied with the understandings I have reached.

My actions as well as my attitudes have begun to shift in certain areas. I am able to perceive, receive, and respond to love in a much more open way than I did a few weeks ago. There is greater ease with respect to my dealing with and responding to my sexual energy. I seem to find it much easier to contact my feelings and, as appropriate, to express them.

Perhaps the most important after-effect has been the indwelling experience of affirmation about what I am doing. There is a sense of correctness; even when feeling muddled and unclear about what is happening, I know at a very deep level that I am moving in the right direction. However dark the path, however many shadows may appear, there is a light within me that provides warmth, illumination, and nourishment. My awareness of this indwelling light and my increased clarity of my sense of purpose has been greatly enhanced by my experience with Adam.

My First Sense of Not Being Paranoid

33-year-old male, graduate student

Set: self-exploratory, therapeutic

Setting: friend's home, with one other participant, two guides

Catalyst: 150 mg. plus 50 mg. MDMA

I went into the experience seeking greater empathy for the child I once was and still am, and to know my own emotional needs well enough that I could begin clearly to distinguish my needs from those of others. I intended to explore the feelings I had in early childhood, particularly in reference to being abandoned by my mother at five, in order finally to begin to rid myself of the burden of this depression.

I also wanted to explore the issue of work and financial survival, of how I could work at a job—to earn money—without falling prey to that kind of depression that comes from not having my needs met while serving the needs of others. This has always led to an exhaustion that I have found crippling and deeply discouraging. How am I to earn money and have my deeper emotional needs met?

The issues of emotional differentiation from my mother and of financial solvency/independence are very closely related. The connection was and is a major issue for me to explore.

For the first twenty minutes or so of the experience I felt considerable fear. I felt myself lowering down into a softer and more vulnerable place. I could feel the layers of fear peeling off of my torso and moving away into space. I felt immersed in fear for a time. Soon after ingesting the second capsule, I dropped below the fear and contacted a warm and supportive baseline feeling, a place of support that was totally without fear. This gave me my first sense of what it is like to not be a paranoid, to be like other people.

I did not return to childhood memories as I thought I would. Instead I remained in the present and experienced my issues in condensed form within the context of my current relationship. My issues of fear, financial survival, and emotional dependency all fell within the relationship. I felt very clear that I didn't want to return to childhood, that there was no need to do so. I didn't feel that I was resisting or avoiding anything; I needed and wanted instead to contact the heart and to establish an ongoing connection with it. This did happen.

When I listened to the tape of my experience I discovered that I have indeed been carrying out the intentions I had during the Adam experience. As long as I remain in contact with the heart and am open and honest with my relationship partner, I know that my childhood pain will continue to surface and to resolve itself within a context of healthy mourning, and at a pace that the bodymind will decide is appropriate to my capacity. My partner understands and accepts this.

Now I Feel the Pain as an Ally, not as an Enemy

45-year-old male, writer, arthritis sufferer

Set: therapeutic, to heal arthritis

Setting: at home and outdoors, with partner

Catalyst: 100 mg. plus 50 mg. plus 50 mg. MDMA; series of sessions

During the past three years I have been afflicted with a very painful case of spinal arthritis. Until recently there had not been a day when the pain was not present in most parts of my body. At times it has been so debilitating that I could barely move for days at a time. I have tried a number of prescribed drugs, including Motrin, but none has had the noticeable, long-term effect of easing the pain and the attendant worry, concern, and even depression.

Until recently. In February, 1984, I began to use MDMA, with the idea of easing the constricting arthritic pain. Within only a minute or so of my ingesting the substance there was a noticeable decrease in pain. As the day progressed, I felt my body become less and less constricted. For some months I had hardly been able to walk more than a few feet at a time. Now my body began to move freely; doubts and fears connected with the disease dissipated. I felt a new sense of hope as the "arthritic crystals" appeared to be breaking up, releasing the very tight constriction. For several days the pain, while not altogether gone, was greatly alleviated. For the first time, I had real hope that, with the aid of MDMA, I could reverse the pattern of living in constant pain.

Other sessions followed, with similar results. At times my body felt so free and light that I began to dance and move quickly with a suppleness that I had not known for years. On June 9 I ingested the substance and, again, within a minute, I began feeling elated, and the spinal-arthritis pain that had been great before was alleviated.

On June 23 there was another session. Seven minutes after the initial dosage the pain in my back began to disappear. Then I began to focus in on a healing spot for my arthritis—a point at the lower back that, when pressed, relieved pressure. The muscle constrictions became less and less, and I felt I was really beginning to be in touch with my body, which was in a state of fluid motion. I felt that there was a healing effect surrounding my body. Then I went into a frenzy of movement and I felt the heaviness and constriction leave the body. The hard stiffness in the lower back and knees loosened up.

During this experience time stood still as I looked at Taos Mountain with a sense of Oneness, stillness, quiet. The stillness of the mountains and the mesa became absolute, the only reality, as a consuming inner heat began to burn. I began to focus on a healing spot for my arthritis, an acupressure point at the lower right back, lower chakra. After applying thumb pressure there, I began to expand and I felt love energy from the mountain enter my heart chakra.

I felt a strong connection with space and the planets. I was part of them. My origins lay there. I played Gustav Holst's "The Planets." The music of Mars coursed through me. I was in space again, the Void. I was at home, free. Mars, the bringer of war. I saw conflagration, the history of the world in battle, but it was a cleansing. From the conflagration came a period of understanding, wisdom, and love. Pockets of deep understanding amidst the fire and conflagration.

I felt a tremendous closeness to my friend, and a great warmth. Space surrounded me. Both my friend and I were still there. We were part of space without time. I felt us billions of years in the past and billions of years in the future. We were part of the universe. A great love permeated me. My friend was a large part of it, but so are the world, universe, and beyond.

I focused in on myself and felt like a different person: consumed by warmth, with a wonderful feeling. My body was in a state of fluid motion; muscle constrictions dwindled, and I was in touch with my body.

Touching the earth and reaching for the sky had a healing effect on my arthritis. Warm, free, beautiful. Dancing, free-flowing body movements, a frenzy of movement, then quiet. I felt the body freeing up. I was literally blowing heaviness and constriction from my body. Energy was caught in my throat. The body was really free. There was a sensual feeling about it. The hard stiffness in my back began to loosen up. Energy was running up my spine, loosening the stiffness in the spinal column. I was literally bouncing to the music.

I felt the presence of space beings all around me. They were trying to impart some message, but I was not open enough yet to receive it. I felt that we all have a benevolent tide of extraterrestrial beings surrounding and protecting us. They want us to grow, to expand.

My body felt like it was opening up to something, like a clear channel. Energy attacked the jaw. I felt the beings trying to get through my body.

Still no message, though. I felt the night sky, covered with stars. I felt a real closeness to the *aliveness* of space. The arthritic pain returned; I felt a slight headache as I came down.

An additional session followed one week later. Within ten minutes of ingesting the drug, there was a considerable lessening of the back pain. Later I again went into a frenzy of movement as insights began to appear as to how to begin to control the energy flow within my body. There was a very rapid movement of my hands, and the arthritic constriction in the hands, knees, and back loosened considerably. My body moved very freely, and I felt much better. For the first time I really believed that I could be cured. Somehow I felt I was beginning to integrate a new me, free of pain. The arthritis in the knees and legs disappeared, and the back pain rapidly decreased.

During this experience I moved with awareness into my body. I felt that my body was a temple that I had desecrated. I wanted to let the body go, but I realized that I couldn't. It was telling me that it would continue to rebel. I felt as though the body were ready to explode in all directions. It felt heavy. I was very much in a "the-body-is-not-me" mode. I felt powerful eruptions from the inside. I felt I needed to go through a death experience—symbolically, I hoped, but great fear was there.

Then I felt comfort, a joyous knowing that there was no death. The body became much freer, though the arthritis pain was still there. I began a frenzy of actual, physical self-flagellation: a very rapid movement of hands, a loosening of arthritis in my hands, my knees, and my back. I lost consciousness while going through fast movements. My hands shook and I could not write. I shook violently and began to exhale rapidly; I was close to hyperventilation. My body moved exceedingly freely, my legs in particular. My body really fired up. I could tell that there was still some arthritis there.

Ferocious anger set in, and my hands started trembling again. My legs shook frantically again, particularly my knees, where the arthritis pain is centered. I breathed heavily, and I felt very, very hot. I felt that I was burning up. A feeling of death surrounded me, but a certain uneasiness and fear prevented me from experiencing it. Still, somehow I knew there was nothing to fear.

I suppose what frightened me was the feeling that I didn't want or need the body any longer. Yet I was stuck with it. Still, I was not my body. I felt an unsuspected confusion, but the fear subsided. I began to feel the eternalness of things, unseen things, the *real* things. A roar was bearing down on me, like a freight train. I felt that I wanted to do something dramatic, but I was not sure what. Consuming fire burned me, I felt that my body could burn away. I thought of spontaneous combustion.

There was something present that I had to break through. I felt that this could be the key to loosening completely the arthritic "crystals." I almost lost consciousness in another frenzy of movement and self-flagellation. I beat my breastplate. The energy had loosened considerably, and I felt much better physically. I still felt some remnants of the arthritis and it pissed me off. I was going to beat the son-of-a-bitch if I had to flagellate myself to death. Beating myself seemed to help, and now I was beating myself with a regular broom. Energy had left the breast-heart area and travelled to the back. My friend beat my back and shoulders with the broom. This brought a big improvement, and my energy freed up.

For the first time I really believed that I could be cured. I felt anger at myself and at my body, and I beat myself with a whisk broom. I felt as though I were caught in the middle of a battle, and I was determined to win. I was fighting the bastard and this felt good. The fire was burning me up, consuming me. I felt exhausted, I was coming down. There was much improvement in the body, but each little pain made me angrier at not being able to let go completely.

My body then shook fiercely, and my exhalations became heavy. I lay on the floor and frantically flailed my hands. I grasped the flesh around my midsection and pulled hard. I beat my butt against the floor, hard, shouting as it hit. Energy travelled up the body to the throat. I grasped my throat and shoulder as though I wanted to rend the flesh from my body.

I felt very hot again, and I feel great anger at myself. Damn it! I wanted to flail the body, beat it into submission if necessary. Then there was quiet. I began to feel a love of myself, for myself, course through my body. It was very, very freeing. Some pain was still there, but I was determined to get it. The pain returned to my back, and I sat in it and just felt the pain. Tears came to my eyes. There was a feeling of sadness, and perhaps of loss. Somehow I had to face this and find out what it was. I was fearful because, perhaps for the first time, I saw that I was destroying my body. Somehow that had to be overcome, for otherwise I was in danger. Perhaps that is what the earlier closeness to death was trying to tell me.

The clouds were so still and quiet. I felt a powerful oneness with space; I wanted to leave my body and join that oneness. Death felt closer and closer, and I felt resigned to it, but I drew back. I had to discover what this thing was in me that wished to die. I knew only that my body was not important, but that I couldn't drop it yet. What was this death inside me? Where was the life? Perhaps both were the same. I felt that there was a connection, a kinship between them. I felt I must experience death, symbolically, but I was afraid that it might turn into a "real" death.

I began to try to feel the death experience. I felt great sadness at first, then body movement. Surprisingly the fear left and, briefly, I passed beyond the portals of life. An encompassing, beautiful white light radiating love surrounded me and, for the first time, I knew that death was not to be feared. It was not the end-all. It was a beautiful, new beginning, a rebirthing. My friend gently massaged my back, pushing the energy up into my spinal column.

The pain is not all gone, but for the first time I know that it will be. I feel a renewed sense of life and purpose. I realize now that I had got to such a point where I was either going to let the negativity and pain kill me or else I was going to rid myself of it. I feel strongly that I have chosen the latter, though more work still needs to be done.

Oh, God, the glory of feeling, the love. For the first time I feel the pain as an ally and not as an enemy. I can use it for insight and understanding, and not for self-destruction. I no longer feel the pall, the aura, of death around me. The pain is telling me that it will disappear completely only after I have pushed that invisible "integration" button. Why? The answer comes as tears flow, and the heart, as it expands, seems to *know*. *Using* the pain with love and understanding instead of constantly fighting it with deep animosity will enable me to end it. A "bolt" from my heart caresses my pain and, strangely, I feel a deep love *for* the pain. It is my teacher. By accepting rather than rejecting it, wonderful, soothing clarity about it pours into me.

On July 18 I had an experience very similar to MDMA, without taking the substance. My feelings and actions were very much the same, however. The energy began to move through my body and I began to move—stretching, pulling, shoving, guiding the energy somehow. It did not blast through the arthritic blocks but appeared to dart around, over and under them. I felt great relief. Later in the day I began to breathe in the cool, wet, soothing wind. It had a comforting, even healing, effect on the arthritis. I exposed both my front and my back to the wind, and the effect on the pain and constriction was noticeably good, and healing. For five full days I was almost completely free of the arthritis pain—the longest stretch of pain-free time in three years!

On July 23 I had still another MDMA-like experience without ingesting the substance. Once again my body moved at a rapid pace and the constriction loosened. I seemed almost to push the constriction down and out of the body through the gut area, which became loose and free. Then I began physically to pull the arthritic pain from the lower back. It worked. The energy went to other areas of the body.

Meditation and Remembering the MDMA State

32-year-old male

Set: therapeutic

Setting: at home, with therapist/guide and two friend/participants

Catalyst: 100 mg. plus 50 mg. MDMA

I've waited a week to put my thoughts and feelings down on paper; I am just now coming out of the euphoria of the experience. This past week I have been happy, contented, loving, concerned, easy to get along with, and at peace with myself. I've made a concerted effort (and it hasn't been that hard) to retain the self I was put in touch with.

Regarding the experience itself, I had no awareness of the passing of time. Throughout I was comfortable personally and I was completely at ease with everyone present. The physical sensation was a combination of warm heaviness and mental clarity. I was totally involved in the conversation and interaction with my friends. All inhibitions and defenses were stripped away, so that I was directly in touch with my feelings and my ability to express them. My thoughts flowed with reason and purpose. I felt a genuine warmth and affection for my friends and a strong desire to express my love and concern for them. I was able to say the words I've saved for so long for fear of prying or of hurting them.

The greatest reward was the positive feedback I received, the respect for who I am and what I have done, and this has given me a far greater feeling of self-worth. Seeing myself through others' eyes has enabled me to see more clearly the good that I have to offer, and it is now easy for me to throw off the cynicism I've been hiding behind. I want to build on a new foundation of trust and openness and to accentuate the positive forces within me. I would hate for this to sound like the gushings of a Polyanna or of a recent convert to the latest cult. I honestly feel that I was given a rare opportunity to look inside myself and to gain a profound understanding of who I really am.

I feel that through self-revelation and the comments of my friends I gained a greater awareness of my strengths as an individual. The session brought out my positive aspects and these overshadowed a negative self-image. It was a profound, delightful experience that I continue to benefit from.

The experience has stimulated my interest in self-discovery. I now feel that I have a great deal of potential that is untapped. I have begun reading books of a spiritual and philosophical nature to help develop this potential. I have resumed meditation after a lapse of about six years; it has a calming, centering effect that helps me remember the MDMA state. I hope to continue meditation on a daily basis and go farther into it than I have in the past. MDMA has helped me to find my center while meditating.

I have taken steps to increase my self-awareness, and I have re-evaluated my needs for love. I think my self-confidence has increased due to the improvement in self-esteem.

MDMA Experiences
Have Saved My Relationship

37-year-old male, businessman

Set: enhancing communication, relationship

Setting: at home, with partner

Catalyst: 150 mg. MDMA

What is the experience like? I address this by describing what my partner and I do. Mainly we sit on the floor facing each other and gazing into each others' eyes—MDMA is the eye-contact drug. Physical contact is also maintained, so we have eye contact, hand holding, gentle caressing of hair and face. Skin surfaces and hair feel incredibly soft (a feeling that persists well beyond the four hours). One is impressed with the preternatural beauty of one's partner. No one has ever been so fine, delicate, exquisite, or full; the sense is that she is all and everything, "I have been looking all my life for you."

I believe that the love experience on MDMA is the Divine Love spoken of by the saints. There is suddenly an openness to giving and receiving unconditional care and adoration, one feels privileged and blessed, nor do one's ordinary fears and defenses rise to quelch these powerful positive feelings. Without question the experience is powerfully intense—powerful, but unlike the overwhelming experiences on LSD or mescaline.

This intense love for one's partner leads naturally and immediately into sexual areas. I desire to undress myself and to have my partner similarly unclothed. I enjoy touching my own genitals and having them touched, and I enjoy touching my partner's. But all of this seems to be an aspect of a greater love, and the genital contact has a charge that is little different in character and degree from an exchange of glances or a facial caress. The world, too, is observed as clear and profoundly present—here and now, in Gestalt parlance. A color slide of a wall whose paint is peeling appears stunningly beautiful, as though seen for the first time.

One night my partner and I held each other while we watched the full moon rise over the ocean and reflect on the waves. We experienced closeness while we experienced the wonder of the world. In my experience, sexual consummation—that is, orgasm—is impossible until the end or slightly after the MDMA experience. If a distinction can be made between love and sex, MDMA is a love drug, and not a sex drug. This fact, taken along with its raw power, suggests that one would not want this experience with everyone, and one would not want it every day. Experiences of this significance require time to digest, so intervals of two weeks or more between experiences seem appropriate, the positive nature of the experiences notwithstanding. As this is a drug that feels sacred, one does not want to profane it by mundane usage.

Further comments are called for on the interactive qualities of MDMA, particularly on the verbal level. Conversation emerges spontaneously and comfortably from the contact and closeness. My partner and I were able to express total love for each other, and the level of articulation is reminiscent of classical love poetry: "A loaf of bread, a jug of wine, and thou . . ." The accumulated grievances of a stormy five-year relationship paled into insignificance. We didn't forget them; indeed, we talked freely about them. Yet the unpleasant memories, the laundry list of hurts, had no charge; it was just so much data, like yesterday's weather. And most touching of all are the expressions of gratitude for the gift of this beautiful life and for each other. It is this receptivity and appreciativeness that Catholic mystics call Grace.

A handful of MDMA experiences have saved my relationship. My partner and I had actually broken up, in each others' and in the world's eyes (an announcement had been made). We had been falling apart despite our love for each other, a rich family life, and an adored infant child. Under the MDMA we reconnected with our mutual caring and love, with what was important to us, and with the place of our love in the larger religious and spiritual nature of things. The lessons we learned carried well past the drug session. We have a look that we give each other that instantly takes us back to the caring place. The MDMA experiences are centerpieces of our common mythology. They are shared peak experiences. Sex is better than before.

Peace with Great Energy, Tangible, Expansive

53-year-old male, minister

Set: spiritual exploration

Setting: outdoors, desert/mountain, with two friends

Catalyst: 120 mg. MDMA

On the morning of August 18, in the presence of two others, who also took MDMA, I drank 120 mg. of MDMA. Prior to taking the substance I was handed a rose, freshly cut, and I was made to feel loved, safe, and secure. Even so I was a bit anxious, because, except for a single encounter with a psilocybin mushroom, I had never ingested a psychedelic.

After a few minutes I began to feel numb from my head to my toes. I became frightened and I looked to the rose for reassurance. The numbness gave way to a sensation of great energy. It felt as though every molecule and atom of my body had a powerful motor, and for the first time every one was turned on. The great surge of power and energy was overwhelming and I began to have second thoughts about taking the substance, but I knew that it was too late. I was at the highest peak of the roller coaster, about to descend with the speed of a falling rock. Great excitement and fear held me, and once again I looked at the rose and felt reassured.

All of this had the feeling of me versus it, and it was winning and was very much in control. Then, at some point, the struggle and fear vanished and a great feeling of peace came over me. It was not the kind that comes from not having problems or stress, but peace with great energy, super peace, tangible, expansive, a real thing, and highly prized. I sat until I was sure this state would not dissolve. I felt as though I were breathing for the first time in my life.

All the while I had been looking at the desert sand beneath my feet. Occasionally I would raise my eyes and look at the pile of wood stacked neatly beside the garage. If the wood appeared so fascinating and wondrous, what must the mountains, which were at my back, be like? I thought perhaps if I turned to look at them, that I would surely be overcome by their great beauty. So I turned very slowly, each glance being a bit longer, taking in more of them with every turn of my head until I felt confident enough to stand and have a panoramic view of the whole range. They were spectacular and *breath-taking*—literally. I was filled with joy.

I went over to my fellow travelers, with much excitement, and I exclaimed, "I knew that there must be such places as this, I knew it, I knew it." Part of this realization was from having read about such states of consciousness, but the larger part of it was that I felt at home, like the birds or fish who migrate thousands of miles because somehow they know and are called by an inner prompting to a place where they have never been, have never seen, but at last find.

Then came a flood of connections. I felt connected with some master plan. Everything seemed to have a purpose and a plan, a reason why, and I felt caught up in it and was thrilled. Life seemed to have been conspiring to get me here to this moment, to this place of love, beauty, goodness, and truth. There was no uncertainty about any of this. "Only the fool, fixed in his folly, thinks that he turns the wheel on which he turns." The greatest freedom is to have no freedom but to go where we long to be. I had been migrating for fifty-three years in order to be home at last. I knew that I had done something as great as the birds and the fish.

As the heart quickens the closer you approach your destiny, so I saw the connection between the fact that my body had uncontrollably quivered the day I had interviewed as a possible candidate for this experience, and the greatness of the experience to which I felt called and which was now part of me. I felt as though all that I was trying to accomplish in life was somehow confirmed by the experience that I was undergoing. It was a premonition, and a confirmation. I was being caught up in the mystery, and the providence, and I was able to know the feeling and the certainty of it all.

I looked at my friend and I knew that he must be an emissary for a new way of living. The feeling was one of destiny. I was enjoying my destiny for the first time. It was real and I was realizing it.

I wanted to explore, to walk out into the desert, to stand alone in that vast panorama of beauty. A few hundred yards from the house I found a huge stone, about five feet high, into which the wind had carved a seat. I climbed onto the rock ("tu es petros"—you are the rock) and sat there in the hot morning sun, looking up into the blue sky, breathing wonderfully clean, warm air, surrounded by overpowering mountains, great rock formations, and ancient boulders that, I had been told, were 25 million years old. I knew what consciousness was about. I thought of the destiny of mankind. We were going to the stars.

I walked back to the house filled with awe and wonder. I asked whether we could go swimming in the spring-filled pond, which was down a gentle slope, a few acres from the house. We nestled there amid three- and four-story-high rocks and boulders of great beauty. Here in this idyllic setting of monoliths and cattails, desert and lush vegetation, I decided that I wanted to be baptized, without ceremony, ritual, or words.

Coming out of the cool spring water I felt refreshed—cleansed inside and out, totally alive and especially privileged.

The rest of the day was spent hiking and mountain climbing, eating rich, hot soup and being fully into the here and now. The intensity of the morning had drifted into a pleasant transition of fun, closeness to one another, and to the events as they unfolded.

Sitting at night under the stars and distant lightning I knew that I had come into an awareness as unique as life and into the promise of scripture, "I have come that you may have life—*and have it more abundantly.*"

Seeing into the Beauty of One's Being

35-year-old female, businesswoman

Set: therapeutic, self-exploratory

Setting: at home, with therapist/guide

Catalyst: 200 mg. MDMA

Sunday morning; not quite 24 hours since my encounter with Adam. A new day is beginning. I feel soft. I feel present. And I am filled with my spirituality.

In many ways yesterday was a spiritual experience. I am moved by my love and by my connections with God. I think for quite some time I've been somewhat out of touch with that. I remember one morning not too long ago, as I was putting on my nylons and heels and my silk business suit, my "armor," as I refer to my work presentation, I said, "I feel like I'm losing myself." Adam was an opportunity to return to self.

It was also a completion of the past in some ways. I am moved by how clearly I saw my mother's death, and how peaceful I am with that. I am very aware of my mother's connection with God, and of her gift of love and appreciation. I'm committed to carrying that forth, and expressing it in the world. And I felt compassion and forgiveness for my father. I am really appreciating who I am in all of this, my experience of love and how all right everything is with me.

I remember when the power of Adam was at its peak, I felt that I would be carried away, that I would go unconscious. The guide told me to lie down, and I wouldn't. Maybe I didn't surrender? I felt like I was holding on. And I gripped the pillow and the sofa. What would have happened if I let go? I had intense body sensations at the peak. I felt like my brain was going to explode through the top of my head. My jaw chattered and clamped, and I chewed the inside of my mouth and the sides of my tongue with my clenched teeth. I felt for sure I was going to throw up. I remember perspiring. My face and hands were wet.

The intense part seemed quite brief. There was a fast and steep climb from the beginning to the climax and then a rather gentle and long denouement with the end coming around ten in the evening, when I went to sleep. I took the tryptophan, but I did not sleep well.

I'm more aware than ever that I have a particular model of the world. Suffering is something I'm grappling with. Yesterday I saw that my view of the world is just that, a view. Yesterday created an opening for me, an opportunity for me to shift my map of the world. Yesterday was also a completion around my experience of being a woman. This male/female thing has been an issue in my life. There's something I saw that allowed me to appreciate being a woman in a way I never had before. Again, there's an opening, and it has to do with being fully powerful, and being a woman. I also experienced compassion for men. I remember saying, "God made men, too, so they must be O.K."

I go back to work tomorrow after being off for two weeks. I feel apprehensive. This opening of the heart is lovely. As I said before, I feel soft. I have the thought that this is too vulnerable a position to be in, that I seem to need to harden up, to get my armor on, in order to go out and function in the business world.

I want to stay "opened," full of heart and love. This is where the joy is, and the possibility of life as celebration. As E.E. Cummings says, "Since feeling is first, he who pays any attention to the syntax of things will never wholly kiss you . . ."

Monday evening: I got through Monday. I felt quite emotional most of the day. I suspect it has something to do with having had an experience of Heart, of being in touch with that which we're really all about, something of essence, of spirit, of source, of our deep sensitivities, our humanity, as contrasted sharply with that which most of us interact with on a day-to-day basis: concerns about making money, treating each other shallowly, dealing with numerous seemingly unimportant details, playing political games, driving in rush hour traffic, not "connecting." What I need to do is *be* in whatever environment, whatever circumstances, full of heart, and love, and spirituality. To bring peace and joy to whatever situation. To have a light heart, an open heart.

Tuesday evening: I had a great day. Nothing particularly special happened in terms of circumstances. I realize that when I have a "bad" day, or things are not going right, I wonder to myself, "What's wrong with me?" And when I have a good day, I take it for granted, as if that's the way it's supposed to be. Today I decided to take credit for having a "good" day. Today, three days after Adam, I would say that what stands out for me is the potential Adam has as an aid in breaking up one's reality, and for seeing into the beauty of one's Being. I want to underline the importance of the context created for the experience. It would not be the same experience without a wise and loving guide.

Thursday evening: I've had a fantastic past few days. I'm really loving this new appreciation of being a woman. Something actually happened for me: I am done with trying to prove something. There's still some unsorted stuff in this area, but I do think I've shifted things. There's something I know about being a woman that I didn't know before. And this impacts on one of my goals: to appreciate myself and express myself more fully.

Springs of Enchantment

26-year-old female, student

Set: relationship communication and bonding

Setting: outside in nature; with partner

Catalyst: 100 mg. plus 50 mg. MDMA

I discovered Adam when I started an affair with this psychologist, who was using it in therapy. I broke off with my boyfriend, from whom I felt estranged and distant, even though he was very hurt and convinced that we were meant for each other. My sexual feelings became re-awakened, after a long slumber.

A few weeks later I moved to a holistic health retreat in the country, where I obtained a job, and began to study hypnosis. My former boyfriend was also there. I didn't want anything to do with him at first, even though he was very needy. Then after a while I thought it would be good if we took Adam—maybe it would help him, and it would make it easier for both of us to accept our separation.

During the session we became very close again, and I saw how he was right: we really were supposed to be together, and learn to work together. So we fell in love again. I called the psychologist friend, who was expecting to see me again, and I told him what had happened. Now he felt hurt and rejected.

He said the Adam experience reminded him of the enchanted springs in the magical forests of Arthurian legend. There was a spring, according to this legend, such that if you went there and drank from it, you would fall asleep, and when you woke up, you would fall in love with the first person you saw. There was also another enchanted spring nearby, with the opposite effect: if you drank from it you would fall asleep, and when you woke up, you would fall out of love with whomever you were infatuated with at the time.

Chapter V. A Guide for Users

When Heisenberg developed the "Uncertainty Principle" in physics, he might as well have been talking about the effects of psychoactive substances. There is no way to predict with certainty the course of an MDMA session.

Careful planning can help push things in the desired direction, but what actually occurs can vary greatly. The design of an MDMA session, therefore, is an art rather than a science. Each of the major factors which blend together to make the whole cloth of the MDMA experience might be thought of as threads. In this chapter, I will try to organize these procedural threads so that future weavers may create more elegant experiential tapestries.

Although not completely predictable, MDMA is a remarkably reliable catalyst of mental experience—especially when compared to the effects of the major psychedelics. The duration of action and required dosage vary little among users. The alternative state of consciousness produced by MDMA is quite consistent and does not depart much from our ordinary consensus consciousness.

There are differing goals for using MDMA. These objectives define the types of MDMA sessions. Each of these sessions has its own regimen and guiding principles. These session types include: (1) therapy-oriented sessions; (2) self-actualization oriented sessions, (3) creativity-enhancement oriented sessions; and (4) recreational sessions. I will discuss each of these briefly.

Therapy-Oriented Sessions

Sessions designed for therapeutic purposes must have the most careful planning, experienced guides, and controlled environment of any of the session types covered here. Obviously, people who have mental problems need more secure structures and safeguards when given a psychoactive drug.

In addition, proper screening must be done to eliminate those whose mental and/or physical conditions contraindicate the use of MDMA.

Psychotherapists, as noted in the previous chapters, have already begun work with MDMA. Of individuals who pursued experimental MDMA therapy, the only practitioners who have written extensively on work specifically with MDMA are George Greer and Requa Tolbert, from whose pilot study I have already quoted. Their papers on the conduct of therapeutic MDMA sessions remain unpublished as of this writing.

In addition to Greer, Rick Ingrasci, while testifying at the Scheduling Hearings, commented briefly on therapeutic procedures. Before going on to sketch out Greer's and Tolbert's procedure, the following is the methodology outlined by Ingrasci:

> (1) The patient or couple fasts for 4-6 hours prior to the ingestion of the MDMA.

> (2) The patient receives between 100-120 mg. MDMA in 4 ounces of orange juice.

> (3) After the onset of action of the drug (usually 45-60 minutes after ingestion), I encourage the patient or couple to talk about what they are thinking and feeling in the present moment. This gentle, non-directive process continues for the next two hours.

> (4) Following the formal therapeutic session with me, I have the patient spend the next two hours with their spouse and/or family members or with a close friend, someone with whom the patient would like to talk to or with in an open, intimate way. With couples, I either leave them alone to be with each other for the next two hours, or I have their children and/or other family members join them for a heart-to-heart discussion.

> (5) All patients are asked to write down their MDMA experience within 24 hours of the session.

> (6) Most patients require only one MDMA session, although some benefit from a second session 4-6 weeks after the initial session.

George Greer has written two papers on MDMA therapy procedure, "The Legal, Safe and Effective Use of MDMA," in 1984 and, with Requa Tolbert, "The Clinical Use of MDMA" in 1985. Both outline similar methodologies based on work done by Greer and Tolbert which I will attempt to present in an abridged form.

Greer and Tolbert used a rigourous screening procedure to select clients for therapy. First, they sent the prospective client a questionnaire, "informed consent" information, and an essay stating their philosophy about psychoactive medicines. The questionnaire evoked personal, medical, and psychiatric history, as well as information about the prospective client's drug use patterns. This material is also designed to orient the person toward having such a session. Questions of this type include: "What is your purpose in having a session with MDMA?" and "What are your expectations/fears of what will happen?"

After reviewing the questionnaire and finding no strong contra-indications to the session, Greer and Tolbert conducted a screening interview in their own home, where they also held most of the MDMA sessions. The screening interview comprised both a final screening and preparation for the session.

There are both physical and psychological problems which preclude the use of MDMA for therapy (or for any other purpose). Greer lists these exclusionary problems in his "Legal, Safe and Effective Use of MDMA" paper:

> MDMA should not be taken by people with the following physical conditions: hypertension, heart disease, seizures, hyperthyroidism, diabetes mellitus, hypoglycemia, glaucoma, diminished liver function, actual or possible pregnancy, and breast feeding . . .
>
> People may experience a recurrence of any psychological problems they have ever had in the past. Those with a history of panic attacks have had recurrences both during and after sessions. For this reason, MDMA is not recommended for people who have ever been unable to function socially or vocationally due to psychological problems unless 24-hour care by trained people is available. The person should also be fully willing to experience whatever may happen during or after sessions. This is the most important factor in screening clients. People who are not ready for anything to happen should not take MDMA because that mental set predisposes one to having a difficult time without benefiting from the experience.

It should be noted that Greer's exclusion of people with severe psychological problems does not mean that MDMA cannot be beneficial to these with psychoses or major mood disorders. We saw earlier that Wolfson used MDMA successfully with these types. What Greer is emphasizing is the need for constant supervision.

During the in-depth interview, the facilitators give an account of their personal histories and experiences, and relate the reasons why they are doing work with MDMA. Then a series of explicit agreements are made to establish a setting in which "clients must feel free to lose complete emotional and behavioral control, within ethical and safe limits." The set of agreements that Greer recommends includes:

(1) Everyone will remain on the premises until all agree that the session is over and that it is safe to leave (including safe to drive); (2) Clients will engage in no destructive activities towards self, others or property; (3) There will be no sexual contact between facilitators and clients or between clients who are not already sexually involved; and (4) The clients agree to follow any explicit instruction given by the facilitator.

The dosage for individual sessions depends on several factors, especially the client's history of sensitivity to other psychoactive compounds. For first sessions by individuals, 75-125 mg. is the specified range. Clients can choose a "low, medium or high" dose as desired, and be given 75, 100, or 125 mg. respectively. Larger doses are recommended for single persons "wishing to explore inner space," and smaller ones for couples who wish to spend time together. A supplement of 50 mg. is offered when the effects subside, somewhere between 1½ and 3 hours after ingestion.

Greer also comments, "Sometimes Inderal (propranolol) at 40 mg. can be given every 4 hours (up to 120 mg. total dose) to partially relieve some of the side effects such as muscle tension. Inderal prevents the heart from beating faster during physical exertion, so clients may feel short of breath if they exert themselves."

In this type of therapeutic session, the facilitator does not take the drug with the client, and maintains a non-directive attitude—not attempting to work with the client, but available in case of difficulties.

After ingesting the compound, the client is asked to lie down and put on eye shades and stereo headphones. Music is played. Greer and Tolbert always recommend instrumental music except for vocal pieces in foreign languages (in some sessions of this type, clients are allowed to choose their own favorite musical selections). The style of music may be either classical, ethnic, or modern, and is based on the intuitions of the therapist. The client may decline a particular piece, or choose to have silence.

Couples or groups are encouraged to initiate their experience in different rooms, allowing them to attend to individual issues in the

MDMA state. Later in the session, after one to two hours, the couple or the group members come together for a sharing of experiences and insights.

If the clients attempt to engage in a "rambling monologue" with the facilitator, they might be asked to stop talking, or to talk into a tape recorder. It is recommended that the client make no commitments while in the altered state, nor engage in activity with outside people (making phone calls or going to public places).

Clients should have no work or social obligations scheduled the next day. This is to permit recovery from the fatigue that may result from the session as well as to allow for integration of the psychological rumblings of the previous day.

Greer gave his subjects a "Peak Experience Profile," authored by Walter Pahnke, Stanislav Grof and Francesco DiLeo, as well as a follow-up questionnaire, to be completed within three days. A facilitator was, as well, made available on a 24-hour basis for the following three days.

An anonymously written fact sheet simply titled "General Information: MDMA" has been circulated by a Santa Cruz, California group called the Psychedelic Education Center. This short, but wise essay was offered as a guide to the conduct of legal MDMA therapy in the pre-Schedule I period.

This fact sheet, from which I will excerpt passages in this chapter, outlines procedures quite similar to those of George Greer and Requa Tolbert, including the use of eye-shades and headphones, and a therapist who refrains from taking MDMA.

This sheet also recommends an alternative procedure:

> The second method is as follows: the person who is leading the experiment participates in the taking of MDMA along with his clients. No one remains outside the experiment. The amount given initially is 120 mgs., and the supplement offered, at about 1-½ to 1-¾ hours is 40 mgs.
>
> It should be noted here that just as it is generally understood by the intelligent and informed therapist or leader that under no circumstances should any person be persuaded or pressured to take MDMA, so must it be understood that there should never be any urging or persuasion regarding the taking of a supplement. The client's instincts and intuitions regarding his or her own state of body and mind are to be regarded as correct and must be respected.

In this second method, which we personally prefer, there is no isolation with earphones and music, although it is understood that anyone involved in the experiment may do anything that he or she wishes to make the experiment enjoyable and comfortable, within the obvious limitations presented by the surroundings and the circumstances.

Generally, talking and sharing insights and feelings goes on continually as desired.

Self-Actualization-Oriented Sessions

The climb up the self-actualization mountain differs in many respects from the climb out of the valley of psychological despair. Instead of the client/therapist relationship, your co-participants in the experience might be a trusted guide (for first-timers), a friend, a lover, or sometimes nobody except yourself. And your goals are not measured in freedom from symptoms, but in degrees of growth.

Screening of individuals for self-actualization-oriented sessions should observe the same rules for excluding physical ailments as in the therapy-oriented category. Presumably, self-actualizing people are free from mental disorders, and so there should be no concern in this regard.

Environments for experiences with this purpose can also be less restricted, especially after the first few sessions. A setting in nature, for example, would not normally be used in a therapy session, but could be suitable for self-actualization-oriented experiences.

As mentioned in this book's Preface, my own experience with MDMA progressed through what I perceived to be stages of growth. Perhaps future cartographers can develop precise maps of such stages for those pursuing self-actualization as a goal. Also, the use of established descriptions of psychological growth from Eastern schools like Zen Buddhism, or Western paths such as Jung's model of stages of self-realization, can be of help.

Creativity-Enhancement-Oriented Sessions

Creativity and peak experiences are not far apart. As I noted in the fourth chapter, creativity often occurs in an alternative state of consciousness and taps the wellspring of the unconscious mind. Thus, much of the same guidelines that were discussed in relationship to self-actualization-oriented sessions also apply here.

There are two methods of MDMA use that may help elicit creativity. In the first, the creative task is attempted during the MDMA session. In the second, the MDMA session is used to generate ideas that later may be applied to the creative task.

In the first method employed in George Greer's and Requa Tolbert's pilot study, a small dose of MDMA, 50 to 75 mg., is taken by one or more individuals. This reduced dose allows the individual to remain closer to their ordinary state of consciousness. After taking the substance, the experient or experients might spend some time "coming on" to the drug, processing through any initial psychological issues that might surface.

Then the experiment turns to a chosen task, which could consist of painting, writing, sculpting, music, or other endeavors to which a creative hand and mind might be applied. There would be no problem with visual distortions, as on major psychedelics, expecially at such a low dose. Also, coordination—including eye-hand coordination—is not impaired; so tasks that require such dexterity could still be accomplished.

In the second method, a full dose (125 to 175 mg.) of MDMA is taken, and the participant or participants refrain from any active involvement with their selected media. If one person is involved in the session, the person could choose to listen to music on headphones or perhaps examine past creations or masterpieces in the chosen creative area. In a pair or group, there might be some kind of "brainstorming" or idea-generating discussion which could loosen the soil of the fertile imagination.

Then, when the effects of the MDMA have subsided, creative ideas or images are applied to the final product. This type of session is particularly valuable for dealing with creative logjams, such as "writer's block." I should mention my own experiment in creativity with regard to the writing of this book, during a time when I felt somewhat blocked. I took a small dose (75 mg.) of MDMA with the idea of working on Chapter III during part of the experience. This was my first time taking the substance alone. I first went on a run along a road that follows the ocean, which is close to my house. An athletic friend had told me that he likes to run and bicycle on low doses of MDMA because it enhances his experience of his body and performance. I had decided previously that I would begin my experiment with my usual evening run to the Santa Cruz Lighthouse and back (about 4 miles).

The run was exhilarating. I completed the distance in a shorter than normal time, returned home, and immersed myself in a cedar hot tub.

A little over an hour and one half into the experience, I sat at my typewriter and attempted to write some of Chapter III. However, the most well-intentioned plans for drug experiences often have to be revised. I began to feel emotional and decided to write a letter to a close friend in Connecticut as a way of expressing the feelings I was having (as there was nobody around, and I had decided to receive no phone calls).

The letter ran to about four typed pages (single spaced). Then I returned to the planned chapter, and wrote a few paragraphs—and felt the block. I began to look over the entire draft of what I had written, however, with a feeling of precision and clarity.

Then I wrote a few more paragraphs and lost interest in writing entirely. I decided to do some reading, and soon was asleep. The next morning, I awoke and set about writing the chapter with renewed energy. What appeared like large granite blocking stones the day before were reduced to pebbles!

My experiment was not quite scientific, and certainly not a pure form of either of the two methods that I have outlined. It was its own kind of creation, as is each session. I look to future rigorous studies to see if what seems subjectively true actually occurs.

Recreational Sessions

Scenario I. The three friends sat holding hands on the sandy beach cove. An almost full moon lit the landscape as the three talked animatedly. Suddenly, they stopped talking and just sat. Waves broke on rocks. The air seemed charged with calm electricity. Their eyes met in wonder. They shared a new depth to their friendship that they had not previously realized.

Scenario II. The stereo filled the large living room with music and a group of partiers gathered together to participate in a spontaneous round of improvisations. Several of the people were theater-arts majors at a local college, and were teaching the rest of the group to do spontaneous skits. It was a special "creative-fun" moment for all of those there, as laughter alternated with applause.

Scenario III. The two lovers sat holding each other. As each looked at the other's naked body, it almost seemed that they could see streaks of energy flowing on the surface of their skin. Touch was highly sensitive and completely free of lustful grasping. Each felt that they were merging with the other yet becoming fully themselves simultaneously.

What do these three scenarios have in common? In all of them, the minds of each of the participants had been set on a new consciousness level, and relations between them were intensified by the recreational use of MDMA.

Recreational drug use has almost become a dirty word in 1988 America. Nancy Reagan's campaign against drug abuse is really a national campaign against any recreational drug use. Marijuana, heroin, and MDMA are not differentiated.

Intelligent use is not distinguished from insane abuse. Yet, if we were to compare the above now-illegal scenarios with similar situations in which the participants were strongly intoxicated on alcohol, we would perceive quite a contrast. Behavior on MDMA would appear more calm, peaceful, and sensitive.

If the three friends in the first scenario were stoned on alcohol, they might stagger along the beach, talking past each other, rather than really listening. The alcohol party might be highlighted by a drunken brawl rather than creative theater skits. And the lovers would be grasping at each other's anesthetized body in inebriated lust, rather than the aesthetic love-dance of the third scenario.

Because MDMA is now illegal, I cannot propose that you use this substance. However, from what we know about the drug underground, it is sure that many of you will.

In the following section, broad guidelines will be given for the use of MDMA. These can be applied to any of the uses of MDMA, including recreational use. Then, when I turn to "Future Potentialities" in Chapter VI, I will propose a more intelligent way for society to handle the use of recreational drugs through education and licensing.

What Determines the Outcome of an MDMA Session?

Returning to our earlier metaphor, if an MDMA session can be thought of as a piece of fabric, then the "set" and "setting" are that cloth's warp and woof. *Set* refers to what the drug taker brings to the situation, her or his enduring personality, as well as earlier imprinting and learning, individual history, emotional and intellectual tendencies, motivations and intentions, the procedure (preparation and programming for the session), philosophy and techniques of the therapist or guide, and the immediate expectations about the experience. *Setting* refers to the actual environment of the experience, both physical and interpersonal (social and emotional milieu), and to the concrete circumstances under which the drug is administered.

The importance of set and setting was first shown by two social psychologists, Schacter and Singer, who demonstrated that the same drug could produce two different effects depending on the set and setting. The drug they used was amphetamine, a simple stimulant. When the social situation was set up to be tense and uptight, the drug produced anger in their subject; when it was made pleasant, the same drug produced euphoria.

Each of the various types of MDMA sessions would have its own particular appropriate set and setting. Part of the set obviously is the purpose for which the substance is taken. Goals chosen have an important influence on where you end up. Fortunately, MDMA experiences tend to be positive and the substance can oftentimes brighten a previously dampened perspective.

As I mentioned before, settings for therapy-oriented sessions must be more secure and protected than for other purposes. The same is true for first-time experiences. Preparation is also part of the requirements of set, and will be disussed later in this chapter.

Settings should be comfortable and aesthetically pleasing to the MDMA taker, and should convey a sense of intimacy and warmth. Items in the environment should be chosen for the influence they might have. For a first-time user, a good setting would be his or her own home, where he or she is surrounded by familiar sights and sounds.

Included in the setting are the other individuals present during the session. The key issue in regard to these others is trust. You *must* trust the persons present with you when you take any psychoactive substance for the experience to be positive. Drug reactions can often amplify any suspicion or mistrust that is present in various session participants.

Perhaps the most important individual present is the person who occupies the position of session leader (sometimes called the guide or therapist). As with all those present in any session, you should trust this individual. The session leader influences the course of the session by his or her particular philosophical model with respect to MDMA sessions, the techniques they use in guiding the session, and how they conduct themselves during the course of the experience.

Finally, the number of people present can greatly influence the outcome of a session. For a first-time experience, the various guides published unanimously recommend taking the substance with one other person or, at most, a partner and a guide (or therapist). More experienced users may prefer to take MDMA by themselves or sometimes in groups. In the next section, a method for group experience will be explored.

Group Experiences

When groups of people take MDMA together, the interpersonal magic of this empathogen is often multiplied in proportion to the number who take the substance. Used for therapy, MDMA group sessions intensify the group-therapy process. An MDMA party can generate unique social forms and facilitate bonding of people for friendship or romance.

One of the best guides for the use of MDMA in groups was issued by the Psychedelic Education Center of Santa Cruz, California. It is based on observations of many group experiences.

> XTC [MDMA] has enormous potential as a tool for connecting and unifying groups of people. Although there are endless possibilities for application of this tool within a group setting, the following guidelines have proven invaluable in terms of creating productive sessions. People seem to get higher if the sessions are directed and organized. We see these guidelines as a point of possible departure, open to change and interpretation but of enough importance to pass this information along . . .
>
> A session is organized as the result of one person's decision to host the event. The host invites friends over, and prepares a space for the session that is clean, attractive, warm and safe.
>
> The participants begin by expressing their hopes, reservations and expectations for the session.
>
> As the effects unfold, all participants are encouraged to share their experience and insights with the group as an entity.
>
> Private conversations tend to disconnect the group and should be minimized.
>
> Shared silence is exquisite.
>
> Having pencils and papers on hand at all times allows people to retrieve information for use at a later time.
>
> Getting together the following day for a debriefing after the experience has dissipated is helpful to bind the things learned during the session into normal operating consciousness . . .
>
> If the session is successful, and the group wishes to get together again, a new host volunteers to provide the space for the next one, and sets a date.
>
> This procedure seems to work best if the majority of the participants are already familiar with the XTC experience, and first-timers are held to a few.
>
> Provision of the XTC itself works well if all participants bring their own supply to the session as much as possible. This relieves the host or any one person from the burden of providing for all, and tends to make the experience more

collective and easier to get together for repeats.

As mentioned in the "Reflections on the Nature of XTC and Guidlines for Its Use" [a companion set of guidelines covering more general principles], it is possible for people to have very difficult trips on XTC, although this occurrence is rare. Individuals most likely to react in this fashion are people with strongly suppressed negative emotions who act as if they aren't hurting when they are hurting badly. People with rigid personalities and belief systems can also have difficulties when their operational foundations crumble. Should a negative reaction occur in a group setting, the participants can best handle the situation by extending love and compassion to their brother or sister who is in trouble. What does this mean? It means supporting them in feeling whatever they're feeling, even if it's negative. On the other side of all negative emotions is love.

Experience has shown that these people often stand to gain the most from these experiences. The act of releasing themselves allows them to be reborn as more sensitive and understanding people, infused with new vigor for life. If possible, try to initiate these people in a small private session, rather than a group session, if the potential for difficulty can be recognized ahead of time. This occurrence is rare, but does happen and should be considered. It can be very intense.

XTC is a a tool for reaching out and touching others in soul and spirit. If responsibly used, strong bonds of unity and love can be forged that strengthen everyone involved.

Claudio Naranjo, in a private communication, describes his work with MDMA in groups, a decade after the experiments in *The Healing Journey.*

On most occasions my scheme of work has involved the following stages:

1. Individual interviews with those group members I have not met before.

2. Preparatory group sessions devoted to personal information, for sharing the expression of interpersonal emotions and for the clarification of individual expectations on the occasion of the session.

3. Group rules and general indications—of which the most important are:

3.1 Seeking a balance between spontaneity and non-interference.

3.2 No sexual intercourse during the psychedelic session and the night after.

3.3 Waiting for the effects of MDMA in an attitude of self-observation and goalless restful effortlessness.

3.4 Seeking not to establish contact with other group members before a sufficient time devoted to "self immersion" (ecstatic or painful).

4. Distribution of MDMA, followed by ingestion: waiting for the effects in a meditative attitude, and the psychedelic group session proper—six to eight hours in duration.

5. An "integrative" session, on the following day, for the retrospective sharing of experiences, group feedback and my comments or supplementary therapeutic intervention.

I usually work with 12-16 people, and meet for about eight hours after ingestion of MDMA and some four hours on the following day . . .

I will describe my manner of intervention during the MDMA therapy session proper briefly and only say that:

1. I rotate part of the time among group members, listening, sharing insights, occasionally using gestalt therapy techniques, giving advice or suggestions for group experiments (such as approaching such and such in such and such an attitude). In the course of years I find myself becoming less directive and less confrontative on this day.

2. I mostly come to people who come to me or call me, and rarely to those who seem to be avoiding me.

3. I am more a "father" than a "mother": I give my attention and perceptions but seek to mediate in such a way that the usual thirst for body contact of participants in the course of regression is satisfied by proximity to those group members who are at the time undergoing the typically warm and contactful MDMA peak experience.

Some of the things I have observed throughout my experience with MDMA groups consist of things that can be observed in individual MDMA therapy as well:

1. "Simple" peak experiences.

2. Peak experiences coupled to psychological insight.

3. Experiencing of hitherto repressed psychological pain.

Claudio Naranjo, M.D., author of The Healing Journey.

4. Age-regression experiences.

Though I have sometimes felt after sessions with "occasional" groups that some individuals might have been helped better through one-to-one MDMA therapy, on the whole I can say even these sessions proved very helpful to many, particularly when preceded by individual appointments and sufficiently long preparatory and integration sessions. Still, I have found work with more coherent groups and families most fruitful. It is particularly in these cases that it may be said that what is lost in individual attention from the therapist (in comparison with one-to-one therapy) is compensated by group dynamic factors. I have also seen in the training structure a satisfactory alternative to individual MDMA therapy.

I have on occasion brought together multiple couples groups: two families (two brothers and their wives, and a brother and sister with their spouses), one joint meeting of these two families and a multiple-team group, constituted by couples and associates. This, together with the experience of two ongoing teams (of psychotherapists) has constituted the most satisfactory part of my MDMA psychotherapy experience. The experience of teams is of a similar quality to that with couples and families, for quickly the team becomes a sort of family, and, indeed, my two groups came spontaneously to call themselves such. In all these instances, persons engaged in ongoing relationships are helped by the potential of MDMA for couples, who were helped through an enhanced ability to express themselves nonmanipulatively and to listen nondefensively to each other.

Having practiced LSD group therapy in the '60s and experimented with multiple substance groups (in which LSD, harmaline or MDA were given to different group members), I have for long appreciated the value of psychedelic group therapy, yet I can say that MDMA group therapy is that which I value most for its specifically psychotherapeutic results.

Though I would question MDMA sessions without the therapeutic context, I think that the properly prepared and properly elaborated MDMA group session is better than any therapeutic group experience that I have witnessed.

I have no follow-up study to present, no before and after testing, no statistics. I am well acquainted with the difficulties and limits in the evaluation of psychotherapy, and have neither been funded to set up that research nor motivated to undertake it without institutional support. I am consoled a bit, however, thinking that most forms of psychotherapeutic practice have been communicated through no more than the activity itself and the sharing of clinical impressions.

Session Preparation

Irrespective of the goal of an MDMA session, careful planning and both physical and mental preparation are important. Experimenters who take the time to prepare for a session will enhance the chances of a positive experience, and much more of almost all the benefits that can be gotten from such an undertaking will be attained.

Experimenters would usually plan to have the experience when participants will be free from any kind of obligations—or other constraints—on their time for the period of the session and for the next day as well, so that, while on the drug, their full-time attention should be on the experience and not on any competing task. Afterward, they will need time to integrate what has been learned.

The experience is something like a retreat. The MDMA experience is neither trivial nor casual. It can be a life-transforming experience.

George Greer says of this period, "Thorough psychological preparation before the session cannot be overstressed. The first and most important question to be answered is, 'Why do I want to take MDMA at this time in my life?' This is the most important preparatory step. This conscious purpose, along with the open willingness mentioned above, is the foundation of a client's mental set for the session."

Ralph Metzner and Sophia Adamson, in their paper, "The Nature and Role of the MDMA Experience" from the yet unpublished anthology, *Forbidden Fruit*, advise us:

> The single most important foundation for a beneficial experience is intention or purpose. One should ask oneself, and discuss with the therapist or guide, "What is my purpose in entering into this altered state of awareness?" Typically, people approach the experience with fundamental existential and spiritual questions ... In addition there may be more personal and therapeutic questions . . . Some

people prefer to declare an intention to explore certain areas
or topics rather than posing questions. In either approach, it
is a good practice to release the questions or intentions to
one's higher self or inner guide, just prior to ingestion. In
this way, one is not too intent merely on problem-solving
which can, on occasion, tend to limit one's experience.

In addition, these authors make some other important recommenda-
tions. They suggest either meditation or some basic relaxation prior to
the session. Those with shamanic bents might like to bring "objects"
such as feathers, crystals, etc. Photographs of parents and other family
members might be helpful in triggering early childhood memories.

In regard to physical considerations before taking MDMA, a good
sleep the previous night is advised, just as is generally good physical
health. It would not be a good idea to take MDMA to attempt to "heal"
influenza or a cold, as the stress to the body will probably worsen the
condition. Exceptions to this rule are terminal illnesses like cancer,
where positive psychological benefits outweigh possible negative
effects.

It would be advisable to have a lot of liquids—fruit juice, soft drinks,
pure water, etc.—available for the session. MDMA increases the need
for fluids. Participants would need to try to drink more than usual during
the experience. Also, they would be advised not to each much food for
about six to eight hours before a session. Food in the stomach will
inhibit the absorption of the drug, or make its effects manifest
unevenly.

Ingesting The Drug—Pharmacological Considerations

Before taking MDMA, one should be certain that the substance is
really MDMA. Someone involved in FDA-sanctioned experimentation
or therapy would have no worry here. A person who has gotten the
drug from black market sources would have more need for concern. It
would be wise to know and trust the individual who supplies any
MDMA. Buying a drug on the streets from somebody courts trouble.
There are cases of substitution of MDMA with MDA or, even worse,
with LSD, PCP, or even "China White."

In 1985, Analysis Anonymous reported that 58% of samples received
contained only MDMA. However, now that MDMA is illegal, the
percentage of MDMA samples cut, adultered, or misrepresented with
other psychoactive compounds will probably rise sharply.

MDMA is usually a white crystalline powder. A reddish or brownish tint is sometimes seen, and indicates the presence of manufacture by-products. The smell of the powder also gives a clue to these by-products. The strong smell of solvent indicates that the material still is damp with ether from manufacture, and the smell of sassafras indicates isosafarole that hasn't been converted into MDMA. However, experience has shown that these two impurities have little impact on the potency of the drug. Different ways of making MDMA result in crystals of various sizes, up to the size of very course rock salt. The crystals are normally ground up before marketing to a fine powdery consistency.

In addition to the crystal form, occasionally MDMA is buffered and pressed into tablets. Normally, a tablet is a single dose. The dosage specified is often not the real dosage, but there is no way of measuring this, because of the buffering material. Crudely made crystal MDMA can be disguised in a buffered pill.

Any unknown drug can be sent to a drug-testing company. The best one we know of is S.P. Lab, 5426 N.W. 79th Avenue, Miami, Florida 33166. They ask for a sample wrapped in foil or plastic, enclosed in an envelope, with a slip of paper telling the alleged content, cost and any undesirable side-effects noticed—$25.00 per sample—and a five-digit number to identify the sample. After 14 days, call (305) 757-2566 for the result.

If the drug is indeed MDMA, and it is not buffered with anything, the experimenter would need to decide on the dosage, in terms of the specific purpose the drug is being taken for and in relationship to the body weight of the individual who is using it.

The average dose for MDMA is somewhere between 125 mg. and 180 mg., depending upon weight. The more you weigh, the more you must take to have the same effect. A complicating factor is that each individual responds idiosyncratically to a given dose of MDMA. Some are very sensitive, while others might be resistant to having an effect on even very high doses. This may be due to variations in metabolism or to psychological factors.

The purpose of the session also enters into the dosage equation. A person taking MDMA for reasons of working creatively might take 50-75 mg., a threshold dose (the smallest amount that has a psychological effect). A person taking the drug for communicating with others might find a moderate dose—between 125 mg. and 160 mg.—to be appropriate. For self-exploration of inner spaces, doses in the high range of about 180 to 200 mg. would be called for.

MDMA is a peculiar drug in that there is a small ratio between its threshold dose and a dose that is too large. A larger dose than 200 mg.

will produce an MDMA experience, but one more like that of amphetamine—a jittery, anxiety-provoking stimulant high.

The paradoxical effects of the drug are lost at these higher doses. Furthermore, a very high dose might be physically harmful or even lethal. *Under no circumstances should anyone take a dose over 250 mg.*

After the initial dose, a "booster dose" can be used to prolong the experience. This dose can range in size from 40 mg. up to the size of the initial dose. A dose between 75 mg. and 100 mg. has been used. The booster is usually taken about one hour after the onset of the first dose's effects. Sometimes a second booster dose is taken in another hour.

But a second booster usually does not have the desired effect of enhancing the experience. Instead, the taker is often made to feel anxious, jittery, and sometimes confused by this third dose, with little of the pleasant effects of the first two. This characteristic is one of the best reasons why MDMA is not subject to abuse.

George Greer says of dosage size, "Many people feel they learn more from lower doses than high ones." This could be because their state is only slightly altered, so that the insights gained are more realistic and applicable to their usual state of consciousness.

Taking MDMA orally is the most usual and probably the best way to ingest it. It can be put in a capsule and swallowed. A more efficient way to take MDMA is to put it in a spoon and place it under the tongue— the sublingual route of administration. This allows for faster and more complete absorption into the blood. However, MDMA tastes terrible, and this practice is certainly not for everyone. A good compromise is to put it in juice or a carbonated beverage and drink it.

An alternative route of taking MDMA is nasally. This is popularly called "snorting" the drug, a slang term picked up from the cocaine subculture. Unlike cocaine, however, MDMA does not numb the nasal passages. Instead, it is quite irritating. Some people cannot tolerate the burning sensation that ensues upon snorting the drug. The effects of nasal inhalation are a shorter onset of action, with an almost immediate effect. The duration seems to be shortened, though, and the psychological impact of the experience seems less than that of an equivalent amount taken orally.

For MDMA to be taken nasally, the crystal must be chopped into a fine powder. This allows for proper absorption in the mucosa. Another method of ingesting MDMA is to inject it into either a vein (intravenous), or a muscle (intramuscular), with a hypodermic syringe. This method is rarely used, mainly because it has little advantage over the oral route. The main reason that drugs such as cocaine, amphetamine, and heroin are injected is that their psychological effects seem predicated on the rate at which the concentration in the blood is increased. This is called the cocaine "rush" or the "flash" with regard to heroin. However, MDMA does not produce a "rush" based on its rate of increase in the blood. Its "rush" is instead part of its course of action. The only difference between swallowing it and injecting it into a vein is the time it takes to feel the initial effects and the required dosage level.

Injecting shortens the time of onset and decreases the dosage requirement, mainly because no MDMA is lost in the digestive tract.

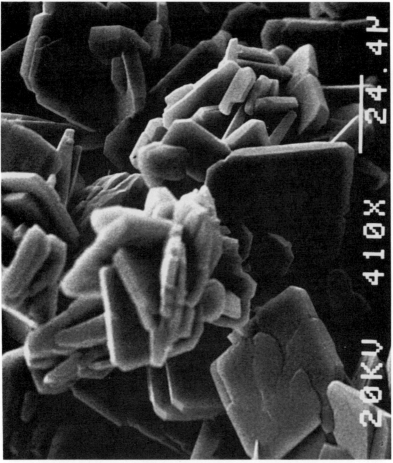

MDMA crystal magnified by electronic microscope (410 times).

Stages of a Typical Session

It has been said that no two people are exactly alike. The same individuality can be ascribed to MDMA sessions. However, in comparison to psychedelic drugs, MDMA's duration, required dosage, and psychological effects are remarkably consistent from session to session and from user to user. With this in mind, I can offer a portrait of the typical MDMA experience.

Coming on (first half hour)

As I mentioned in my Preface, and in Chapter II, the initial portion of the MDMA experience is the most profound. This period is colloquially termed the "rush," the "hit," or the "come-on."

Unlike major psychedelic substances, in which the effects appear mild and gradually become more intense, the transition to the peak of an MDMA experience happens very rapidly—about 30 to 45 minutes after the substance is taken. Its duration is between 15 and 30 minutes, followed by a gradual descent back to normal consciousness.

At the beginning of the typical positive session, there dawns a sudden clarity and intensification of experiencing. Outwardly, everything seems brighter and crisper. Inwardly, there is a feeling of ecstasy and utter happiness. Everything is perfect just as it is; everybody is lovable just as they are.

Unless you are in a therapy session, blindfolded and isolated, there is a tendency to verbalize what you are experiencing. Psychologists use the strangely awkward term "pressure of speech" to describe this phenomenon.

This increased talkativeness can be a real delight. Along with it comes a dropping of the normal defenses which we put on what we say. Many unexpressed ideas or feelings can come forth at this time. There may be a feeling of sharing your true self with others, of deep empathetic contact.

This period, if used for introspection with blindfolds or just being by yourself, can be a different kind of experence. There may be a rapid flow of ideas or emotions. Along with it, the same ecstatic awareness as in the more extroverted session may be felt. One may have a noetic perception of the world, now viewed in a completely fresh new light.

On rare occasions, there is a build-up of psychic tension, instead of the usual initial "rush" as described above.

Within 10 to 15 minutes, however, reasons for this negative experience are acknowledged, and the effects of the MDMA become apparent. This is sometimes referred to metaphorically as "bubble bursting." It is usually not experienced during any subsequent session.

The reason for the resistance involved in a negative experience is usually the surfacing of some traumatic memories. In therapeutic sessions, when the reason for giving the MDMA is to allow the individual to deal with ongoing psychological problems, the encounter of negativity in the initial session is much more common than in other session types. Many victims of violence or rape, as well as individuals with terminal disease, have a difficult time comprehending why MDMA ever was named Ecstasy.

In a therapeutic session, the therapist may encourage the encounter and reliving of traumatic episodes. But in other types of sessions, people who resist the positive effects of the substance are best told to relax, let go, and surrender to the experience.

Plateau (one half hour to 3 hours after initial effect)

Like a flat expanse on the top of a prairie plateau, there is a leveling off of experience after the initial rush. This can manifest as a peaceful calm awareness and affinity with others. The same qualities that were intensely felt at the beginning continue on. These feelings can deepen into a profound stillness, which some have likened to the realization of the goals of meditation.

During this period, coordination and movements are not impaired. It is transitions between states of consciousness that are the most dramatic manifestations of drug experience. Here, a steady new state of consciousness has been achieved. Freed from the initial "noise" of the rush, the MDMA user can now begin to explore this state's parameters.

One suggestion for using the MDMA experience for later benefit is called "future pacing." Here you conjure up, while in your alternative state, a mental image of people or situations which you would like to experience in an open and empathetic way. Then you construct an image, visual, auditory, and/or kinesthetic, of an experience of being in the MDMA state while with those persons or in that life situation. In the days ahead, your experience of that person or situation focused on might change as a result of this exercise.

Coming Down (3 to 6 hours after initial effect)

The psychological effects of the MDMA begin to shut down after about 2 ½ to 3 hours of action. The stimulant qualities of the substance can sometimes linger on for another 2 or 3 hours. For this reason, it is best if the session can be planned for the entire day or early enough in the evening that 6 or 7 hours can elapse between the taking of the drug and going to sleep.

There can be some disappointment and other negative emotions experienced at this time. This is probably best explained psychologically as the contrast between the MDMA state and baseline (ordinary) states. Physiologically, both fatigue (the result of any stimulant) and depleted neurotransmitters can account for this low after the high.

To minimize this physiological component of post negativity, some nutritional supplementation would be useful. Upon coming down from an MDMA experience, one might take 1000 mg. tryptophan before going to sleep. Then, upon rising, one might take 1000 mg. of tyrosine. Both amino acids are available at most health food and vitamin stores. These amino acids will replenish some of the neurotransmitters *suspected* to be depleted by the action of MDMA.

Psychologically, it would be a good tactic to recall the most positive moments of the experience. Looking back on these highlights and insights would help you reaccess the positive state and dispell psychic darkness.

Afterglow (the day after the session)

This is a period when you feel tired, relaxed, and open to others. There persists a residual mental clarity and positive emotional state from the previous day's empathetic and entactogenic adventure. This is sometimes called the"afterglow" and may persist for days or even weeks after a particularly beneficial session.

You might feel either somewhat fatigued or perhaps energized by the previous day's experience. As mentioned earlier, it is best to leave this day free of obligations for the reintegration of the material generated by the session into normal awareness, as well as for continued exploration of the openness you may be feeling. My own preference was to spend most of the next day at home with some time allotted to naps. In addition, I liked to get out to a public place to walk around and interact with people. I found it fascinating to see how my perceptions of people changed after an MDMA session.

Side-Effects and Adverse Reactions

There are a number of common side-effects of MDMA. These include (from a list by George Greer): jaw-clenching, eye wiggle (nystagmus), muscle tension, nausea, decreased appetite. Occasional side-effects reported less frequently are: difficulty in walking, chills, sweating, biting the inside of the cheek, headache, fainting, inability to reach orgasm, and vomiting. Also, psychosomatic symptoms can occur and these can take many forms.

This list of possible side-effects may sound horrible. However, most people find them tolerable, given the highly rewarding main effects of MDMA. None of the symptoms on the list occur in all those who take the substance.

The listed side-effects are most probably not products of the mind, but a direct result of the physiological effects of MDMA. Yet they can be minimized with psychological techniques.

As an example, take the most commonly noted side-effects—jaw-clenching and muscle tension. A good method to allay these negative symptoms is as follows. First, get a moistened washrag, and place it between the teeth of the sufferer. Tell the individual to close his or her eyes and on the count of ten, to progressively tense every muscle in her or his body and to bite down as hard on the washcloth as they can. Then slowly count to ten, instructing them to make their muscles "more and more tense" and their jaw "tighter and tighter." You might talk about the tension in each specific muscle group between counts. Then finally, on ten, tell the individual to "relax completely."

Done in a hot tub, this exercise can be doubly effective.

Hot springs and saunas would be very useful for MDMA sessions, because they help tight muscles to unwind. George Greer disagrees with me on this. He fears that hot tubs might lead to faintness or even cardiac problems.

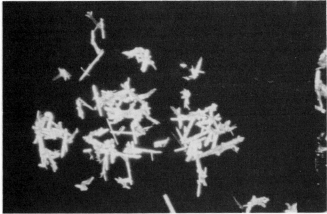

MDMA crystals.

Another technique for relieving jaw tension is to chew gum during the session.

The prescription drug Inderal (chemically known as propranolol) at a dosage of 40 mg. every 4 hours, including a dose shortly before the initial dosage of MDMA, is also helpful. Three doses is probably a good cut-off point. Inderal can relieve some of the side-effects, including tremor and muscle tension. However, Inderal is a blood-pressure medication, which prevents the heart from beating fast; so there may be shortness of breath during any activity requiring exertion.

As mentioned above, the pain of unfinished grief, or early traumatic epidodes, can arise as negative psychological bubbles that burst, transforming into an ecstatic release of tension. Sometimes, an adverse reaction will last the entire session, with no release at all. Greer, in "The Legal, Safe and Effective Use of MDMA," comments:

> The most common undesirable emotional symptom is anxiety. Depression, emotional lability, racing thoughts, confusion, and grandiose thoughts can also occur during or after the session. These other symptoms are not common. It is safe to assume that any psychological disturbance could occur.
>
> The facilitator running the session should be very exper- ienced at handling such reactions and helping clients use them for therapeutic growth. Any physical or psychological reaction can be utilized beneficially if all parties are committed to that endeavor.

It always should be remembered that it is best not to consider sessions as "bad" and "good" sessions, but rather as "difficult" and "easy." An experience that is filled with difficult material can often prove quite useful to an individual, showing him or her areas of their *psyche* that they have repressed and avoided. By opening up to these dark sides of oneself, psychological growth is promoted.

Because these difficult sessions almost always occur during the first few exposures to MDMA, it is important to have a guide or "sitter" who will be there for support and to help the beginner through any possible negative manifestations.

Claudio Naranjo, in the Preface of *The Healing Journey*, discusses what he calls "The Healing Power of Agony and Ecstasy." Naranjo compares experiences on psychoactive substances to the situation in Dante's *Divine Comedy*, a guided tour of heaven and hell. Both the heavenly and hellish types of journey can be useful for psychological growth. The heavenly ones give you a glimpse of your potentials in growth, and the hellish sorts point to what has been repressed from conscious awareness. In terms of the *Divine Comedy,* Naranjo depicts the role of the session's guide:

> For practical purposes, though, it seems clear that the best that the therapist can do is stand by the traveler in hell as Virgil did by Dante, reminding him of his goal, giving him the courage to step ahead and see, pushing him even when he wants to retreat in fear. I believe that the realization that hell is no hell must come from inner realization and not from well-intentioned reassurance and brainwashing, so I find myself saying to patients again and again, "Stay with it." Staying with it is the best way of going through it, whatever it is.

The Changing Nature of the MDMA Experience

Of those that try MDMA, there are some who abide by the words of one fellow who remarked, "When you get the message, hang up the phone." These individuals feel that they have learned what they needed to on their initial sesion and don't need to repeat it. Some comment that they now hope to recapture the feelings they experienced without having to take a drug. Others initiated into the empathetic and entactogenic world are eager to repeat the experience as soon as possible.

This, of course, leads to the question: "How often can you safely use MDMA?" As mentioned earlier, MDMA cannot be taken repeatedly, or it loses its main effect and becomes a bunch of increasingly annoying side-effects. This is due to a phenomenon known as tolerance. Tolerance is the tendency of a person to build up a resistance to the effects of a psychoactive substance when taking it repeatedly. MDMA shows a type of tolerance called tachyphylaxis, which means that tolerance rises rapidly upon subsequent administrations.

Tolerance to a substance decreases with the passage of time. Physically, MDMA can be taken again in two or three days. However, the effects appear to flatten out when taken this often.

There seems to be a need to mentally digest the experience at all levels of the *psyche.* Once per week is the most often MDMA can be used without diminished effect. More sensible would be using it perhaps once per month. This would give sufficient time to integrate all the material uncovered by the experience.

One comment I have heard repeatedly is: "I never have MDMA experiences anymore like my first one" (or first ten sessions). I have noticed from my own series of sessions, over eight years, that while none of my experiences had quite the overwhelming impact of my first few, there were occasions when MDMA again seemed to break me through to a new level of communication, or self-understanding, that I had never before achieved.

This loss of quality in repeated usage might have either physiological or psychological causes. A physiological explanation, for example, is that the long-term tolerance is the result of some permanent change in the way that receptors, at the synapses of brain neurons, react to the MDMA after repeated exposures. Perhaps more likely are possible psychological explanations.

It may be that the experience becomes much more familiar and therefore does not impress us as much. Or it could be that as we integrate the state of consciousness achieved on MDMA into our ordinary state of consciousness, the difference between the two states becomes smaller. Since it is dramatic shifts in consciousness which are noticed most, these repeated experiences are perceived as more commonplace.

If sessions are taken far enough apart, there will be an upward spiraling progression from experience to experience. I leave it for future explorers to find and delineate the patterns that this psychological evolution might take.

Synergy with Other Drugs

Noted architect Buckminster Fuller developed the concept of synergism—"The simultaneous action of separate agencies which, together, have greater total effect than the sum of their individual effects." Many of you know of common synergies, both positive and negative, in the realm of recreational drugs.

A famous example of a negative synergy is the mixing of barbiturates and alcohol. Just small amounts of the two taken together—neither one of them by itself high enough to be dangerous—can combine to kill.

Combinations of MDMA and other drugs most often demonstrate the positive effects of drug synergism. One of the most important discoveries of this kind was that of the benefits to be derived from taking MDMA prior to ingestion of a major psychedelic.

When taken by itself, LSD is quite non-specific in its effects. Set and setting are critical variables in determining which direction an LSD experience will go. But because MDMA is more specific and mainly positive in its effects, using MDMA either shortly before or simultaneously with LSD can usually ensure a positive, short-term psychological set for the LSD experience. For those who normally experience some anxiety prior to taking LSD, the de-stressing, anti-anxiety effect of MDMA can be an enormous boon toward ensuring a positive initial direction to the LSD experience.

This synergistic effect of MDMA and LSD can be quite useful in LSD-assisted therapy. This sort of therapy—which has demonstrated benefits in the treatment of neurosis, alcohol and substance abuse, and terminal cancer patients—can now be practiced with a greater probability of eliciting a positive psychedelic reaction.

MDMA has been combined experimentally with another new psychedelic substance, 2-CB (2,5-dimethoxy-4-bromo-phenethylamine). Alexander Shulgin described 2-CB at a 1983 Conference, "Psychedelics and Spirituality," at the University of California, Santa Barbara:

> 2-CB . . . is a tool . . . which ties the mental process directly and constructively into the physical soma.
>
> The analgesic effects experienced with many, if not most, psychedelic drugs, are not present with 2-CB. On the contrary, there is increased body awareness of every kind, including skin sensitivity, heightened responsiveness to smells, tastes, and sexual stimulation.
>
> One experiences increased consciousness of physical health and energy, or, on the other hand, sharpened awareness of any body imbalance or discomfort.
>
> 2-CB allows for rich visual imagery and intense eyes-closed fantasy without the cluttering up of the mental field with too much elaboration . . . It is a superb tool for learning and growth.

2-CB, as of this writing, is still a legal compound (aside from the "analogs law," which is constitutionally questionable) and has been used by both psychotherapists and self-experimenters. At high doses (above 30 mgs.), 2-CB is intensely hallucinogenic, and, like any major psychedelic, can be frightening for certain people. In small doses, it becomes a mild sensory enhancer but does not have the strongly empathogenic qualities that MDMA has.

Perhaps the best use that has been found for 2-CB is as a synergist with MDMA. When taken together, the MDMA pushes the non-specific 2-CB reaction in a more warm and empathetic direction. Because

2-CB is a psychedelic drug, and therefore not fully predictable, its action can take the user in many different directions. But if the set and setting are right, 2-CB can enhance the desire for sexual orgasm during an MDMA experience. The synergy of the two substances can on occasion be a true aphrodisiac.

What about MDMA in combination with common recreational drugs, such as alcohol, marijuana, and cocaine?

While on MDMA, people can drink a lot of alcohol and not be affected as they would normally be. This is probably due to MDMA's stimulant quality. Observing recreational sessions, I have sometimes noted copious consumption of alcohol. This is not recommended—for two reasons. First, alcohol acts as a depressant, impedes MDMA's action, and produces a stupor state that interferes with MDMA's clarification of thought processes.

Second, the day after MDMA and heavy drinking is bound to be rough. It is a combination of the fatigue of Adam, mixed with the hangover of too many drinks that weren't noticed, that hits you like a ton of bricks.

The most intelligent way to use alcohol with MDMA is to have one mixed drink or a glass of wine after coming down, as a way of calming any residual anxiety.

What was just said about alcohol could almost be applied verbatim to marijuana. Sometimes, however, a small amount of marijuana can be a useful adjunct during the session, as a method of dampening the stimulant qualities of the MDMA. Remember that over-smoking marijuana can dull the experience as well as lead to post-session fatigue.

Since they are both stimulants, MDMA is sometimes compared to cocaine. But there are many important distinctions between them. Cocaine's duration is much shorter, and its effects differ greatly from those of MDMA. Cocaine is not truly empathogenic, leading to talkativeness but not real contact between people. Cocaine is euphoric, but usually does not lead to any authentic self-insight. Many cocaine abusers find regular, though relatively infrequent, use of MDMA as a way of escaping their addiction. They report that the MDMA experience was what they were looking for with cocaine, but never got.

Cocaine truly is addictive. It can be injected or smoked (as a free base), and this will produce a euphoric rush due to the rapid rise of concentrations in the blood. Tolerance builds up, but subsequently larger doses will still produce the rush. A long string of successive dosings is possible.

MDMA and cocaine should never be used together. There are

indications in the MDA literature which suggest that cocaine is negatively synergistic with MDA. Until research can be done, the combination of these two drugs should be avoided.

Chapter VI. Future Potentialities

"The time will come when we'll separate all our senses and capabilities—the visual from the auditory, the tactile from the sense of smell, as well as wit, intellectual capability, creativity— and [be able] to enhance them with drugs."
—Alexander Shulgin (in "Future Drugs," *Omni* magazine)

The controversy and promise of MDMA is part of a larger issue facing our society—the possibility of accessing new states of mind through the intelligent use of drugs and potential non-drug methods, as well as our freedom to do so. The development of tailor-made drugs with more specific effects will continue, as the above quote from Shulgin suggests. Our understanding of the brain, both of its chemistry and structure and of its relationship to thought and feeling, will expand as we enter the 21st century.

Only science fiction, with its broad powers to speculate and extrapolate on current trends, can touch what will someday become our reality. Now I will make an attempt to explore these possible directions, as well as point to coming choices that might lead down very different roads. A possible model for using MDMA in a more rational and less hysterical manner, to make best use of its potential, will then be proposed.

Roots in the Past

However, the future must rest on the present and the present on the past. The introduction of MDMA into our society as a popular intoxicant is part of a historical process in which every ten or twenty years American culture embraces a new drug which reflects the avant-garde ethic of its time, including its art and music, its literary style and street slang.

When someone mentions the "Roaring Twenties," for instance, we think of hip flasks and flappers dancing the Charleston. The speakeasies were packed with multitudes imbibing a very illegal drug called booze.

Then there was the amphetamine boom during World War II. The Germans developed amphetamines in the 1930's and used them to wage the "Blitzkrieg" or "Lightning War." The German slang expression for "speed" was "blitz." Their bomber pilots could stay "wired" for their long-distance runs over England.

But the American military, not to be outdone by the Germans, started packing "crank" (slang for amphetamine) into ration kits of the G.I.'s. The total use during World War II amounted to one pill per soldier per day.

In the 1950s there were the Beatniks. Beats "dug" jazz and jeans and sweatshirts and cool, reciting marijuana-inspired poetry in coffee houses and urban lofts. And they learned Indian chants with a bitter peyote after-taste. The leaders of this new movement challenged the Valium culture of Eisenhower, with its conformist in the grey flannel suit. Their drug of choice was marijuana.

Although he died in 1963, young John Kennedy—with his plans for a New Frontier, his easy-going hedonism and visions of peace—laid the groundwork for the explosive decade of the 'Sixties. The Kennedy spirit found its legacy in the flower-power of the Hippie upheaval and the anti-war sentiment that grew as the decade developed. The drugs of choice of the young and bold of those times were the psychedelic drugs—mushrooms, mescaline, LSD.

Then, the repressive atmosphere of Vietnam warrior and law-and-order champion Nixon led in the 'Seventies, and soon we had the Arab oil cartel setting off a world-wide recession. "Looking out for Number One," the self-assertive ethic of the decade, replaced the mind-expansion and laid-back ways of the previous ten years. So it came as no suprise that cocaine was chosen as drug of the decade.

During this same decade, our friend Adam (aka MDMA) was born as a social phenomenon as part of a new generation of psychoactive compounds. After a relatively quiet childhood, Adam emerged in adolescence as just the right antidote to 'Eighties paranoia.

But Adam's passage to adulthood has been troubled. Adam was branded a renegade in the anti-drug political climate of the times. When Ronald Reagan took over in the White House, he declared "War on Drugs." His wife Nancy chose to turn this war into her Holy Crusade. In this atmosphere colored by fundamentalist politics, in which any drug aside from alcohol is considered sinful, it is difficult to contend that any new substance might be benevolent and useful.

Adam's future is hard to predict. Will he grow up to be a career criminal or a therapist? What about Eve, or the next generation?

Prospects for the Immediate Future

The DEA appears determined to keep MDMA illegal, and any MDMA research frozen. It appears that the DEA intends to keep MDMA in Schedule I. Every recommendation by an independent judicial body to place MDMA in a lower schedule has been rebuffed by the DEA.

The Omnibus Drug Bill of 1986 included "the Controlled Substance Analogue Enforcement Act of 1986," popularly called the "Analogs Act." The bill lists felony penalties for the distribution and manufacture of substances that have a chemical structure substantially similar to that of a controlled substance in Schedules I or II, or which have hallucinogenic, stimulant or depressive effects which are substantially similar or greater than that of a controlled substance.

With the passage of this bill, a whole new tack has been steered with respect to drug policy. The government is sailing full-tilt into dangerous waters where laws ban states of consciousnesss rather than specific drugs.

Thus the prospects for Adam and his friends for the near future appear bleak. Unless the voices of therapists and researchers, who are a small yet vocal minority, can be heard, the anti-drug hysteria sweeping our land may succeed in throwing the baby out with the bathwater. Laws designed to curb dangerous designer drugs, like a synthetic heroin substitute that has produced Parkinsonian symptoms, will also be used by the DEA to repress the radically different sort of drugs being developed to expand human functioning.

A Model for Rational MDMA Use

Thomas Kuhn, in his *The Structure of Scientific Revolutions*, noted that it takes about one generation for a new theory to be accepted by the scientific establishment. The same is more or less true of many new ideas and practices in society.

A good example of this is gambling. A generation ago, lotteries run by the "mob" were called the "numbers racket." Today, many states run numbers rackets of their own, calling them "state lotteries."

It should also be noted that commonly accepted drugs today—such as alcohol and coffee—carried penalties in some past cultures more dreadful than that given for heroin or cocaine in our own society.

Matthew Huxley, articulate son of the late novelist Aldous Huxley, discussed the possiblities of the development of a "socially sanctionable drug" in a 1976 issue of *Interdisciplinary Science Reviews*, which I will examine later in this chapter. In a recent interview in the December 1985 issue of *Futurist Magazine*, Huxley comments on the present situation in this country with respect to drug use:

> Under this administration, hysteria about drug use is back again, much as it was in the late 1950s and 1960s. This is a reflection of the views of many of the administration's supporters, such as born-again Christians. I do not know how long the hysteria will last before a sensible approach can be taken. Let us remember that McCarthyism lasted all too long and seems, alas, to be reappearing.
>
> I do not see a trend against drug use in America, particularly among the middle-aged and the young. In fact, drug use has grown by leaps and bounds. It is the small, conservative, "moral" groups—some of whom have the ear of the administration—who are pressing for draconian enforcement measures.

If Huxley's view is accurate, then it seems inevitable that sooner or later we will have a loosening up of social restrictions on the use of drugs. As the harsh drug measures and billions of dollars poured into armies of drug enforcement personnel fail to stop drug use, the views of the man-on-the-street about how to deal with drug abuse may change dramatically.

People may begin to understand that education, rather than criminalization, is the best way to temper drug use. As I have mentioned earlier in this book, the failure to distinguish between proper use and abuse of drugs—as well as the more fundamental error of not distinguishing between drugs that are safe when used properly and dangerous drugs—led to our present mess with respect to drug use. Classes which teach young people what each drug does and how to use the more benevolent drugs—including the study of such topics as the influence of set and setting on drug exprience, the use of proper dosage, and drug purity—could help enormously in irradicating the present ignorant misuse of drugs.

Our culture is certainly not the first to use powerful mind-altering substances. The use of potent plant-derived compounds has existed in many cultures around the globe and since the beginnings of our species. Powerful psychedelic drugs like psilocybin mushrooms, for example, have been used by Indians in southern Mexico as an adjuct to healing. Shamans called *curanaderos* conduct nighttime ceremonies guided by chanting and drumming. Many other examples of tribal use of powerful intoxicants could be given.

Yet nowhere in any of these cultures can you point to drug-abuse problems that are so prevalent in Western industrial societies. The reason is that the use of drugs in tribal communities is institutionalized, and respect for the powerful sacraments of healing and religion is taught early.

To harness the potential of the newly developed mind-changing compounds, schooling on the proper use of drugs would provide a good first step. Education might be accomplished within the present educational institutions.

But even more innovative would be the development of new institutions for training people to use psychoactive compounds as well as conducting basic research in this area. These would be the central feature of a new model for the use of MDMA as well as other mind-altering tools. Within this new institution—which might be called a Psychological Exploration Center—we might see the integration of many of the growth techniques developed by humanistic and transpersonal psychologies during the past twenty-five years, drug as well as non-drug.

Licensing for the use of drugs would be part of our model for the solution of the drug problem. People would be required to take a course at school or in the Psychological Exploration Center—which might include classroom computer and video simulations of drug experiences, readings, lectures and guided drug sessions to learn to use MDMA responsibly. Then, after taking a comprehensive exam, they would be certified to use MDMA on their own.

This licensing has precedent in the way that our society presently handles the operation of a motor vehicle. Certainly there are many more people killed each year driving cars than using MDMA. There have been only five substantiated cases of human death related to the use of MDMA (all in individuals with heart arythmias and in several cases complicated by multiple drug use). Car accidents are the largest non-disease related cause of death in the United States. As mentioned in Chapter I, there are few if any individuals mentally damaged by MDMA. In spite of the hazards of operating an automobile, there is no draconian ban on the use of cars. Instead, we use education and licensing to make driving as safe as possible. This is because automobiles are tremendously useful for transportation. Society sees the casualties as an acceptable risk when balanced against its benefits. MDMA and some other new compounds, in a similar way, can be seen as useful tools for human mental development.

Licenses for various drugs would require different amounts of training. MDMA would entail a fairly simple course of study compared to the more demanding requirements for mastering of a drug like LSD.

To train and research the mastery of altering consciousness safely, a new specialization—the "Self-Exploration Guide"—might emerge from the fields of psychiatry and psychology. These individuals would be experts at managing and directing the new mental energies and behaviors catalyzed during drug sessions.

Possible Futures

When we speak of "Psychological Education Centers" and "Self-Exploration Guides," we begin to take leave of the dominion of science and enter into the more speculative realm of science fiction. Instead of describing the future of MDMA and mind-altering drugs, it might be better to talk of possible futures—each of them described in terms of potentialities rather than certainties.

In 1973, the United States Government's National Institute on Drug Abuse issued a small booklet which was quite unusual for an agency which normally publishes literature delineating the dangers of using drugs. *Drug Themes in Science Fiction*, by science fiction-author Robert Silverberg, is a short but fascinating work which begins with a lively essay on the book's topic, giving a short history of drug themes in the genre, discussing the "two distinct attitudes toward the use of mind-related drugs" (cautionary and visionary), and listing the various descriptors that are used in the book's Annotated Bibliography. These categories for drug-related science fiction stories include "Drugs as Euphorics," "Drugs as Mind Expanders," "Drugs as Panaceas," "Drugs as Mind Controllers," "Drugs as Intelligence-Enhancers," "Drugs as Sensation-Enhancers," "Drugs as Reality-Testers," Drugs as Mind-Injurers," and "Drugs as Means of Communication."

Of these categories, "Drugs as Euphorics"—"Drugs that give pleasure in simple unstructured ways through release from depression and tension, much as alcohol does in our society" [although alcohol is not, strictly speaking, a euphoric, of course], and "Drugs as Means of Communication"—"Drugs that have the specific property of opening hitherto unknown channels of communication between minds," would begin to suggest the effects of MDMA, which was virtually unknown when this booklet was written.

Silverberg states in his introduction:

> A drug is a kind of magic wand; but it is a chemist's magic
> wand, a laboratory product, carrying with it the cachet of
> science. By offering his characters a vial of green pills or a
> flask of mysterious blue fluid, the author is able to work
> wonders as easily as a sorcerer; and by rigorously examining
> the *consequences* of his act of magic, he performs the
> exploration of speculative ideas which is the essence of
> science fiction.

Each of the alternative scenarios listed in Silverberg's cartography of
possible futures describes yet another effect a drug might have on mind
and civilization. Some of these are quite amazing, and give us some
sense of possible future shapes our humankind may be molded into by
chemical influence. Yet somehow none of the compounds we have
examined in this book appear to be accurately predicted by any of those
works listed in Silverberg's book.

Perhaps the person who came closest to predicting some of the
functions of the empathogens/entactogens is Aldous Huxley. Huxley,
one of the great novelists of the 20th century, developed a deep and
abiding interest in mind-altering drugs, including their effects upon the
**individual and society. As described in Appendix I of this book,
Huxley's academic interests became more worldly with his introduction**
into the altered landscape of mescaline intoxication by Humphry
Osmond in 1954. After that time, Huxley took infrequent but evidently
illuminating psychedelic journeys until his death in 1963. During that
time he also lectured widely, often on the topic of visionary experience
or human potential, which included extensive discourses on mind
drugs.

In a 1962 talk entitled "Human Potentialities" at Esalen Institute
(recorded by Big Sur Tapes), Huxley made the following prediction:

> One day, somebody may discover a really good euphoric.
> We all know that happiness is one of two conditions that
> cause people to function at a high level (the other being
> crisis). Happy people do their work well. A good and
> completely harmless euphoric, one that works its effects
> without damaging the physical organism, might be
> developed which would make people happier and more
> contented.
> Such a drug would lower the barriers between the

conscious mind and the preconscious, the ego and the creative self, leading to the production of great works of art or literature. The euphoric might also have another effect, to make people more moral. Bertrand Russell was fond of pointing out that contented and happy people are more virtuous and kindly toward one another than unhappy people. And here again, we may find the pharmacological tools contributing to the realization of greater potentialities.

Following this path first forged by his venerable father, Matthew Huxley has also written about the possibilities of our culture developing and legitimizing new socially sanctionable drugs which he calls "Soma." The Soma—or, in this case, Somas—of the future would be different from the ancient Soma of the *Vedas* or the Soma envisioned by Aldous Huxley in his novel *Brave New World*.

In his paper "In Search of a Socially Sanctionable Drug," published in *Interdisciplinary Science Reviews* (Vol. 1, No. 2, 1976), the younger Huxley presages the development of new drugs which would be engineered to have specific effects and which would be safe for both the individual and society.

There might be several of these new Somas, each with differing purposes. A Type I Soma "should, like alcohol, be able to enhance social situations by disinhibiting emotional expression, elevating mood, reducing anxiety levels and the like." Sounds a bit like MDMA, doesn't it?

A Type II Soma would foster "the introspective, ideational, contemplative state of consciousness in individuals alone, or in very small groups," while Type III would be sought as a mechanism for "explorations" of the sensory universe. All three types would be engineered for precise duration of effects, be fully tested and approved, and have a way to turn off the effects when doing so would be desirable. They would also be restricted in their use by sanctions on "purpose, person, place, and provider."

Understanding Consciousness and the Nervous System

Another science-fiction author who has made psychoactive drugs a part of his literary repertoire is Norman Spinrad. Spinrad, in an article in the now defunct *Head* magazine, says, "psychochemistry [has] created states of consciousness that had never existed before." His view is that "psycho-chemicals are a declaration of independence from the minds we were born with," and that hence "we will no longer be able to count on our 'naturally evolved' brain chemistry as a benchmark of sanity."

Spinrad is touching here on the idea developed in Chapter II that there exist many alternative states of consciousness, and that our ordinary state is not necessarily the only state in which we can be considered mentally healthy. The intervention of a drug into the nervous system means that different patterns of brain activity are set up, with each compound producing its own distinct mode of experiencing.

Building upon this theme is the work of psychologist Timothy Leary. In his fascinating book *Exo-Psychology*, Leary explores a model of human psychological growth in which each individual turns on and uses a series of brain "circuits" during his or her life. These circuits are distinct states of what Leary calls "contelligence" (consciousness + intelligence). Each succeeding circuit activated is a quantum leap to a new and different level of contelligence, but rests upon the foundation of the preceeding circuits.

He also postulates that humankind is itself evolving through a sequence in which much of our species will soon operate at higher levels of neural functioning. Leary states, "The person who can dial and tune the circuits of the nervous system is not just more intelligent but can be said to operate at a higher, more complex level of evolution."

The last part of this millennium may see dramatic advances in the areas of neurophysiology, psychopharmacology, and consciousness sciences. The new understandings and resultant technologies will shape future human psychological growth.

In neurophysiology, the brain is at last beginning to yield its secrets. In the last twenty years, psychobiologists have begun to describe the chemistry of brain neurons, the synapses that separate them, and the way in which signals travel through both. A number of neuro-transmitters have been isolated and studied, and their relationship to the various neuron circuits in the brain are starting to be understood.

The function of various types of neurons have also begun to be comprehended, as have ways that more complex structures in the brain act to regulate sensation, thought, feelings, and behavior.

Psychopharmacology has emerged as a distinct science during the last thirty years. Alexander Shulgin, in a talk at a 1983 Psychedelics Conference at the University of California, Santa Barbara, speculated on the implications of some discoveries in this field:

> Let us look at the history of other areas of psychotropic chemistry.
>
> A few decades ago, it was marveled on that past drugs

such as the opiates, including morphine, heroin, meperidine, could have such an exacting influence on the brain's integrity. Then it became known that there were natural factors in the brain that had these actions, and there were specific sites in the brain which were pre-designed to respond to them.

There were the enkephalins and their fragmented portions, known as the endorphins, which were derived from the cephalic process, and related to morphine; these met the person's need for the suppression of pain.

Perhaps there are the enkedelics (from the psychedelics) and the specific enescalines (from mescaline) yet to be discovered that are related to these communicative factors— which might be natural and which might be connected, eventually, to the natural receptor sites, for transcendental communication.

We can speculate that there are also receptors in the brain for MDMA, and that these have something to do with the way that empathy is expressed in the structures of the nervous system. In the future, we may find many compounds that control almost every aspect of human thought, feeling, and behavior. From the random and haphazard ways we function now, the future may see each of us as a musician playing the keys of a magic synthesizer. What may be commanded from our fleshy instrument is not just sound, but all the qualities of human experience.

In addition to our understanding of the hardware of mental functioning, we will soon learn more about the states of consciousness associated with the neurological structures. Psychologists such as John Lilly, Kenneth Pellitier, Ken Wilbur, and Timothy Leary have proposed complex maps of human consciousness and intelligence. Valle and von Eckertsberg have compiled a book listing more than a score of these maps which they call *Metaphors of Consciousness.*

Each of these systems is built on concepts drawn from science, art or religion, and sometimes from combinations of the three. They attempt to use metaphors from these fields to build models of how the human mind actually processes information and, even more mysterious, how it becomes aware of itself.

Beyond the tentative threads of today may lie a true science of consciousness, and when integrated with neurophysiology, a real scientific psychology may emerge.

Altering States of Consciousness

From the new knowledge of the nervous system and consciousness will come more powerful and precise technologies for changing the functioning of the nervous system and producing altered states of consciousness. Not all of these new technologies will be limited to pharmacological compounds, but will probably include a wide range of methods. Nor will each of these new technologies be used exclusively, but may be combined to vastly increase their effectiveness.

One of these new technologies will be biofeedback. Back in the 'Sixties, when biofeedback was first introduced, it was touted by some as the path to instant meditation, or as an "electronic LSD." Small machines that produced alpha brainwave feedback were marketed that did nothing more than convey electrical noise made by people moving their eyes.

Biofeedback devices pick up electrical waves from the surface scalp by the use of electrodes taped on the head. A device called an E.E.G. (an electroencephalograph) measures the brainwaves, which are then presented back to the person being monitored by sound (a tone, for instance) or visually (some new biofeedback devices have video monitors).

The early disillusionment with biofeedback as a method of altering consciousness may have resulted because the ultimate promise of this method could not be matched by the technology of the time. With the advent of the microcomputer, biofeedback might again move to fulfill its original potential.

Computers may help us find out exactly what electronic changes occur in response to changes in states of consciousness, and to use feedback to help make desired changes. Some of the possibilities of human/computer linkups are a future when we could buy ROM-discs which contain previously recorded desirable experiences, play them on a machine, and have the experiences. This might eventually replace movies as a form of entertainment.

Another use of biofeedback is close in its reported effects to that of MDMA. Psychologist Jean Millay has done experiments with a biofeedback device which places the brainwaves of two individuals into synchronization. Some have reported increased empathy and even telepathy while making these connections.

Other experiments being done with altered-states technologies include new ones—such as electronic brain stimulation using electrodes taped to parts of the heads to induce altered states—and older methods—such as hypnosis presented in new and more powerful ways.

Recently, "brain spas" have appeared which feature machines which alter the brain in different ways, as described in Michael Hutchison's book *Megabrain*. While there are many who claim to have been helped by these machines, it is probably best to see these as early prototypes of what will be truly useful devices ten or twenty years from now.

If present trends continue and are allowed by the conservative forces in our society to manifest, the future may see a blending of the various new altered-state technologies to radically transform the way humans function psychologically. We may find even more advanced generations of specific psychoactive drugs, electronic interfaces with computers and biofeedback devices blended with ancient methods, such as meditation and yoga, to allow individuals the freedom to change their states of consciousness at will, as well as freedom from negative states of mind.

Violent individuals might find ways to control their impulses.

Creative artists may find ways to augment their craft.

Humanity may find a key to ecstasy.

Understanding Ecstasy

Ecstasy is a transcendent emotional experience and an altered state of consciousness. The root meaning of the word comes from *ex-stasis*, literally out of, or released from, a fixed or unmoving condition.

MDMA certainly can lead to the attainment of its unique version of ecstasy. Novelist Thomas Pynchon, author of *Gravity's Rainbow*, says of the action of MDMA: "the circuits of the brain which mediate alarm, fear, flight, fight, lust, and territorial paranoia are temporarily disconnected. You see everything with total clarity, undistorted by animalistic urges. You have reached a state which the ancients have called nirvana, all seeing bliss."

Nirvana and ecstasy are here synonyms for an experience that is often attained through the prudent and responsible use of MDMA. Robert Masters, head of the Institute for Mind Research and author of *Varieties of Psychedelic Experience* (with his wife Jean Houston), compares MDMA to the mythic drink of the ancient Greek gods, *Nepenthe*—the banisher of sorrows. The state of transcendent ecstasy temporarily dispels our psychic darkness, filling us with the light that heals. The therapeutic effects of this modern *Nepenthe* has its origin in the capacity to banish the mental traumas and depressions that cloud minds, giving us a glimpse of what it's like to be truly happy.

Appendix I.
MDMA's Family Tree:
Chemistry & Physiological Effects

The family tree to which MDMA belongs is large and varied, heavy with psychoactive drug fruit of every description. The main trunk is alkaloid drugs and, further up, the tree forks. We follow up the branch of the compounds called phenylalkylamines and, still higher, the tree branches again into the phenylisopropylamines. The methoxylated phenylisopropylamines are found on a small top branch from which hangs a cluster of MDA-like fruit—including MDMA as well as a bud or two.

MDMA is a semi-synthetic drug. It is related to several substances found in plants, but is also a member of a large family of psychoactive compounds that are synthesized in chemical laboratories.

The vegetative ancestry of MDMA is found in the essential oils of more than half a dozen familiar herbs, roots, and spices, which contain substances from which MDMA and its relatives can be derived. The list of plants containing these precursor volatile oils include nutmeg, mace, sassafras, saffron, calamus, crocus, parsley, dill, and vanilla beans. Of these, nutmeg, mace, and calamus have long histories of use as psychoactive plants.

Calamus (botanically *Acorus calamus*) contains the active essential oil asarone, which is a natural precursor of the psychedelic TMA-2, which will be discussed later in this section. Because of this psychoactivity, calamus under other names such as "rat root," "sweet flag," etc., has been used by many cultures—including those of India and China—as a medicine, and by the North American Indians for the relief of fatigue and in their puberty initiation rites.

Peter Stafford, in his *Psychedelics Encyclopedia*, recounts some of the lore surrounding nutmeg and mace:

> Nutmeg, which in the U.S. is mainly used as a garnish during Christmas festivities, is the dried kernel of *Myristica fragrans*, a tree native to the Spice Islands, near New Guinea. Now cultivated in many places, the tree grows to about fifty feet high and bears seeds for up to sixty years. Its fruit looks much like a peach, and contains a brownish-purple, shiny

kernel encased within a bright orange-red or red covering. The covering, or aril, is used for production of mace; the seed, dried in the sun for about two months and turned over each day, becomes nutmeg. Both the kernel and its covering contain psychoactive components within their oils.

Most of the natural substances that contain compounds similar to MDA have a history of use for their medicinal properties and their psychoactivity. The *Ayurveda* of ancient India refers to nutmeg and mace as *made shaunda*, generally translated as "narcotic fruit." An 1883 *Materia Medica* from Bombay records that "the Hindus of West India take Myristica as an intoxicant." Nutmeg has been used for centuries as a snuff in rural eastern Indonesia; in India, the same practice appears, but often the ground seed is first mixed with betel and other kinds of snuff. Restrictions on hashish in Egypt have brought about periods when nutmeg was used as a substitute.

Nutmeg appears in the Hindu Pharmacopoeia as a treatment for fever, asthma, and heart disease. Since the seventh

Nutmeg, a psychoactive spice, is the dried seed within the fruit of an East Indian tree, Myristica fragrans.

century A.D., Arab physicians have used it for digestive disorders, kidney disease, and lymphatic ailments. Yemeni men are said to consume nutmeg to increase and maintain their sexual vigor.

Nutmeg and mace weren't known to the Greeks or Romans. They were not introduced to the West until 1512, when the Portuguese reached the Banda, or Nutmeg, Islands. The earliest record of nutmeg's mental effects comes from 1576, in the description of a "pregnant English lady who, having eaten ten or twelve nutmegs, became deliriously inebriated" (she was lucky not to have died).

In the seventeenth century, nutmeg became an important article in the spice trade which the Dutch monopolized for a long while with their naval superiority.

Use of this commonly available substance as an inebrient has continued into this century. "Confirmed reports of its use by students, prisoners, sailors, alcoholics, marijuana-smokers, and others deprived of their preferred drugs," write Shultes and Hofmann in *The Botany and Chemistry of Hallucinogens*" are many and clear. Especially frequent is the taking of nutmeg in prisons, notwithstanding the usual denial of prison officials."

Nutmeg's essential oils include safrole, which is similar to MDA, and myristicin, which is related to MMDA. Conversion of these non-amine oils in the presence of ammonia into the amine forms (e.g. MDA and MMDA) has been demonstrated in the laboratory, giving rise to speculation that a similar process occurs in the body to produce mental effects.

In the chemical laboratory, these essential oils can be aminated (converted to the amine form) to produce their semi-synthetic relative. notably *Myristica fragrans* (nutmeg) can be aminated to make MDA. Indeed, the simplest chemical process for manufacturing MDA is to combine safrole with the basic gas ammonia. There are some other, more complicated laboratory methods for the making of MDA—including the manufacture from Heliotropin, used in the perfume industry to make the scent of hyacinths.

These semi-synthetic compounds are part of a larger family of chemicals known as the alkaloids. Shulgin, in his chapter "Psychotomimetic Drugs: Structure-Activity Relationships" in *Handbook of Psychopharmacology, Volume 11*, states:

These are basic, nitrogen-containing organic chemicals from the plant kingdom, and they represent a bewildering array of structural variations. A consistent theme found through most of the alkaloids is the separation of the nitrogen atom from an aromatic system, by two carbon atoms.

This relationship can be found through most of the known family of alkaloids and has been the mainstay for

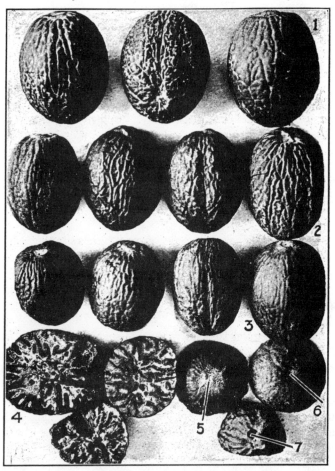

Myristica (nutmeg): 1, Penang nutmegs. 2, Round West India nutmegs. 3, Banda nutmegs. 4, Longitudinal, cross and a broken surface of the seed. 5, Upper part of the seed. 6, Base of the seed. 7, Wormy seed.

the thousands of synthetic drugs that have been based on some alkaloid model.

From the alkaloid trunk, there are many branches reaching skyward. Among them are two branches of compounds, the phenylalkylamines and the indolealkylamines, which have within them most of the drugs variously called psychedelic.

The phenylalkylamines are alkaloids with a simple benzene ring in the position of the aromatic system. The indolealkylamines are alkaloids with the more complex indole ring in the position of the aromaic

Sassafras is a botanical source used in synthesizing MDA-like compounds.

system. On the phenylalkylamines branch (also sometimes called the substituted phenylethylamines) are also a number of stimulants and our friends, the empathogens. The indolealkylamines fork into three branches—the tryptamines (of which psylocybin, the active ingredient in magic mushrooms, is a prototype); the lysergic acid derivatives (of which LSD is the prototype); and the beta-carbolines (of which harmaline, the most active ingredient of the South American vine from which the psychedelic drink *yage* is made, is the prototype).

Structure/Activity Relationships

Structure/activity relationships are the ways that (1) the members of

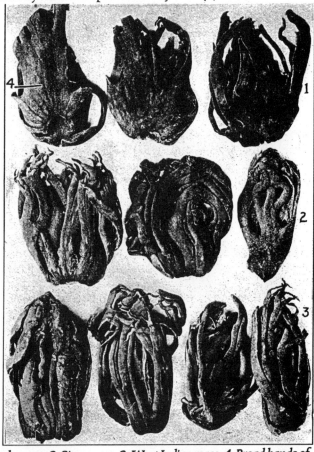

Macis: *1, Banda mace. 2, Siam mace. 3, West Indian mace. 4, Broad bands of Banda mace.*

a family of compounds compare structurally to each other, and (2) correlation of these differences with observed differences in the potency and the effects of the compounds. What is amazing is how slight changes in a position of a carbon atom on a benzene ring, for example, or the addition of an "alpha-methyl tail," can make such dramatic changes in the nature of the "high" or the duration of the experience of various psychoactive substances.

These structure/activity relationships have been systematically mapped by chemists and pharmacologists. For those who would like more technically detailed descriptions (I can imagine some readers objecting that all of this is already too technical), I suggest looking at Roger Brimblecombe and Roger Pinder's *Hallucinogenic Agents*, or Alexander Shulgin's "Speculations on Structure/Activity Relationships" as noted above.

Among the indolealkylamines as a class, structure/activity relationships have been mapped with some success. But the greatest demonstration of the significance of variations has been with the phenylalkylamines. Shulgin divides the phenylalkylamines into two subgroups, the phenethylamines, of which mescaline is the prototypical example, and the phenylisopropylamines, of which TMA is the primary representative.

Mescaline and the Phenethylamines

On the bottom of the phenylalkylamine branch is 3,4,5-trimethoxyphenethylamine, commonly known as mescaline. Mescaline is the prototype of the phenethylamines. Mescaline is a psychedelic drug and the primary active component of the cactus *Lophophora williamsii*, generally known as peyote. This small cactus has been used for perhaps as long as 3,000 years by the Mexican Indians in religious rites and healing ceremonies. Mescaline was first isolated from peyote in 1897 by Arthur Heffter, and first synthesized by Ernst Späth in 1919.

Mescaline is normally taken as a sulphate or hydrochloride (chemical forms that make it active when taken by mouth).

The compound appears as a powder composed of long white needle crystals. The active dose is about 400 mg., and the inebriation lasts for about 12-15 hours. Perhaps the most influential account of a mescaline experience was by novelist Aldous Huxley, in his short book *Doors of Perception*, published in 1954. Huxley reported on his initial mescaline experience and speculated on the nature of such radical mental transformations.

One individual who "took a day from my professional work in

industry to explore the catalytic effects of mescaline" was Alexander Shulgin. Shulgin comments, in his chapter "An Ever-Changing Quest," in Grinspoon and Bakalar's *Psychedelic Reflections,* on this experience:

> The impressions of the experience are best expressed in the flow of events that followed that day. There began what might be called a quest of curiosity. I realized that the mind, and the senses that provide inputs to the mind, were all grossly under-utilized faculties in the study of the world around us; and that it was irrational to ascribe to a small quantity of chemical the intrinsic power to provide this sensory augmentation. I found it hard to accept that such a simple, unsophisticated molecule, containing barely 30 atoms, could carry within its structure such complexities of thought patterns, of sensory license, of visual magic.
>
> It was inescapable that the molecule didn't do anything itself, but rather, allowed the human mind to make these changes. It could only serve as a catalyst, unleashing and promoting channels of mental processes that were native, that lay inculcate in the normal brain. And why should a modest cactus contain such an effective catalyst, expressible only in man?
>
> Psychologists might be able to dissect the nature of the changes, and physicians might be able to define the sites of action, but my background in chemistry and biochemistry limited me to the atoms and bonds of this catalyst, and the compelling inquiry into their function by the simple strategy of changing them and observing the changes in effect that resulted. I felt that by providing in a single process both the structural change and the subjective evaluation of the results of such change, a pattern might emerge that would tie together the definitions of the catalyst and the process being catalyzed.

Alexander Shulgin's methodical investigation—changing various parts of the molecule related to his initial catalyst, mescaline—has yielded many new psychoactive compounds, members of MDMA's extensive family tree. Many of these new compounds are much more potent and have quite different effects than the prototypical mescaline. As we will see, Shulgin has been the discoverer of almost all of them.

Shulgin developed several noteworthy compounds in the same classification of substituted phenethylamines as mescaline. These include escaline, which has a substituted ethyl group and proscaline, which bears a substituted propyl group, both in the "four position" on the benzene ring—demonstrating how changing things at this important place in the molecule can increase the potency of a compound. Both have effects almost identical to those of mescaline, but escaline is about five times as potent and proscaline ten times as potent as mescaline. Their durations of action are also somewhat shorter than mescaline.

Two other substituted phenethylamines with potential for clinical and other applications are the substitition variants of mescaline, 2-CB and 2-CD. These are also known chemically as the 2-carbon homologs of the phenylisopropylamines DOB and DOM. In Chapter V, I discuss 2-CB in more depth, describing its usefulness in combination with MDMA.

There are several more active compounds in this group, some with potencies greatly exceeding mescaline and some with bizarre mental effects.

TMA and the Methoxylated Phenylisopropylamines

On one branch higher up on our psychoactive tree, we find phenylisopropylamines. One bunch of drug-fruit on this branch are the methoxylated phenylisopropylamines. The prototype of this cluster is the first psychedelic drug to evolve from a planned and systematic use of the principles discovered in the study of the relationship between chemical structure and biological activity—TMA (3,4,5-trimethoxy-phenylisopropylamine). First synthesized in 1947 by Hey, his enthusiastic report on the euphoric properties of the substance provoked Perez and a group of Canadian coworkers to investigate further. They discovered that the experience on low dosages was pleasant and there were no complaints aside from some initial nausea. Later experiments with higher doses showed TMA to be a "hallucinogenic drug with some undesirable features." What was important, however, was the two-fold increase in potency due to the connection of an alpha-methyl group to the nitrogen in the mescaline molecule.

The addition of the alpha-methyl group to the nitrogen atom in phenethylamine gives rise to the compound amphetamine, a powerful stimulant. Thus, many of the compounds that have this transformation have, in the past, been called psychotomimetic amphetamines or psychedelic amphetamines.

But the name "amphetamine" properly belongs only to one

Chemical Structure of Mescaline and the Phenethylamines.

substance, 2-amino-1-phenylpropane—the well-known stimulant. There are many psychoactive substances in this group, and many of them have effects very different from those of the stimulant amphetamine. Instead, let's call this class of substances the phenyl-isopropylamines.

The number of psychoactive substances in this group is large. There are, for example, six types of TMA. I will mention only the most noteworthy.

In 1962, Shulgin aminized the essential oil asarone, contained in calamus—with TMA-2 (2,4,5-trimethoxyphenylisopropylamine) being the result. It had been synthesized earlier, but Shulgin was the first to discover its psychoactive effects. What he found was that the re-arrangement of the molecule from the configuration of mescaline to a different substitution pattern (2,4,5 instead of 3,4,5) had increased the potency ten times over that of the first TMA! Reports of extensive nausea during the experience should deter use of this strong hallucinogen.

DOM and the Alkylphenylisopropylamines

A second dangling collection of psychoactives on the phenyliso-propylamine branch is the alkylphenylisopropylamines, represented by their prototype DOM (2,5-dimethoxy-4-methyl-amphetamine). DOM was first synthesized in 1963. In 1967, a new drug was introduced to the counterculture under the name STP. Although this fact wasn't clear for some time, STP and DOM turned out to be the same drug. 5,000 tablets of STP, 10 mg. each, were distributed at the first hippie "love-in" in San Francisco's Golden Gate Park.

The experience was intensely hallucinogenic, and there were a number of panic reactions. Some claimed that the experience lasted for three days, although later studies indicated that it can last only up to around 24 hours. STP rapidly lost popularity after this rocky debut.

Actually, DOM, taken in the dosages that Shulgin and his colleagues first used in exploring the compound (around 3 mg.), has euphoria and enhancement of self-awareness as its main effects, while being free of strong physiological changes or perceptual distortions. But the first doses of street STP contained 20 mg. of DOM, later halved to 10 mg. At this dosage level, DOM becomes a powerful hallucinogenic drug lasting up to 24 hours. A chemical relative of DOM, DOET (2,5-dimethoxy-4-ethylphenylisopropylamine) is very similar in its effects to DOM, but is experienced as milder until it reaches dosages that would be hallucinogenic for DOM. At dosages around 4 mg. the effects are similar

Chemical Structure of MMDA Series.

MDMA

MDE

MDA

MBDB

MMDA

Chemical Structure of MDMA and it Variations.

to those listed above with low dosages of DOM.

MDA and the Methylenedioxyphenylisopropylamines

Do you find the above word a tongue-twister? Now you know why I put this discussion at the back of this book.

MDA (3,4-methylenedioxyphenylisopropylamine) was first synthesized by German chemists G. Mannish and W. Jacobson in 1910. Yet it wasn't until 1939 that the first animal studies were conducted, when the team of Gunn, Gurd, and Sachs became interested in the substance while conducting adrenaline studies. Two years later, another team— Loman, Myerson, and Myerson—thought this compound might alleviate Parkinsonism, but abandoned the concept when the single patient tested experienced muscular rigidity. Also about this time, MDA was rejected as a possible weight-reduction agent and as an antidepressant by the Smith, Klein, and French Co., because pronounced though not "hallucinogenic" effects interfered after a few days with the patients' ordinary routines.

Then, in the mid-'Fifties, Gordon Alles, the UCLA researcher who had discovered amphetamine in 1927, became interested in MDA and a related compound because of their similarity to ephedrine, the standard drug for testing central nervous system stimulation during the 1930s and 1940s. Peter Stafford, in his *Psychedelics Encyclopedia* describes the details of Alles' examination of MDA:

> He decided that he would conduct what he called a "double-conscious" test of these substances—meaning he would synthesize, measure, and take them himself in order to compare their effects with what he knew about how ephedrine affected him. "I was quite well-calibrated," he remarked later, "with 50 mg. doses of ephedrine and with similar doses of amphetamine."
>
> After tests with dogs, which indicated that these two compounds were one third to one half as active in their peripheral effects as mescaline and amphetamine, Alles swallowed 36 mg. of MDA. During the following two hours, he noticed neither physical nor mental sensations. He then took an additional 90 mg.
>
> Within a few minutes, he "realized that a notable subjective response was going to result." The muscles of his neck became markedly tensed, and he was closing his jaws tightly and grinding his back teeth. He perspired quite a bit

and noted a slowed respiration rate. His pupils were "markedly dilated . . . I had never seen such dilation of the pupils in animals or man to such an extent."

About 45 minutes after the second dose, smoke rings filled the air, moving in slow motion about him. In a closed room on the sixth floor of a university building, there "was no possible source of smoke rings." Yet,

> an abundance of curling smoke rings was readily observed in the environment whenever a relaxed approach in observation was used. Visually, these had complete reality; and it seemed quite unnecessary to test their properties because it was surely known and fully appreciated that the source of the visual phenomena could not be external to the body. When I concentrated my attention on the details of the curling gray forms by trying to note how they would be affected by passing a finger through their apparent field, they melted away. Then when I relaxed again, the smoke rings were there.

Talking about these smoke rings later, Alles commented, "I was as certain they were really there as I am now sure that my head is on top of my body." These visual effects only introduced what lay ahead.

Looking at his "almost entirely black eyes," he had been fearful momentarily but thereafter had "a general feeling of well being," accompanied by a switch in his perception of the location of his consciousness.

> When I was very relaxed, my thinking became introspectively speculative. Awareness of the body and of its functionings became subject to a detached spatial consideration, and the reality of the place of detached observation for a time seemed clearly transposed out of the body and to a place above and to the right rearward. I was compelled to turn my head several times and look into the upper corner of the room in wonder at what part of me could be up there and observing the subjective situation and behavior as if from that point. I observed this phenomenon from where I was seated.

Alles recounted this experience before a Josiah Macy Jr.
Foundation conference in 1957. In 1959, his account was
published as part of the proceedings of the conference as
Neuropharmacology: Transactions of the 4th Conference (edited
by Harold Abramson).

By the mid-'Sixties, MDA began to show up in the subculture—
nicknamed "the Love Drug" or "the Mellow Drug of America." Because
of its high profile at the time of the Comprehensive Drug Abuse
legislation of 1970, it was placed in Schedule I.

As I noted above, safrole, the essential oil in a number of plants, most
notably *Myristica fragrans* (nutmeg) can be aminized to make MDA.
Indeed, the simplest chemical process for manufacturing MDA is to
combine safrole with the basic gas ammonia. There are a some other,
more complicated laboratory methods for the making of MDA—
including its manufacture from Helitropin, used in the perfume industry
to make the scent of hycacinths.

MDA is actually two distinct drugs. Each is a mirror image of the
other, and thus classified by the direction in which they bend light. The
dextro,or right-handed, version and the *levo*, or left-handed, form of
MDA each exhibit unique drug effects but are often blended together in

Gordon Alles, discoverer of the psychoactive effects of MDA.

a 50% mix called "racemic" MDA.

Clinical studies performed by Shulgin have shown that the *levo* isomer of MDA possesses properties that occur with the use of the racemic mixture. On the other hand, the *dextro* isomer of MDA does not possess such properties, but rather has been characterized by Shulgin as "more benign and peaceful," when compared with racemic MDA.

The pharmacologically equivalent dosages for the first three forms are 70 mg. for the *levo*, 125 for the racemic, and 225 for the *dextro*. It is clear that the *levo* isomer is responsible for most of the activity of the racemic mixture.

It has been noted that discoveries in science often occur at about the same time to two or more researchers working independently of one another. Another case of such synchronous discovery is the production of MMDA (3-methoxy-4,5-methyldioxyphenylisopropylamine) by both Gordon Alles and Alexander Shulgin, at about the same time. Both produced MMDA through the aminization of another of the essential oils of nutmeg, myristicin.

MMDA is effective as a hydrochloride salt at 120-150 mg. In addition to the original MMDA, there are five other MMDAs numbered in a manner similar to the six TMAs and varying molecularly in somewhat the same fashion (although there is no MMDA corresponding to MMDA 6, but, instead, a MMDA-3a and MMDA 3b). Each of these MMDAs has its own distinct set of effects, and these vary in potency, with MMDA-2, MMDA-3a and MMDA-5 with the highest potencies, about three times as powerful as MMDA.

Now we reach the top of the tree, stretching high to grasp two globes of fruit at the end of a small top branch. Does it not seem odd that these two "N-methyl derivatives of the phenylisopropylamines" have been called Adam (MDMA) and Eve (MDE)—two fruits from the tree of wisdom in our psychotropic garden?

It is structurally analogous to MDA in the same way that methamphetamine is analogous to amphetamine. This "N-methylation" of MDA shortens the course of the experience, increases the required minimum dosage, and changes its effects in the ways already described.

MDMA (N-methyl-3,4-methylenedioxyphenylisopropylamine), the focus of this book, is one of these two deri005ivitives of MDA.

Like MDA, MDMA has both a right-handed and a left-handed version. However, it is the *dextro* or right-handed isomer that is active, while the *levo* or left handed version is substantially without activity. David Nichols, who discussed this topic at length during 1986 MDMA hearings, has speculated that it is "N-methylation" (the addition of an N-methyl group to MDA) that makes the action of MDMA so different. Nichols goes on to suggest that the N-methylation renders the *levo* isomer inactive while leaving the *dextro* isomer unaltered in its effects. This would account for the lack of a hallucinogenic component to MDMA's effects.

MDE (N-ethyl-3,4-methylenedioxyphenylisopropylamine) has come into some prominence since the banning of MDMA—under the nickname "Eve." Still an unscheduled substance as of this writing, MDE is somewhat similar to MDMA, but is slightly faster-acting and shorter-lived than MDMA. According to Shulgin, its action is just about completed at the end of the second hour of its action. It is also said to be 25% less potent than MDMA. Eve has been described by some users as lacking MDMA's ability of unlocking the emotions. Instead, it is said to be more of a stimulant than a feeling-enhancer.

One largely unexplored fresh bud on a branch at the very top of our tree is the newly reported compound MBDB, or N-methyl-1-(1,3-benzodioxol-5-yl)-2-butanamine. David Nichols has described MBDB in a paper in the proceedings of the 1986 MDMA Conference held in Oakland published in the *Journal of Psychoactive Drugs* with the long but informative title, "Differences Between the Mechanism of Action of MDMA, MBDB, and the Classic Hallucinogens: Identification of a New Therapeutic Class: Entactogen."

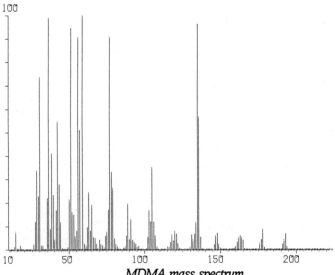

3,4-METHYLENEDIOXYMETHAMPHETAMINE HCL

MDMA mass spectrum.

Although less potent than MDMA, MBDB has qualitative effects in humans very similar to MDMA. Furthermore, it has the *dextro*-isomer that was more active, similar to MDA and in contrast to the hallucinogenic amphetamines. In rats trained to discriminate LSD from saline, MBDB did *not* have LSD-like actions.

MBDB represents a structure that combines two separate structural features that abolish or attenuate hallucinogenic activity: N-methylation and alpha-etheylation. All the logic of structure-activity relationships derived from substituted amphetamines argues that the synergistic attenuation provided by these two structural features should render MBDB totally inert as a hallucinogen. Yet, MBDB *is* biologically active. It generally has the same effect on emotion and empathy as MDMA. Clearly, one is not dealing with the pharmacology of hallucinogens anymore, but with some different category of psychoactive drug.

Inasmuch as MBDB represented the first molecular structure that could definitely be placed outside the structure-activity definitions of the hallucinogenic amphetamine class, it was designated as the prototype of a new pharmacological class. That is not to say that MDMA—or even MDA—does not exert this same action to some degree, but only that MBDB is the clearest example, based on a structure-activity relationship argument that cannot be classified as a hallucinogen.

Nichols goes on to name this class of psychoactives the "entactogens." MBDB has been reported by early users to be milder in its action than MDMA because it lacks the stimulant-like euphoria at the beginning of the experience. Instead, the experience is a more subtle yet purer version of the empathogenic-entactogenic qualities attributed to MDMA.

MDMA and the Brain

The question of what MDMA does in the brain remains largely unanswered at the present time. Much more is known about the psychopharmacology of psychedelics, such as LSD, and stimulants, such as amphetamine.

Only one paper has thus far been published on the subject of MDMA's brain activity, by David Nichols and others in the *Journal of Medicinal Chemistry*. In this study, the release of serotonin, a brain neurotransmitter, was studied in "whole rat brain synaptosomes." The results suggested that MDMA's activity might be due to the release of the serotonin transmitter.

In order to understand what this means, I should tell you something about the brain and the way psychoactive drugs work in them.

Brains are made up of neurons, cells which transmit electrical signals through them and to one or more other neurons with which they are interconnected. These chains and networks of neurons make up the circuitry by which the brain does such complex tasks as receiving sensory information, thinking and reasoning, and sending commands to muscles.

The way that neurons transmit this information is complicated, but what is important here is that their transmission involves an electrical charge traveling down the length of the neuron and triggering the release, at the end of the neuron, of a bunch of chemicals into a gap (called a synapse) between the transmitting end (dendrite) and the receiving end of the next neuron (called an axion).

The chemicals, called neurotransmitters, then travel across the gap and fit into little molecular keyholes (imagine that the neurotransmitters are keys) called receptor sites. When these keyholes are fitted with keys and "turned on" they trigger a charge to be passed down the stimulated neuron to other dendrites. These stimulated neurons might then, in turn, trigger other neurons, this process continuing to form long neural cirucits, networks of activated brain cells.

Many of these neurotransmitters resemble psychoactive drugs. The two principal neurotransmitters for one of the neuron systems (the cholinergic system), dopamine and norepinephrine, are similar to the prototypical mescaline of the substituted phenethylamines. Serotonin, the principle transmitter of the indolic system, looks an awful lot like the powerful psychedelic drug DMT and its close relative psilocybin.

Psychoactive drugs can affect systems of neurons in several different ways. They can imitate the neurotransmitters themselves and plug into receptor sites just as the neurotransmitter native to the brain might. This could stimulate a firing of the affected neuron, or it might just tie up the receptor, keeping it from being activated by the brain's native neurotransmitters.

Psychoactive drugs can also keep neurotransmitters from being recycled once they are used. This is called blocking "reuptake." Or they might stimulate the brain's natural neurotransmitters to be released.

It is this last possibility that Nichols and his colleagues are suggesting occurs with regard to MDMA. They also have contrasted this action with that from MDA, which they speculated may stimulate neurotransmitters directly affecting receptor sites.

The neurotransmitter systems affected may also differ between MDA, MDMA, and MBDB. Both MDA and MDMA have significant effects on dopamine pathways in the brain, while MBDB does not. However, MDMA's effect is an order of magnitude less than that from amphetamine. Thus, MDMA and MDMB cannot be considered stimulants as amphetamine is.

MDMA and the Human Body

One of the most often expressed fears about the use of MDMA centers on its effects upon the body. Indeed, what does MDMA do to our fragile human shells?

Since MDMA has not undergone the usual trials required by the FDA for approval of a new drug, there is little hard information to report. The controversy surrounding the possibility of brain damage has already been discussed at some length. I have also noted some of the short-term psychological side-effects that may occur during an MDMA session in Chapter V. In that chapter as well are listed medical conditions with which MDMA should not be used. The most important of these is heart arythmia, to which five human deaths have been attributed.

The only physiological study of MDMA was reported by Joseph Downing. This report is summarized by Rick J. Strassman, M.D., in MDMA:

> He (Downing) describes the effects of MDMA (0.8-1.9 mg./pound), given orally, to 21 experienced MDMA users as well as their responses on a screening questionnaire. All subjects were free of significant medical and/or psychiatric disturbances. Ages ranged from 20 to 58 years (with an average of 31), with educational experience being, on the average, four years of college. There were 13 men and 8 women. During the drug administration part of the study, various physical parameters were monitored. Cardiovascular responses, including an increase in systolic and diastolic blood pressure, and an increase in heart rate, usually occurred with minimal levels attained within 30-60 minutes.
>
> No subjective symptoms were noted in this regard. Blood pressure was less than pre-drug values within six hours, and often was less than pre-drug values 24 hours after drug

exposure. No hypotensive reactions or complaints were noted. No effects of MDMA on blood chemistry were noted.

From the report itself, here are some excerpts of the study's conclusions:

> This experimental situation produced no observed or reported psychological or physiological damage, either during the twenty-four hour study period or the three-month follow-up period. Thus, while our subjects are in no way typical of the general population, our findings support the general impression among knowlegeable professionals that MDMA is reasonably safe, produces positive mood changes in users, does not cause negative problems, is used sparingly and episodically, and is without evidence of abuse.
>
> Certainly, any drug that causes ataxia and elevates blood pressure and pulse is potentially unsafe. We can say little about "safety" when we study effects and side-effects for twenty-four hours, then obtain blood cytology after three months. "Safety" must exclude long-term toxicity. DES and Thalidomide were safe in acute toxicity studies, but had

An unusually large MDA crystal grown in ethanol.

serious long-range toxicity. We do not know enough about MDMA's long-range effects other than random anecdotal evidence supplied by unselected and unsupervised users.

From the information presented here, we can only say that MDMA, at the doses tested, has remarkably consistent and predictable psychobiological effects which are transient and free of clinically apparent major toxicity. The experimental subjects believed that MDMA is both safe and beneficial, but there is insufficient evidence to judge accurately either harm or benefit . . .

APPENDIX II

RISK ASSESSMENT
The FDA and MDMA Research
by Rick Doblin

This brief review of the history and current status of the neurotoxicological research concerning MDMA is intended to familiarize the interested non-neurologist with the latest information about MDMA neurotoxicity. There are many open scientific questions concerning MDMA, yet current research is almost exclusively focused on whether or not MDMA produces any neurotoxicity. Though this is an important and interesting area of investigation, it will prove, I believe, to be one of the least fascinating areas of MDMA research. Yet assessing safety is a necessary first step prior to any initiation of more wide- ranging investigations into the therapeutic aspects of MDMA-assisted psychotherapy, or into MDMA's remarkable ability to affect attention, emotion, pain, meditation, and physical healing.

Initial Observations

In 1984, in the University of Chicago laboratory of Dr. Charles Schuster, Dr. Lewis Seiden, and Dr. George Ricaurte, a study was conducted with MDA that was to open up a new direction of neurological research, one which is currently engaging research teams around the country. Dr. Ricaurte noticed that MDA, when injected into rats in various doses twice a day for four days, resulted in varying amounts of nerve terminal degeneration, affecting only the serotonin nerve terminals.

Gene Haislip of the Drug Enforcement Administration discussed this research with Dr. Schuster when they were both guests on the Phil Donahue show in April, 1985, and seemingly judged MDMA guilty of being a very serious public health problem. One month later, the DEA placed MDMA in Schedule I on an emergency basis, partially justifying their action by citing this study and the potential danger of brain damage to human users of MDMA. Also in May, 1985 an Expert Committee of the World Health Organization, to which Dr. Schuster was a consultant, recommended MDMA for international scheduling, weighing very heavily the risk of neurotoxicity.

There are three basic questions that must be asked concerning the question of brain changes from MDMA. First, is it temporary or permanent? Second, when it does occur, does it produce any observable functional or behavioral effects, good or bad? Third, does it occur at human dosage levels?

Nerve Terminal Degeneration But No Cell Death

In an attempt to evaluate varying levels of exposure to MDMA for possible harmful physical effects, the MDMA therapeutic community funded a 28-day animal toxicity study in dogs and rats, conducted by Toxicology Pathology Associates. Different dose levels were administered orally to several groups of animals, for 28 consecutive days. The observable toxic effect on their bodies was minimal, even at extremely large doses taken in a manner that bears little resemblance to the human therapeutic use. In terms of brain damage, Dr. Charles Frith, the principal investigator, concluded "It is of significance that neuropathological changes were not evident in either species, since that was the primary reason for performing the study. It may be that more sophisticated methods, such as the silver Fink-Heimer stain, which was used by Dr. Ricaurte in demonstrating certain MDA-induced changes in the CNS, may be necessary for the demonstration of neuropathological changes."

The seeming contradiction between the studies of Dr. Frith and Dr. Ricaurte bring us to a very important question. If there is damage in humans, is it temporary or permanent? After 28 consecutive days of exposing animals to MDMA, Dr. Frith's study failed to detect any cell death, the usual marker of permanent brain damage. Dr. Ricaurte's study had looked at the animals two weeks after dosing and used the Fink-Heimer stain, which detects only degenerating nerve terminals and/or cell bodies. There actually is no contradiction between the two studies because degenerating nerve terminals are not detected by the methods used by Dr. Frith's study, and cell death does not occur at the doses used.

Neurotoxicity is Temporary and Not Permanent

In monkeys, Dr. Ricaurte has recently seen degenerating nerve terminals, and inclusion bodies developing in the soma of the cell. Initially, it was suspected that these inclusion bodies might lead to cell death. To the surprise of some of the researchers, when the primates were looked at ten weeks after dosing with MDMA rather than two weeks, the inclusion bodies disappeared as the nerve terminals regenerated. Although the significance of the inclusions is unclear, the important point is that there is no evidence at all of cell death. Therefore, at the doses used, it seems MDMA damages only nerve terminals. Some researchers have even speculated that MDMA may not be able to kill cells, but can only damage nerve terminals. Furthermore, up to the middle of 1988, all the available evidence to date indicates that the cells do recover. Studies in monkeys have shown partial recovery of depleted serotonin levels over a period of several months, while one study in rats by Dr. Battaglia, et. al. shows total recovery after a period of a year.

Lack of Gross Functional Effects From 90% Reductions

Another essential question concerns the functional effect, if any, of serotonin reductions, when they occur. Preliminary studies in primates that have had their serotonin reduced by 90% failed to distinguish the treated animals from the controls (personal communication). Even with massive 90% serotonin reduction, there was no observable effect. This finding is both encouraging and complicating. Millions of doses of MDMA have been taken by humans within the U.S., without one single documented case of permanent harmful neurological consequences resulting from its use. While this seems to indicate the safety of MDMA even if there is temporary serotonin depletion, there may still be asymptomatic effects on the serotonin system. For example, Parkinson's disease often does not manifest until there are 95% reductions in dopamine.

Evidence From Other Drugs

The social use of MDA in the turbulent 'sixties also sheds some light on the fears of latent damage from MDMA. MDA is roughly twice as neurotoxic as MDMA, and its use began over twenty-five years ago. Though there has been no systematic effort to locate and examine past users of MDA, no cases of MDA-related neurotoxicity have been identified. The current medical use of fenfluramine, an FDA-approved drug used in children on a daily basis for months or for years at a time, also offers indirect evidence for the safety of MDMA. Fenfluramine causes similar types of neurotoxicity as MDMA in approximately the same dose ranges, and yet has seemingly been safe. No cases of fenfluramine-related neurotoxicity have been identified and the Physicans Desk Reference does not even mention neurotoxicity as a potential side-effect.

If there are asymptomatic changes in humans now, will there be some significant delayed reaction which might not manifest itself for twenty years or so? This would be a more likely if brain cells were weakened and died over an extended period of time, falling below a certain limit and triggering symptoms. While this is possible, the demonstrated evidence for nerve terminal regeneration, the total lack of evidence for cell death, and the lack of observed neurological complications linked to MDMA, MDA or fenfluramine use make this seem unlikely.

Neurotoxic Effects Disappear at Human Dose Levels

One can also legitimately wonder if there are any neurotoxic effects in humans at all. When primates are given single oral doses of MDMA, the effects on the serotonin system disappear at levels relatively close to the human therapeutic dose. At 5.0 mg/kg given orally in a single dose to primates, no effects on serotonin levels were found two weeks after dosing in most areas of the brain, though significant effects were still found in the thalamus and the hypothalamus. Looking at the dose response curve, one can hypothesize that 2.5 mg/kg given orally in a single dose to primates would cause no effect on serotonin levels two weeks after dosing. This indeed appears to be the case in the two monkeys tested. Since the relative sensitivities to MDMA of the primate brain and the human brain can only be estimated, animal studies alone cannot provide a conclusive answer as to where the human no-effect level actually is.

Evidence from Human Studies

The primate studies do, however, give us an important lead for further studies. Reductions in brain serotonin levels were found to be associated with reductions in cerebrospinal fluid levels of brain neurotransmitter metabolite levels. This is the link that leads to human studies. Subjects who had used MDMA and were sufficiently motivated by the quality of their MDMA experiences to volunteer for spinal taps came to Stanford from all over the country to participate, assisted by the Multidisciplinary Association for Psychedelic Studies (MAPS).

In human studies at Stanford University conducted by Dr. Ricaurte, 34 MDMA users volunteered for spinal taps and had their cerebrospinal fluid analyzed for 5HIAA levels, the serotonin neurotransmitter metabolite. The group has taken MDMA an average of about 60 times, and has also taken other psychedelics as well as other drugs. Interestingly enough, there is a subgroup of 9 people in the study that have taken MDMA almost exclusively, 5 over a hundred times. Neurotransmitter metabolite levels will be compared to those of a control group of non-drug users who were already having spinal taps due to back pain. This study is still in process.

A published study by Dr. Peroutka tested only five subjects, and concluded that MDMA does not significantly affect human serotonin metabolite levels. His group averaged taking MDMA about 15 times, and their use of other drugs was minimal. Dr. Peroutka used literature controls, and intends to continue this research in more subjects.

Methodological Problems

Both of these studies have significant methodological problems. The major problem is that the initial neurotransmitter metabolite levels of the MDMA users is unknown. The data is very difficult to draw meaningful conclusions from since baseline levels vary quite widely between individuals, with some peoples' normal levels being about 300% more than others. Also, an individual's levels can vary by around 15% within a twenty-four hour period due to a wide variety of influences such as diet, rest, stress, etc. Serotonin level changes that may be occurring may be missed, or differing levels that occur may be attributed to MDMA when they actually are due to other factors.

Another problem relates to the control groups. In Dr. Peroutka's study literature controls are used, and this is not conclusive since the laboratories where the studies were conducted may be calibrating their equipment differently, or using control groups that are composed of different sorts of people. There seems to be as much art as science at the forefront of neurotoxicological brain research, and all conceivable extraneous variables that can be controlled should be.

In Dr. Ricaurte's study the control group is not composed of normals, but of people with back pain. Though some studies indicate that this does not affect neurotransmitter levels, other researchers have their doubts. 5HIAA levels can also vary according to personality factors, and neither control group nor MDMA group was given any personality tests prior to testing. Another potentially confounding variable that makes conclusive interpretation of the results impossible is that the people in the MDMA group also used other drugs, with varying frequency and variety. Control spinal fluid should ideally be run at the same time in the same equipment, and taken from age, sex, health, drug use patterns and personality matched subjects.

Furthermore, the relationship between a study of serotonin levels of repeated users of MDMA, who averaged about 60 doses, and the likely effect on serotonin levels when MDMA is used in therapy for usually a maximum of 3 times, is also unclear. This initial study was designed in an attempt to find a drug effect, if there is any. If an effect is found, extrapolations back to the therapeutic use pattern are needed to more realistically assess risk.

For better research design and more conclusive results, subjects should serve as their own control. In other words subjects need to be tested first prior to their being exposed to MDMA, and then tested again afterwards. The FDA is presently denying permission to researchers interested in doing this work on the grounds that the animal studies are not yet completed, and that though no evidence for functional neurotoxicity has occured in over fifteen years of human use there may still be some danger of longer term effects. During this War on Drugs in 1988, the FDA has even denied permission to researchers to investigate MDMA in terminally ill patients for whom any long term toxicity, even if it did occur, would be unlikely to matter much.

Tryptophan Challenges and Neuropsychological Studies

Two additional human studies were conducted at Yale. Nine volunteers from the spinal tap study, primarily the subjects with the lowest levels of 5HIAA, were given a tryptophan challenge test. The test is designed to ascertain if their serotonin system is functioning normally. Since there is such a wide variability of normal 5HIAA levels, simply knowing a person's 5HIAA level is not sufficient to determine if their level is normal for them or not. This pilot study is now in the data analysis phase.

In order to gather additional data on the mental health of the volunteers in the spinal tap study, MAPS arranged for neuropsychological studies to be conducted on those MDMA users who underwent the tryptophan challenge test. According to Dr Opsahl, " By and large, these results are striking for the fact that most subjects evaluated had IQ scores in the above average range or higher." This study in users who averaged about 60 doses leaves one with the impression that being exposed to MDMA several times in a therapeutic context would have no observable harmful neuropsychological effect, particularly since the subjects in this test had taken an average of 13 grams of MDMA.

Studies in Progress-Rate of Regeneration and No-Effect Levels

Two fundamentally important studies remain to be conducted. Studies in rats with 90% serotonin depletion have shown total recovery of nerve terminals after a year, and studies in primates with 90% serotonin depletion have demonstrated partial recovery after ten weeks. It remains to be seen if the primates will show total recovery. Accordingly, MAPS has partially funded a study that has recently been initiated at Johns Hopkins. The study will evaluate several groups of 90% serotonin-depleted primates after 10, 20, and 40 weeks. This study will help to determine whether the process of nerve terminal regeneration that has already been shown to occur will completely restore the animals to their baseline levels, and if so at what rate. The hypothesis is that such complete recovery will occur, perhaps by 20 weeks and almost certainly by 40 weeks. Behavioral studies will be conducted on these animals, attempting to identify functional correlates of serotonin reduction and recovery.

Several remaining critical pieces of information will come from a study concerning the no-effect level for neurotoxicity. This study is currently being designed and funded and will be conducted by Dr. George Ricaurte at Johns Hopkins. Results are expected by spring of 1989. A single dose of 2.5 mg/kg was shown to have no effect in two primates. For there to be more convincing evidence for a no-effect level, more animals must be tested. Also, since a 5.0 mg/kg dose did produce an effect in two small brain regions, the question remains as to the precise location of the no-effect level. The preliminary design for a study to clarify a dose response curve calls for primates to be given single oral doses of 2.5, 3.75, 5.0 and 10.0 mg/kg, and then evaluated two weeks after dosing.

An additional aspect of this study will investigate the effect of cumulative dosing. One group of primates will be given 2.5 mg/kg four times, once every two weeks, for a total exposure of 10 mg/kg. It is conceivable that a single dose of 2.5 mg/kg produces a slight effect too small to measure. If this is occuring, the cumulative dosing should produce an effect large enough to be measured. When the data is in from both the single and the multiple dosing experiment, the no-effect level in primates may be identified.

Conclusions

Research concerning the relative safety of MDMA is a particularly important public health question. The non-medical use of MDMA has not stopped with its scheduling and continues at a very significant rate in the United States. By my estimate there are about 100,000 doses per month sold in the United States, and this number is increasing.

At the same time, MDMA has a great but undeveloped therapeutic potential, as the many case histories and anecdotal reports point out. If it can be demonstrated that MDMA-induced neurotoxicity is temporary, and that there is a primate no-effect level above the human dose level, the risk of using MDMA infrequently in carefully controlled research seems very minimal. Even if neurotoxicity does occur, there are presently no behavioral or functional effects that have been associated with it.

Once careful risk/benefit analyses can be conducted, rational decisions can be made concerning future research. If the data comes in as preliminary indications suggest, there can be hope that the FDA will permit direct MDMA research in humans to begin.

APPENDIX III

ANNOTATED BIBLIOGRAPHY OF THE SCIENTIFIC LITERATURE REFERRING TO MDMA

(including a sampling of the popular literature)

Prepared by

ALEXANDER T. SHULGIN, PhD
1483 Shulgin Road
Lafayette, CA 94549

TABLE OF CONTENTS

(1) Chemistry

(2) In Vitro Studies

(3) Biochemistry

(4) Pharmacology
(behavior and drug discrimination studies)

(5) Neurochemistry

(6) Toxicology

(7) Clinical Studies

(8) Analysis

(9) Reviews and Commentaries
(including books and magazine articles)

(10) Legal History

(1) CHEMISTRY

Anon: Verfahren zur Darstellung von Alkyloxyaryl-, Dialkyloxyaryl- und Alkylendioxyarylaminopropanen bzw. deren am Stickstoff monoalkylierten Derivaten. German Patent, 274,350; Filed December 24, 1912, issued May 16, 1914. Assigned to E. Merck in Darmstadt.

A chemical process is described for the conversion of several allyl- and propenyl-aromatic compounds to the corresponding beta- or alpha-bromopropanes. These, in turn, react with ammonia or primary amines to produce the corresponding primary or secondary propylamines. Specifically, safrole was reacted with aqueous HBr, and the impure reaction product reacted with alcoholic methylamine to produce MDMA in an unstated yield. Also described and characterized are MDA and DMA, as well as the corresponding 1-phenyl-1-aminopropanes. No pharmacology.

Anon: Formyl Derivatives of Secondary Bases. German Patent 334,555, assigned to E. Merck. 1920. CA: 17:1804a.

A chemical conversion of MDMA to its formyl derivative, and the properties of the latter, are described.

Biniecki, S. and Krajewski, E. Preparation of DL-1-(3,4-Methyl-enedioxy)-2-(methylamino)propane and DL-1-(3,4-dimethoxyphenyl) 2-(methylamino)-propane. Acta Polon. Pharm. 17 pp. 421-425 (1960). CA: (1961) 14350e.

A chemical procedure is given for the conversion of safrole to the beta-bromopropane with HBr, and its subsequent conversion with alcoholic methylamine to MDMA. 4-Allylveratrole was similarly converted to 3,4-dimethoxy- methamphetamine.

Braun, U., Shulgin, A.T. and Braun, G., Centrally Active N- Substituted Analogs of 3,4-Methylenedioxyphenylisopropylamine (3,4-Methylenedi-oxyamphet-amine), J. Pharm. Sci., 69 pp 192-195 (1980).

Twenty two homologs and analogs of MDA were synthesized and their physical properties presented. Twelve of them were assayed in man as psychotomimetic agents. Three of them were found to be active: MDMA with a human potency of between 100 and 160 mg orally; MDE somewhat less potent at a dosage requirement of 140-200 mg orally; and MDOH, which was similar to MDMA in potency. Some animal pharmacology is reviewed, and a comparison between MDMA and MDA (toxicology, CNS pharmacology, and human effectiveness) is tabulated.

Fujisawa, T. and Deguchi, Y. (Concerning the Commercial Utilization of Safrole). J. Pharm. Soc. Japan 74 975 (1954). CA: 49: 10958i.

The conversion of safrole to piperonylacetone is described, using formic acid and hydrogen peroxide, in acetone. The yield is satisfactory, and this is probably the most direct and efficient conversion of a natural product to an immediate precursor to MDMA.

Janesko, J.L. and Dal Cason, T.A. Seizure of a Clandestine Laboratory: The N-Alkyl MDA Analogs. Paper presented at the 39th Annual Meeting of the American Academy of Forensic Sciences, San Diego, CA Feb. 16-21 (1987). See Microgram, 20 52 (1987).

Several clandestine laboratories have been seized, revealing the illicit preparation of not only MDMA, but the N-ethyl (MDE), the N-propyl (MDPR), the N-isopropyl (MDIP) and the N,N-dimethyl (MDDM) homologues. These were all synthesized by the NaCNBH3 reduction method from the appropriate amine salt and piperonylacetone. Also, the N- ethyl-N-methyl, and the N,N-diethyl homologs were found, prepared by catalytic hydrogenation.

Nichols, D.E., Synthesis of 3,4-Methylenedioxymethamphetamine Hydro-chloride. FDA Master File on MDMA. 1986.

A detailed synthesis of MDMA from piperonylacetone is presented, including all the spectroscopic and physical detail, bibliographies, CVs, and such that define the final product for medical needs.

Shulgin, A.T. and Jacob III, P., Potential Misrepresentation of 3,4-Methylene-dioxyamphetamine (MDA). A Toxicological Warning. J. Anal. Toxicol., 6, pp 71-75 (1982).

The commercial availability and overt misrepresentation of 3,4-methyle-nedioxybenzylacetone as 3,4-methylenedioxy- phenylacetone might well suggest that an unsuspecting attempt to synthesize MDMA may yield a new and unexplored base, 1-(3,4-methylenedioxyphenyl)-3-(methyl-amino)butane. This compound was synthesized, and characterized in comparison to MDMA. The analogous relationship between MDA and its comparable homolog, 1-(3,4-methylene-dioxyphenyl)-3- aminobutane, was also explored.

(2) IN VITRO STUDIES

Battaglia, G., Brooks, B.P., Kulsakdinum, C. and De Souza, E.B. Pharma-cologic Profile of MDMA (3,4-Methylenedioxymethamphetamine) at Various Brain Recognition Sites. Eur. J. Pharmacol. 149 159- 163 (1988).

The affinity of MDMA for various neurotransmitter receptor and uptake sites was studied in vitro, using competition with various radioligands. Comparisons with MDA, MDE, amphetamine and methamphetamine are reported.

Brady, J.F., Di Stephano, E.W. and Cho, A.K., Spectral and Inhibitory Interactions of (+/-)-3,4-Methylenedioxyamphetamine (MDA) and (+/-)-3,4-Methylenedioxy-methamphetamine (MDMA) with Rat Hepatic Microsomes. Life Sciences 39 1457-1464.

Both MDA and MDMA were shown to form complexes with cytochrome P-450 that were inhibitory to its function as to demethylation of benzphet-amine and carbon monoxide binding. Liver microsome studies showed the metabolic demethylation of MDMA and the N-hydroxylation of MDA.

Frye, G. and Matthews, R. Effect of 3,4-methylenedioxymethamphetam-ine (MDMA) on Contractile Responses in the G. Pig Ileum. The Pharma-cologist 28 149 (#318) (1986).

Using the longitudinal muscle of the guinea pig ileum, MDMA evoked dose-related, transient contractions, but failed to reduce contractions produced by serotonin, acetylcholine, or GABA. The MDMA contractions were blocked by atropine, and do not appear to involve serotonin recep-tors.

Gehlert, D.R., Schmidt, C.J., Wu, L. and Lovenberg, W., Evidence for Specific Methylenedioxymethamphetamine (Ecstasy) Binding Sites in the Rat Brain. Europ. J. Pharmacol. 119 135-136 (1985).

Evidence is presented from binding to rat brain homogenate studies. The use of the serotoninergic re-uptake inhibitor, active in vivo, does not antagonize this binding, nor in studies with uptake into striatal micro-somes.

Levin, J.A., Schmidt, C.J. and Lovenberg, W. Release of [3H]- Monoam-ines from Superfused Rat Striatal Slices by Methylenedioxymethamphet-amine (MDMA). Fed. Proc. 45 1059 (#5265) April 13-18, 1986.

The release of tritiated serotonin and dopamine from superfused rat striatal slices was observed for three amphetamine derivatives. MDMA and p-chloroamphetamine were equivalent, and about 10x the potency of methamphetamine. This last compound was, however, some 10x more effective than MDMA in the release of dopamine.

Lyon, R.A., Glennon, R.A. and Titeler, M. 3,4-Methylenedioxymetham-phetamine (MDMA): Stereoselective Interactions at Brain 5- HT1 and 5-HT2 Receptors. Psychopharmacology 88 525-526 (1986).

Both MDMA and MDA, and their respective optical isomers, were assayed as to their affinity at radio-labelled serotonin (5-HT1 and 5-HT2) and dopamine (D2) binding sites. The "R" isomers of both drugs showed a moderate affinity at the 5-HT2 receptor (labelled with 3-H ketanserin), and the "S" isomers were lower. Affinities for the 5-HT1 site were similar, but that for D2 sites were very low. ·Since the "S" isomer of MDMA is the more potent in man, it may not work primarily through a direct interaction at 5-HT receptors.

Nichols, D.E., Lloyd, D.H., Hoffman, A.J., Nichols, M.B. and Yim, G.K.W. Effects of Certain Hallucinogenic Amphetamine Analogues on the Release of [3H] Serotonin from Rat Brain Synaptosomes. J. Med. Chem. 25, pp 530-535 (1982).

The optically active isomers of MDMA (as well as those for MDA, PMA) and the corresponding phentermine analogs, have been evaluated as to their effect on the release of serotonin from rat brain synaptosomes. The (+) isomer of MDMA was the more effective (this is the active isomer in humans) suggesting that serotonin release may play some role in the psychopharmacological activity. The alpha-alpha dimethyl homologues were inactive even at the highest concentrations studied.

Steele, T.P., Nichols, D.E. and Yim, G.K.W. Stereoselective Effects of MDMA on Inhibition of Monoamine Uptake. Fed. Proc. 45 1059 (# 5262) April 13-18 1986.

In the investigation of the optical isomeric difference of activities seen for amphetamine, MDMA, and DOM (the more potent isomers being the "S", "S" and "R" resp.) their abilities to inhibit the uptake of radio-labelled monoamines into synaptosomes were studied. The findings are discussed, and it is concluded that MDMA exhibits stereoselective effects similar to those of amphetamine on monoamine uptake inhibition, a parameter that is unrelated to the mechanism of action of the hallucinogen DOM.

Steele, T.D., Nichols, D.E. and Yim, G.K.W. Stereochemical Effects of 3,4-Methylenedioxymethamphetamine (MDMA) and Related Amphetamine Derivatives on Inhibition of Uptake of [3H]Monoamines into Synaptosomes from Different Regions of Rat Brain. Biochem. Pharmacol. 36 2297-2303 (1987).

MDA, MDMA, and the alpha-ethyl homolog MBDB were found to inhibit serotonin uptake in brain synaptosomes. The conclusions to a broad series of studies were that MDMA and its homologs are more closely related to amphetamine than to DOM in their biochemical actions.

Wang, S.S., Ricaurte, G.A. and Peroutka, S.J., [3H] 3,4 Methylene-dioxy-methamphetamine (MDMA) Interactions with Brain Membranes and Glass Fiber Filter Paper, Europ. J. Pharmacol. 138 439-443 (1987).

Tritiated MDMA appears to give a pharmacological "binding profile" in rat brain homogionate studies, even in the absence of brain tissue. This appears to result from an unexpected binding of the radioligand to glass filter paper. Pretreatment with polyethylenimine eliminated this artifact.

(3) BIOCHEMISTRY

Gibb, J.W., Hanson, G.R. and Johnson, M. Effects of (+)-3,4- methylenedi-oxy-methamphetamine [(+)MDMA] and (-)-3,4- methylenedioxy-metham-phetamine [(-)MDMA] on Brain Dopamine, Serotonin, and their Biosyn-thetic Enzymes. Soc. Neurosciences Abstrts. 12 169.2 (1986).

The optical isomers of MDMA were studied in rats, as to the extent of serotonin and dopamine depletion, and the changes in their respective biosynthetic enzymes TPH (tryptophane hydroxylase) and TH (tyrosine hydroxylase). The (+) was the more effective in reducing serotonin levels at several sites in the brain, and was the more effective in reducing the TPH levels at all sites. Striatal TH was not effected by either isomer.

Johnson, M., Bush, L.G., Stone, D.M., Hanson, G.R. and Gibb, J.W. Effects of Adrenalectomy on the 3,4-Methylenedioxymethamphetamine (MDMA)-induced Decrease of Tryptophan Hydroxylase Activity in the Frontal Cortex and Hippocampus. Soc. Neurosci. Abstr., Vol. 13, Part 3, 1987. # 464.6.

The tryptophan hydroxylase (TPH) activity of rat frontal cortex and hippocampus was found to decrease seven days following an acute large dosage of MDMA. The latter area was spared enzyme loss with adre-nalectomy.

Letter, A.A., Merchant, K., Gibb, J.W. and Hanson, G.R. Roles of D2 and 5-HT2 Receptors in Mediating the Effects of Methamphetamine, 3,4-Methylene-dioxymethamphetamine, and 3,4-Methylenedioxyamphetam-ine on Striato-Nigral Neurotensin Systems. Soc. Neurosciences Abstrts. 12 1005 (# 277.7) 1986.

The chronic treatment of rats with methamphetamine, MDA or MDMA leads to a 2-3x increase of the neurotensin-like immuno-reactivity in the striato-nigral areas of the brain. Efforts to assign neurotransmitter roles led to the simultaneous administration of serotonin and dopamine antagonists. These interrelationships are discussed.

Lim, H.K. and Foltz, R.L. Metabolism of 3,4-Methylenedioxymethamphet-amine (MDMA) in Rat. FASEB Abstracts Vol. 2 No. 5 page A-1060. Abst: 4440.

The metabolism of MDMA in the rat is studied. Seven metabolites are identified from the urine. These are:

4-hydroxy-3-methoxy methamphetamine
3,4-methylenedioxy amphetamine

4-hydroxy-3-methoxy amphetamine
4-methoxy-3-hydroxy methamphetamine
3,4-methylenedioxyphenyl acetone
3,4-dihydroxyphenyl acetone
4-hydroxy-3-methoxyphenyl acetone

Merchant, K., Letter, A.A., Stone, D.M., Gibb, J.W. and Hanson, G.R. Responses of Brain Neurotensin-like Immunoreactivity to 3,4-methylene-dioxymeth-amphetamine (MDMA) and 3,4-methylenedioxyamphetamine (MDA). Fed. Proc. 45 1060 (# 5268) (1986).

The administration of MDA and MDMA profoundly alters the levels of neurotensin-like immunoreactivity (NTLI) concentrations in various portions of the brain of the rat. Increases of up to a factor of 3x are observed in some regions of the brain.

Schmidt, C.J. and Taylor, V.L. Acute Effects of Methylenedioxymeth-amphetamine (MDMA) on 5-HT Synthesis in the Rat Brain. Pharmacologist 29 ABS-224 (1987). See also: Biochemical Pharmacology 36 4095-4102 (1987).

Acute exposure of MDMA dropped the tryptophane hydroxylase activity of rats, and this persisted for several days. Subsequent administration of Fluoxethine recovered this activity, but reserpine or alpha-methyl-tyrosine did not.

Stone, D.M., Johnson, M., Hanson, G.R. and Gibb, J.W. A Comparison of the Neurotoxic Potential of Methylenedioxy-amphetamine (MDA) and its N-methylated and N-ethylated Derivatives.

Multiple doses of MDA and MDMA decreases the level of brain trypto-phan hydroxylase (TPH). The N-ethyl homolog was without effect. It is argued that although the studies here were well above human exposures, the cumulative effects of repeated exposures, the differences between rat and human metabolism, and increased human sensitivity to this drug, could present a serious threat to human abusers of this drug.

Stone, D.M., Hanson, G.R. and Gibb, J.W. GABA-Transaminase Inhibitor Protects Against Methylenedioxymethamphetamine (MDMA)-induced Neurotoxicity. Soc. Neurosci. Abstr. Vol. 13, Part 3 (1987). # 251.3.

The neurotoxicity of MDMA (in the rat) was protected against by GABA-transaminase inhibitors.

Stone, D.M., Stahl, D.C., Hanson, G.R. and Gibb, J.W. Effects of 3,4-methylenedioxyamphetamine (MDA) and 3,4-methylenedioxymetham-phetamine (MDMA) on Tyrosine Hydroxylase and Tryptophane Hydroxylase Activity in the Rat Brain. Fed. Proc. 45 1060 (# 5267) April 13-18, 1986.

The effects of rats treated chronically with either MDA or MDMA on the enzymes involved with neurotransmitter synthesis is reported. The levels of tryptophane hydroxylase (TPH, involved with serotonin synthesis) were markedly reduced, differently in different areas of the brain. The tyrosine hydroxylase (TH, involved with dopamine synthesis) remains unchanged. This is in contrast to the documented reduction of TH that follows high dosages of methamphetamine.

(4) PHARMACOLOGY

Anderson III, G.M., Braun, G., Braun, U., Nichols, D.E. and Shulgin, A.T., Absolute Configuration and Psychotomimetic Activity, NIDA Research Monograph #22, pp 8-15 (1978).

The "R" isomer of most chiral hallucinogenics is known to be the active isomer. This generality includes LSD, DOB, DOM, DOET, and MDA. This assignment has been demonstrated both in rabbit hyperthermia studies as well as in clinical evaluations. With MDMA, however, this assignment is reversed. In both rabbit and human studies, the more potent isomer of MDMA is the "S" form, similar to that of amphetamine and methamphetamine. The summed activity of the individual isomers did not satisfactorally reproduce the activity of the racemic mixture. Also, the addition of an N-methyl to a known hallucinogenic amphetamine routinely decreases the potency (as with DOB, DOM, TMA and TMA-2). The exception again is with MDA, which produces the equipotent MDMA. The relationship between the stimulants amphetamine and methamphetamine is similar. The two drugs MDA and MDMA appear not to be cross-tolerant in man.
It is argued that the mechanisms of action of MDMA must be different from that of MDA and related hallucinogenics.

Beardsley, P.M., Balster, R.L. and Harris, L.S. Self- administration of Methylene-dioxymethamphetamine (MDMA) by Rhesus Monkeys. Drug and Alcohol Dependence 18 149-157 (1986)

In monkeys trained to self-administer cocaine intra- venously MDMA was found, in two out of four, to be an effective substitute.

Beaton, J.M., Benington, F., Christian, S.T., Monti, J.A. and Morin, R.D. Analgesic Effects of MDMA and Related Compounds. Pharmacologist 29 page ABS 281 (1987).

Analgesia of several compounds (including MDMA and several close homologs) was measured by the tail-flick reponse in mice. All produced analgesia, with the (+) (S) MDMA being the most potent.

Bird, M. and Kornetsky, C. Naloxone Antagonism of the Effects of MDMA "Ecstasy" on Rewarding Brain Stimulation. The Pharmacologist

28 149 (#319) (1986).

The lowering of the reward threshold (REBS, rewarding electrical brain stimulation) by the s.c. administration of MDMA to rats (as determined by implanted electrodes) was blocked by naloxone. This suggests that MDMA affects the same dopaminergic and opioid substrates involved in cocaine and d-amphetamine reward.

Braun, U., Shulgin, A.T. and Braun, G. Prufung auf zentral Aktivitat und Analgesie von N-substituierten Analogen des Amphetamin-Derivates 3,4-Methylenedioxyphenylisopropylamin. Arzneim.-Forsch. 30 pp 825-830 (1980).

MDMA, and a large collection of N-substituted homologs, were assayed in mice for both analgesic potency and enhancement of motor activity. MDMA proved to be the most potent analgesic (compared with some 15 homologs) but was not particularly effective as a motor stimulant. The structure and pharmacological relationships to known analgesics are discussed.

Callahan, P.M. and Appel, J.B. Differences in the Stimulus Properties of 3,4-Methylenedioxyamphetamine (MDA) and N-Methyl-3,4- methylenedioxy-methamphetamine (MDMA) in Animals Trained to Discriminate Hallucinogens from Saline. Soc. Neurosci. Abstr., Vol. 13, Part 3, p. 1720 (1987) No. 476.2.

The stimulant properties of MDA and MDMA (including the optical isomers) were studied in rats that were trained to discriminate mescaline or (separately) LSD from saline. "R"-MDA appears similar to both hallucinogens, but the other isomers gave no clear-cut accord to the literature reports of behavioral activity.

Davis, W.M. and Borne, R.F., Pharmacological Investigation of Compounds Related to 3,4-Methylenedioxyamphetamine (MDA), Subs. Alc. Act/Mis. 5 105-110 (1984).

MDA and MDMA, as well as the homologous 3-aminobutanes HMDA and HMDMA, were studied toxicologically in both isolated and aggregated mouse groups. Both MDA and MDMA were of similar lethality in isolated animals (ca. 100mg/Kg i.p.) which was enhanced 3-fold or 4-fold by aggregation. The homologs HMDA and HMDMA were approximately twice as toxic but showed no such enhancement. The prelethal behavior characteristics and the effects of potential protective agents are described.

Evans, S.M. and Johanson, C.E. Discriminative Stimulus Properties of (+/-)-3,4-Methylenedioxymethamphetamine and (+/-)- Methylenedioxyamphetamine in Pigeons. Drug and Alcohol Dependence 18 159-164 (1986).

Pigeons, trained to discriminate (+) amphetamine from saline. Both MDA and MDMA substituted for amphetamine, and both were less potent.

Fellows, E.J. and Bernheim, F. The Effect of a Number of Aralkylamines on the Oxidation of Tyramine by Amine Oxidase. J. Pharm. Exptl. Therap. 100 94-99 (1950).

There were some animal behavioral studies made on the chain homolog of MDMA, vis., 1-(3,4-methylenedioxyphenyl)-3- methylaminobutane. This is the amine that would result from the use of the "wrong" piperonylace-tone in illicit synthesis. In the dose range 10-25 mg/Kg, toxic effects such as tremors and convulsions were seen.

Glennon, R.A. and Young, R. Further Investigation of the Discriminative Stimulus Properties of MDA. Pharmacol. Biochem. and Behavior 20, 501-505 (1984).

In rats trained to distinguish between racemic MDA (and separately, "S"-amphetamine) and saline, MDMA (as well as either optical isomer of MDA) was found to generalize to MDA. Similarly, with rats trained to distinguish between dextro-amphetamine and saline, MDMA and "S"-MDA (but not "R"-MDA or "S"-DOM) produced generalization re-sponses.

Glennon, R.A., Little, P.J., Rosecrans, J.A. and Yousif, M. The Effects of MDMA ("Ecstasy") and its Optical Isomers on Schedule- Controlled Responding in Mice. Pharmacol. Biochem. Behav. 26 425-426 (1987).

The effectiveness of several analogs of MDMA were evaluated in mice trained in a reinforcement procedure. Both (+) and racemic MDMA were 4x the potency of the levo- isomer; all were less potent than ampheta-mine.

Glennon, R.A., Young, R., Rosecrans, J.A. and Anderson, G.M. Discrimina-tive Stimulus Properties of MDA Analogs. Biol. Psychiat. 17, 807-814 (1982).

In rats trained to distinguish between the psychotomimetic DOM and saline, several compounds were found to generalize to DOM (including racemic MDA, its "R" isomer, and MMDA-2). Others did not generalize to DOM (including MDMA, the "S" isomer of MDA, and homopiperylam-ine). These results are consistent with the qualitative differences reported in man.

Glennon, R.A., Yousif, M. and Patrick, G. Stimulus Properties of 1-(3,4-Methylenedioxy)-2-Aminopropane (MDA) analogs. Pharmacol. Biochem. Behav. 29 443-449 (1988).

Rats were trained to discriminate between saline and DOM or d-ampheta-mine. They were challenged with "R" and "S" MDMA, with racemic, "R" and "S" MDE, and with racemic MDOH (N-OH-MDA). The amphetamine-trained animals generalized to "S" MDMA, but not to "R" MDMA, nor to any of the MDE isomers nor to MDOH (nor to homopiperonylamine). N-substituted amphetamine derivatives (N-ethyl and N-hydroxy) also gave the amphetamine response, but not of these compounds generalized to DOM. This study supports the suggestion that MDMA represents a class of compounds apart from the stimulant or the hallucinogenic.

Gold, L.H. and Koob, G.F. Methysergide Potentialtes the Hyperactivity Produced by MDMA in Rats. Pharmacol. Biochem. Behav. 29 645-648 (1988).

The hyperactivity that results from MDMA administration is significantly increased by the methysergide. This latter drug was itself without effect, nor did it potentiate the hyperactivity induced by amphetamine administration.

Griffiths, R.R., Lamb, R. and Brady, J.V. A Preliminary Report on the Reinforcing Effects of Racemic 3,4-Methylenedioxy- methamphetamine in the Baboon. Document entered into evidence Re: MDMA Scheduling Docket No. 84-48, U.S. Department of Justice, Drug Enforcement Administration, October 16, 1985.

In three baboons trained to respond to cocaine, MDMA maintained self-administration at a somewhat lower level than cocaine, d-amphetamine, and phencyclidine. There was the evocation of distinct behavioral signals, which suggested that MDMA had a high abuse potential.

Harris, L.S. Preliminary Report on the Dependence Liability and Abuse Potential of Methylenedioxymethamphetamine (MDMA). Document entered into evidence Re: MDMA Scheduling Docket No. 84- 48, U.S. Department of Justice, Drug Enforcement Administration, October 16, 1985.

MDMA and amphetamine were compared as to locomotor activity in mice, and in reinforcing activity in monkeys as compared to cocaine. MDMA showed a fraction (20-25%) of the stimulant activity of amphetamine, and was substituted for cocaine in some of the test monkeys.

Hubner, C.B., Bird, M., Rassnick, S. and Kornetsky, C. The Threshold Lowering Effects of MDMA (Ecstasy) on Brain-stimulating Reward. Psychopharma-cology 95 49-51 (1988).

MDMA produced a dose-related lowering of the reward threshold, as determined in rats with electrodes stereotaxically implanted in the medial forebrain bundle- lateral hypothalamic area. This procedure has been used as an animal model for drug-induced euphoria.

Kamien, J.B., Johanson, C.E., Schuster, C.R. and Woolverton, W.L. The Effects of (+/-)-Methylenedioxymethamphetamine and (+/-)- Methylene-dioxy-amphetamine in Monkeys Trained to Discriminate (+)- Amphetamine from Saline. Drug and Alcohol Dependence 18 139-147 ((1986),

In monkeys trained to discriminate between amphetamine and saline, MDMA substituted and suggested that there was an amphet-amine-like component to its action. This similarity to amphetamine suggests a dependence potential.

Kasuya, Yutaka Chemicopharmacological Studies on Antispasmodic Action. XII. Structure-Activity Relationship on Aralkylamines. Chem. Pharm. Bull. 6 147-154 (1958).

In vitro studies on mouse intestinal segments were carried out for the chain homolog of MDMA, vis., 1-(3,4- methylenedioxyphenyl)-3-methyl-aminobutane. This is the amine that would result from the use of the "wrong" piperonylacetone in illicit synthesis. The compound shows weak atropine action.

Kulmala, H.K., Boja, J.W. and Schechter, M.D. Behavioral Suppression Following 3,4-Methylenedioxymethamphetamine. Life Sciences 41 1425-1429 (1987).

Rotation in rats was employed as an assay of the central dopaminergic activity of MDMA. At low doses it acts similarly to amphetamine, but at higher doses it appears to stimulate the dopamine receptor directly.

Lamb, R.J. and Griffiths, R.R. Self-injection of d,l-3,4- Methylenedioxy-methamphetamine in the Baboon. Psychopharmacolgy 91 268-272 (1987).

In monkeys conditioned to the self-administration of cocaine, MDMA produced a similar but less potent response. A decrease in food intake was also reported.

Li, A., Marek, G., Vosmer, G. and Seiden, L. MDMA-induced Serotonin Depletion Potentiates the Psychomotor Stimulant Effects of MDMA on Rats Performing on the Differential-Reinforcement-of- Low-Rate (DRL) Schedule. Society of Neurosciences Abstracts 12   169.7 (1986).

This is a study of Serotonin depletion and motor response. The long term depletion following both acute and chronic administration of MDMA to rats, increased activity and decreased serotonin suggests some inhibitory action of this neurotransmitter.

Nichols, D.E., Hoffman, A.J., Oberlender, R.A., Jacob III, P. and Shulgin, A.T. Derivatives of 1-(1,3-Benzodioxol-5-yl-2- butanamine: Representatives of a Novel Therapeutic Class. J. Med. Chem. 29 2009-2015 (1986).

Animal discrimination studies (LSD versus saline) of the alpha-ethyl homologues of MDA and MDMA were performed. No generalization occurred with the N-methyl analogs of either group (MDMA and MBDB), and the latter compound was also found to be psychoactive but not hallucinogenic in man. It was found to be less euphoric than MDMA, but with the same sense of empathy and compassion. The term "entactogen" is proposed for the class of drugs represented by MDMA and MBDB.

Oberlender, R. and Nichols, D.E. Drug Discrimination Studies with MDMA and Amphetamine. Psychopharmacology 95 71-76 (1988).

In rats trained to discriminate saline from either racemic MDMA or dextroamphetamine, the MDMA cue generalized to MDA and to all isomers of MDMA and MBDB, but not to LSD or DOM. The dextroamphetamine cue generalized to methamphetamine, but to none of the forms of either MDMA or MBDB. The "S" isomers of both MDMA and MBDB were the more potent.

Rosecrans, J.A. and Glennon, R.A. The Effect of MDA and MDMA ("Ecstasy") Isomers in Combination with Pirenpirone on Operant Responding in Mice. Pharmacol. Biochem. Behav. 28 39-42 (1987). See also: Soc. Neurosci. Abstr., Vol. 13, Part 3, p. 905 (1987) No. 251.10.

The disruptive effects of the optical isomers of MDA and MDMA were studied for mice trained in a reinforcement schedule, both with and without pretreatment with pirenpirone, a serotonin antagonist. Of the four isomers evaluated, only "R"-MDA behavior responses were attenuated by pirenpirone.

Schechter, M.D. Discriminative Profile of MDMA. Pharmacol. Biochem. Behav. 24 1533-1537 (1986)

Rats trained to discriminate cathinone, apomorphine, tetra-hydrocannabinol, or fenfluramine (each against saline) were challenged with MDMA. The results indicate that MDMA generalizes to both serotonergic and dopaminergically- mediated drugs and, thus, it may act both as a dopamine and as a serotonin agonist. This property is related to its abuse potential.

Schechter, M.D. MDMA as a Discriminative Stimulus: Isomeric Comparisons. Pharmacol. Biochem. Behav. 27 41-44 (1987).

Studies with rats trained to discriminate racemic MDMA from saline, showed generalization with both optical isomers of MDMA, with the "S" isomer being more potent. The chronological observations paralleled the reported human responses.

Schlemmer Jr., R.F., Montell, S.E. and Davis, J.M. Fed. Proc. 45 1059

(#5263) April 13-18 (1986).

The behavioral effects of MDMA have been studied in a primate colony, following multiple acute exposures. There was a decrease in activity, grooming, and food-searching, and an increase in staring. There was a disruption of social behavior that differed from the effects of other hallucinogens.

Thompson, D.M., Winsauer, P.J. and Mastropaolo, J. Effects of Phency-clidine, Ketamine and MDMA on Complex Operant Behavior in Monkeys. Pharmacol. Biochem. Behav. 26 401-405 (1987).

The loss of response to conditioned behavior in monkeys was observed for the title drugs. All were effective i.m., with phen-cyclidine the most potent, and MDMA the least.

(5) NEUROCHEMISTRY

Ali, S.F., Scallet, A.C.,Holson, R.R., Newport, G.D. and Slikker Jr., W. Acute Administration of MDMA (Ecstasy): Neurochemical Changes Persist up to 120 Days in Rat Brain. Soc. Neurosci. Abstr., Vol. 13, Part 3, p. 904 (1987) No. 251.5.

Rats were given 40 mg/Kg MDMA twice daily for 4 days. After 120 days, some regions of the brain (frontal cortex, hippocampus) still had serotonin depletion. There was fighting behavior noted between rats during the dosing and for up to two weeks following it.

Battaglia, G., Kuhar, M.J. and De Souza, E.B. MDA and MDMA (Ecstasy) Interactions with Brain Serotonin Receptors and Uptake Sites: In vitro Studies. Soc. Neurosciences Abstrt. 12 336.4 (1986).

The receptor site uptake of the optical isomers, as well as the racemate, of both MDA and MDMA were measured by separate, selective labelling with appropriate radioligands. The relationships between the isomers depended on whether uptake sites or receptors were involved, and differed at different locations in the brain.

Battaglia, G., Yeh, S.Y. and De Souza, E.B. MDMA-Induced Neurotoxic-ity: Parameters of Degeneration and Recovery of Brain Serotonin Neu-rons. Pharmacol. Biochem. Behav. 29 269-274 (1988).

A number of parameters were studied to define the nature of the neuro-toxic effect on serotonin axions and terminals. Both the size and fre-quency of drug administration resulted in a dose-dependent response. Regeneration of these neurons was also time dependent, returning to control levels in 12 months. Pretreatment with an serotonin uptake blocker (citalopram) prevented the neurodegenerative effects of MDMA. The rat and guinea-pig brain was affected, whereas the mouse brain was not.

Battaglia, G., Yeh, S.Y., O'Hearn, E., Molliver, M.E., Kuhar, M.J. and De Souza, E.B. 3,4-Methylenedioxymethamphetamine and 3,4-Methylenedi-oxyamphetamine Destroy Serotonin Terminals in Rat Brain: Quantification of Neurodegeneration by Measurements of [3H] Paroxetine-Labeled Serotonin Uptake Sites. J. Pharm. Exptl. Therap. 242 911-916 (1987),

Effects of repeated administration of MDMA and MDA on the levels of rat brain monoamines and their metabolites are reported. Only the serotonin-related systems were found to be affected.

Bird, M.P., Svendsen, C.N., Knapp, C., Hrbek, C.C., Bird, E.D. and Kornetsky, C. Evidence for Dopaminergic and Not Serotonergic Mediation of the Threshold Lowering Effects of MDMA on Rewarding Brain Stimulation. Soc. Neurosci. Abstr., Vol. 13, Part 3, p. 1323 (1987) No. 365.13.

An effort is made to determine the rewarding aspect of MDMA by a combination of brain electrodes and specific neurotransmitter inhibitors. It is felt that MDMA reinforcing values may be mediated by the dopamine D-2 receptor rather than the serotonin 5-HT-2 receptor.

Champney, T.H., Golden, P.T. and Matthews, R.T. Reduction of Hypothalamic Serotonin Levels after Acute MDMA Administration. Soc. Neurosciences Abstrts. 12 101.6 (1986).

Cortical, hypothalamic, and pineal levels of catecholamines, serotonin and 5-HIAA were determined shortly following an acute exposure of rats to each of several doses of MDMA. Dose-dependent decreases of serotonin and 5-HIAA were noted in some but not other areas. The catecholamine levels were unchanged.

Commins, D.L., Vosmer, G., Virus, R.M., Woolverton, C.R., Schuster, C.R. and Seiden, L.S. Biochemical and Histological Evidence that Methylenedi-oxy-methamphetamine (MDMA) is Toxic to Neurons in Rat Brain. J. Pharm. Exptl. Therap. 241 338-345 (1987).

MDMA was chronically administered to rats and guinea pigs , and the neurotransmitter levels were assayed in several portions of the brain. Neurotransmitter levels are related to dosage, and to the extent of exposure. Anatomical morbidity is carefully described.

DeSousa, E.B., Battaglia, G., Yeh, S.Y. and Kuhar, M.J. In Vitro and In Vivo Effects of MDA and MDMA (Ecstasy) on Brain Receptors and Uptake Sites: Evidence for Selective Neurotoxic Actions on Serotonin Terminals. Amer. Coll. of Neuropsychopharm. p. 207 (Dec. 8-12, 1986).

MDA and MDMA both showed a relatively high affinity for both 5HT-2 serotoninergic and alpha-2 adrenergic brain receptors, but low affinities for 5HT-1, and for the alpha-1 and beta adrenergic receptors, as well as for dopamine, muscarinic, and opiate receptors. Chronic administration of either drug decreases the number of 5-HT2 receptors in various brain locations.

Finnigan, K.T., Ricaurte, G.A., Ritchie, L.D., Irwin, I., Peroutka, S.J. and Langston, J.W. Orally Administered MDMA Causes a Long-term Depletion of Serotonin in Rat Brain. Brain Research 447 141-144 (1988).

The oral and sub-cutaneous routes of MDMA toxicity to rat serotonergic neurons are studied. Both routes lead to a dose dependent serotonin depletion.

Gehlert, D.R. and Schmidt, C.J. Acute Administration of Methylenedioxy-methamphetamine (MDMA) Results in a Persistent and Selective Increase in 5-HT-1 Receptor Binding in Rat Brain. Pharmacologist 29 ABS-44 (1987)

Acute administration of MDMA in the rat showed an increase in serotonin binding in 24 hours. This occurred in several parts of the brain.

Glennon, R.A., Titeler, M., Lyon, R.A. and Youssif, M. MDMA ("Ecstasy"): Drug Discrimination and Brain Binding Properties. Soc. Neurosciences Abstracts 12 250.11 (1986).

In rats treated chronically with MDMA (trained to discriminate racemic MDMA from saline), radioligand binding studies were conducted with both serotonin and dopamine sites. The Ki values for both 5-HT1 and 5-HT2 receptors were highest for the "S" isomers of MDMA and MDA, with the racemate lower, and the "R" isomer yet lower. There was no particular affinity for the dopamine receptors studied.

Gold, L.H., Hubner, C.B. and Koob, G.F. The Role of Mesolimbic Dopamine in the Stimulant Action of MDMA. Soc. Neurosci. Abstr., Vol. 13, Part 3, p. 833 (1987) No. 234.13.

The administration of MDMA to rats may involve (like amphetamine) the release of dopamine. Test animals with lesions induced by 6-hydroxydopamine showed less motor activity in response to MDMA than control animals.

Johnson, M., Letter, A.A., Merchant, K., Hanson, G.R. and Gibb, J.W. Effects of 3,4-Methylenedioxyamphetamine and 3,4- methylenedioxymethamphetamine Isomers on Central Serotonergic, Dopaminergic and Nigral Neurotensin Systems of the Rat. J. Pharm. Exptl. Therap. 244 977-982 (1988).

The difference of the isomers of MDA and MDMA in their ability to induce neurotransmitter changes and neurotensin immunoreactivity are reported. In general the d-isomers of each were the more potent in affecting neurochemical systems.

Johnson, M.P., Hoffman, A.J. and Nichols, D.E. Effects of the Enantiomers of MDA, MDMA, and Related Analogues on [3H]Serotonin and [3H]Dopamine Release from Superfused Rat Brain Slices. Europ. J. Pharmacol. 132 269-276 (1986).

The study of a series of MDA homologs (MDA, MDMA, MBDB) showed a dramatic dependence between chain length and dopamine release. The longer the chain, the less the release. It is concluded that dopamine release plays a minor role in the human activity of these compounds.

Kalix, P. A Comparison of the Effects of Some Phenethylamines on the Release of Radioactivity from Isolated Rat Caudate Nucleus Prelabelled with 3H-Dopamine. Arzneim. Forsch. 36 1019-1021 (1986).

A number of phenethylamines were found able to release radioactivity from dopamine-prelabelled caudate nuclei. MDMA was not spectacular, as the simplest unsubstituted amphetamine derivatives were the most effective.

Kalix, P., Yousif, M.Y. and Glennon, R.A. Differential Effects of the Enantiomers of Methylenedioxymethamphetamine (MDMA) on the Release of Radioactivity from (3H)Dopamine-Prelabeled Rat Striatum." Res. Commun. Subst. Abuse 9 #1 45-52 (1988).

The S-isomer of MDMA (the more effective stimulant) is more effective than the R-isomer in releasing radioactivity from tritiated dopamine-prelabeled rat striatum. It is about one sixth the potency of S-methamphetamine.

Kopajtic, T., Battaglia, G. and De Souza, E.B. A Pharmacologic Profile of MDA and MDMA on Brain Receptors and Uptake Sites. Soc. Neurosciences Abstrts. 12 336.1 (1986).

Both MDA and MDMA were studied at various brain recognition sites using radioligand binding techniques. The findings suggest that these drugs may express their effects at serotonin receptors or uptake sites and/ or alpha-2 adrenergic receptors.

Logan, B.J., Laverty, R., Sanderson, W.D. and Yee, Y.B. Differences Between Rats and Mice in MDMA (Methylenedioxymethylamphetamine) Neurotoxicity. Europ. J. Pharmacol. 152 227-234 (1988).

A single large administration of MDMA to the rat or the mouse caused only transient changes in serotonin, norepinephrine and dopamine levels (and those of their metabolites). Repeated administrations were reqired to establish long-lasting changes in the rat; the mouse remained relatively insensitive. It appears that both the nature and the degree of neurotoxicity with MDMA is species-specific.

Lyon, R.A., Glennon, R.A. and Titeler, M. 3,4-Methylenedioxy- methamphetamine (MDMA): Stereoselective Interactions at Brain 5- HT1 and 5-
HT2 Receptors. Psychopharmacology 88 525-526 (1986).

The assay of the optical isomers of MDA and MDMA with isolated
receptors of rat brains suggested that MDMA does not work primarily
through direct interaction with serotonin receptors.

Mokler, D.J., Robinson, S.E. and Rosecrans, J.A. Differential Depletion of
Brain 5-Hydroxytryptamine (5-HT) by (+/-) 3,4- Methylenedioxymethamphetamine (MDMA). Pharmacologist 29 ABS-273 (1987).

Specific brain areas have been studied for the serotonin depletion effects
of MDMA. The neuron metabolic activity in the specific areas might be
involved.

Mokler, D.J., Robinson, S.E. and Rosecrans, J.A. (+/-) 3,4- Methylenedioxymethamphetamine (MDMA) Produces Long-term Reductions in
Brain 5-Hydroxytryptamine in Rats. Europ. J. Pharm. 138 265-268 (1987).

Following chronic administration of MDMA to rats, both serotonin and 5-
HIAA became depleted in the brain. It is suggested that MDMA can
function as a neurotoxin.

Mokler, D.J., Robinson, S.E. and Rosecrans, J.A. A Comparison of the
Effects of Repeated Doses of MDMA ("Ecstasy") on Biogenic Amine
Levels in Adult and Neonate Rats. Soc. Neurosci. Abstr., Vol. 13, Part 3, p.
905 (1987) No. 251.9.

MDMA was given to both adult and neonate rats in 10-40 mg/Kg doses
over several days. The serotonin levels were decreased and the dopamine
levels were significantly increased.

Molliver, M.E. Serotonergic Neural Systems: What their Anatomic
Organization Tells Us about Function. J. Clinical Psychopharm. 7 3S-23S
(1987).

A review of the organization of the serotonin nervous system is presented.
The findings associated with the neurotoxic effects of MDMA are used as
instructive tools, and speculation is extended as to the role of these
neurons in the generation of the affective state.

Molliver, M.E., O'Hearn, E., Battaglia, G. and De Souza, E.B. Direct
Intracerebral Administration of MDA and MDMA Does Not Produce
Serotonin Neurotoxicity. Soc. Neurosciences Abstrts. 12 336.3 (1986).

The microinjection of either MDA or MDMA directly in to the cerebral
cortex resulted in no detectable cytotoxicity. This suggests that the
neurotoxicity of both compounds may be due to some metabolite formed
peripherally.

Monti, J.A., Beaton, J.M., Benington, F., Morin, R.D. and Christian, S.T. MDMA and MBDB Potentiate Phorbol Ester- Stimulated Catecholamine Release from PC-12 Cells. Society for Neuroscience, Abstract, for November 13-18, 1988.

The "S" isomer of both MDMA and MBDB are potent in stimulating catechol release from PC-12 cells. The norepinephrin and dopamine release was increased in the presence of phorbol dibenzoate. It is suggested that this release may be mediated by protein kinase-C.

O'Hearn, E., Battaglia, G., De Souza, E.B., Kuhar, K.J. and Molliver, M.E. Systemic MDA and MDMA, Psychotropic Substituted Amphetamines, Produce Serotonin Neurotoxicity. Soc. Neuro- sciences Abstrts. 12 336.2 (1986).

Rats exposed chronically to either MDA or MDMA were found, on sacrifice, to have a reduced number of serotonin axon terminals. This was most evident in cerebral cortex, thalamus, olfactory bulb and striatum, but also occurred in other areas. This may be due to the binding of thse drugs to the uptake sites. The serotonin cell bodies and the preterminal axons are spared.

Peroutka, S.J., Pascoe, N. and Faull, K.F. Monoamine Metabolites in the Cerebrospinal Fluid of Recreational Users of 3,4- Methylenedioxy-methamphetamine (MDMA, "Ecstasy"). Res. Commun. Subst. Abuse 8 125-138 (1987).

Lumbar punctures from five MDMA users with various histories were assayed (some weeks following the last exposure) for the levels of metabolites from the three major neurotransmitters serotonin, dopamine, and norepinephrine. All assays fell within normal limits.

Ricaurte, G.A., Bryan, G., Strauss, L., Seiden, L. and Schuster, C. Hallucino-genic Amphetamine Selectively Destroys Brain Serotonin Nerve Terminals. Science 229 986-988 (1985).

MDA was studied and found to produce long lasting reductions in the level of serotonin, the number of serotonin uptake sites, and the concentration of 5-HIAA in the rat brain. It was suggested that these deficits were due to serotonin nerve terminal degeneration. This was the research report that had been submitted for publication at the time of the MDMA hearings, and that played a focal role in the emergency scheduling of MDMA.

Ricaurte, G.A., DeLanney, L.E., Irwin, I. and Langston, J.W. Toxic Effects of MDMA on Central Serotonergic Neurons in the Primate: Importance of Route and Frequency of Drug Application. Brain Research 446 165-169 (1988).

The toxicity of MDMA was studied in primates both by the oral and the subcutaneous routes, and in single and multiple doses. Multiple doses are more effective that single doses in depleting serotonin, and the s.c route is more effective than the oral route. However, a single, oral administration of MDMA still produces a long-lived depletion

Ricaurte, G.A., Finnegan, K.F., Nichols, D.E., DeLanney, L.E., Irwin, I. and Langston, J.W. 3,4-Methylenedioxyethylamphetamine (MDE), a Novel Analogue of MDMA, Produces Long-lasting Depletion of Serotonin in the Rat Brain. Europ. J. Pharmacol. 137 265-268 (1987).

MDE was qualitatively similar to MDMA in the depletion of serotonin in rat brain, but was only one fourth as potent.

Ricaurte, G.A., Forno, L.S., Wilson, M.A., DeLanney, L.E., Irwin, I., Molliver, M.E. and Langston, J.W. (+/-) Methylenedioxymethamphetam-ine (MDMA) Exerts Toxic Effects on Central Serotonergic Neurons in Primates. Soc. Neurosci. Abstr., Vol. 13, Part 3, p. 905 (1987) No. 251.8.

MDMA was given s.q. twice daily for four days to monkeys, at 2.5, 3.75 and 5 mg/Kg. Post-mortum brain analyses showed serotonin reduction (90%) and axon damage. Some was described as "striking" and involved morphological changes.

Ricaurte, G.A., Forno, L.S., Wilson, M.A., DeLanney, L.E., Irwin, I., Moliver, M.E. and Langston, J.W. (+/-) 3,4-Methylenedioxymethamphet-amine Selectively Damages Central Serotonergic Neurons in Nonhuman Primates. J.A.M.A. 260 51-55 (1988).

The parenteral administration (subcutaneous, twice daily for four days) of MDMA to monkeys of three species produced both brain serotonin depletion and accompanying neuron damage upon autopsy following a two-week waiting period. Considerable microscopic detail is given. The evidence presented could imply, but does not established, that there may be actual neuron cell death. The human pattern of use is oral rather than parenteral, but a warning for prudence is advanced for the human use of either MDMA or (the neurotoxicologically similar drug) fenfluramine.

Scallet, A.C., Ali, S.F., Holson, R.R., Lipe, G.W. and Slikker Jr., W. Neuro-histological Effects 120 Days after Oral Ecstasy (MDMA): Multiple Antigen Immunohistochemistry and Silver Degeneration Staining. Soc. Neurosci. Abstr., Vol. 13, Part 3, p. 904 (1987) No. 251.6.

Both silver degeneration procedures (Fink-Heimer) and immunohisto-chemical techniques have been appled to MDMA- treated rats long after dosing. There are indications of regional differences in recovery, and that some changes may be irreversible.

Schmidt, C.J. Acute Administration of Methylenedioxymethamphet-amine: Comparison with the Neurochemical Effects of its N- desmethyl and N-ethyl Analogs. 136 81088 (1987).

MDMA (and its two immediate homologs, MDMA and MDE) were studied in the serotoninergic systems in the rat brain. There was depletion of cortical serotonin which in the case of MDMA appeared to persist after at least a week.

Schmidt, C.J. and Lovenberg, W. (+/-)Methylenedioxymethamphetamine (MDMA): A Potentially Neurotoxic Amphetamine Analogue. Fed. Proc. 45 1059 (#5264) April 13-18, 1986. Note paper below, Schmidt et al., with this same title.

Rats were administered MDMA s.c. at various doses and sacrificed at three hours. Brain concentrations of dopamine and serotonin, and their major metabolites were determined. The serotonin concentrations were reduced in a dose- dependent manner. Coadministration of a serotonin uptake inhibitor, citalopram, blocked the MDMA-induced decline in striatal serotonin concentrations suggesting a mechanism similar to that of the known serotonergic neurotoxin p- chloroamphetamine.

Schmidt, C.J. and Lovenberg, W. Further Studies on the Neurochemical Effects of 4,5-Methylenedioxymethamphetamine and Related Analogues. Soc. Neurosciences Abstrts. 12 169.5 (1986).

The racemate and optical isomers of MDMA produced depletion of cortical and striatal serotonin. The (+) isomer was the more effective material. MDA was similar to MDMA, but effects produced by the N-ethyl homolog (MDE) were reversed in a week. Whereas all three drugs caused an acute decrease in serotonin concentration, only MDA and MDMA reduced the uptake of tritiated serotonin at the dosages studied (20 mg/Kg).

Schmidt, C.J., Wu, L. and Lovenberg, W. Methylenedioxymethamphetetamine: A Potentially Neurotoxic Amphetamine Analogue. Eur. J. Pharmacol. 124 175-178 (1986). A typewritten draft of this paper was presented to the DEA in conjunction with the legal hearings held concerning the scheduling of MDMA.

Acute administration of MDMA to rats provide selective and long lasting serotonin and 5-HIAA depletion, similar to that produced by p-chlorophenylalanine. There was an elevation of neostriatal dopamine as well as its primary metabolite homovanillic acid.

Seiden, L.S. Report of Preliminary Results on MDMA. Document entered into evidence Re: MDMA Scheduling Docket No. 84-48, U.S. Department of Justice, Drug Enforcement Administration, October 16, 1985.

Rats were treated both acutely and chronically with MDMA, and the study of the decrease of serotonin receptors and the interpretation of neurological staining indicated a neurotoxicity similar to, but less dramatic than, that seen with MDA.

Slikker, W., Ali, S.F., Scallet, A.C. and Frith, C.H. Methylenedioxymethamphetamine (MDMA) Produces Long Lasting Alterations in the
Serotonergic System of Rat Brain. Soc. Neurosciences Abstrts. 12 101.7
(1986).

The chronic treatment of rats with MDMA (orally) produced decreased
levels of serotonin and 5-HIAA. At high dose levels there was a temporary decrease in homovanillic acid (HVA) but no change in dopamine
levels.

Spanos, L.J. and Yamamoto, B.K. Methylenedioxymethamphetamine
(MDMA)-induced Efflux of Dopamine and Serotonin in Rat Nucleus
Accumbens. Society of Neurosciences Abstr't. 12 p. 609 (#169.6)

Following MDMA adminstration to rats, the efflux of dopamine was
decreased but then it quickly recovered. Serotonin depletion does not
recover even after 2 hours, thus MDMA may be neurotoxic.

Stone, D.M., Hanson, G.R. and Gibb, J.W. Does Dopamine Play a Role in
the Serotonergic "Neurotoxicity" Induced by 3,4- Methylenedioxymethamphetamine (MDMA)? Society of Neurosciences Abstract 12 169.4
(1986).

The possibility that the negative serotonin effects of MDMA might be
mediated by dopamine was investigated. Studies involving dopamine
synthesis inhibitors and antagonists suggest less involvement of dopamine than is seen with methamphetamine.

Stone, D.M., Hanson, G.R. and Gibb, J.W. Differences in the Central
Serotonergic Effects of Methylenedioxymethamphetamine (MDMA) in
Mice and Rats. Neuropharm. 26 1657-1661 (1987).

A number of studies as to the brain serotonin responses to MDMA (in
rats) suggest that the duration of exposure might be an important factor in
the estimation of toxic effects. Mice are shown to be less susceptible,
neurotoxicologically, than rats.

Stone, D.M., Merchant, K.M., Hanson, G.R. and Gibb, J.W. Immediate and
Long Term Effects of 3,4-Methylenedioxymethamphetamine on Serotonin
Pathways in Brain of Rat. Neuropharmacology 26 1677-1683 (1987).

The time course for the decrease of markers of central serotonin function
in the rat is reported. Changes were observed at 15 minutes following a
10 mg/Kg s.c. injection, and much recovery was observed at the 2 week
point. Following multiple dose administration of MDMA, significant
serotonin changes were still evident after 110 days.

Stone, D.M., Stahl, D.C., Hanson, G.R. and Gibb, J.W. The Effects of 3,4-
methylenedioxymethamphetamine (MDMA) and 3,4- methylenedioxy-
amphetamine (MDA) on Monoaminergic Systems in the Rat Brain. Eur. J.
Pharmacol. 128 41-48 (1986).

Single or multiple doses of either MDMA or MDA caused marked
reduction in both serotonin and 5-HIAA, as well as in the associated
enzyme tryptophane hydroxylase (TPH). Single injections elevated
striatal dopamine concentrations, although after repeated injections, these
values became normal. Striatal tyrosine hydroxylase (TH) was not
changed.

Takeda, H., Gazzara, R.A., Howard, S.G. and Cho, A.K. Effects of
Methylene-dioxymethamphetamine (MDMA) on Dopamine (DA) and
Serotonin (5-HT) Efflux in the Rat Neostriatum. Fed. Proc. 45 1059 (#5266)
April 13-18, 1986.

Employing electrodes implanted in the neostriatum of anesthesized rats,
the MDMA-induced efflux of dopamine and serotonin was measured.
The serotonin efflux was significantly increased by MDMA, and had
returned to normal by three hours. The dopamine efflux increased
slightly, and then dropped below normal. MDA decreased dopamine
efflux.

Trulson, T.J. and Trulson, M.E. 3,4-Methylenedioxymethamphetamine
(MDMA) Suppresses Serotonergic Dorsal Raphe Neuronal Activity in
Freely Moving Cats and in Midbrain Slices in vitro. Soc. Neurosci. Abstr.
Vol. 13, Part 3, p. 905 (1987) No. 251.7.

A study of the decrease of brain serotonin levels in cats given 0.25-5.0 mg/
Kg MDMA is reported. Pretreatment with p-chloroamphetamine greatly
attenuated the suppressant action of MDMA, and it is suggested that the
action of the two drugs is similar.

Wilson, M.A., Ricaurte, G.A. and Molliver, M.E. The Psychotropic Drug
3,4-Methylenedioxymethamphetamine (MDMA) Destroys Serotonergic
Axons in Primate Forebrain: Regional and Laminar Differences in
Vulnerability. Soc. Neurosci. Abstr., Vol. 13, Part 3, p. 905 (1987) No.
251.8.

The monkey shows a striking brain loss of serotonin terminals following
exposure to MDMA twice daily for 4 days at 5 mg/Kg. The distribution
and extent of this damage is reported.

Woolverton, W.L., Virus, R.M., Kamien, J.B., Nencini, P., Johanson, C.E.,
Seiden, L.S. and Schuster, C.R. Behavioral and Neurotoxic Effects of
MDMA and MDA. Amer. Coll. Neuropsychopharm. Abstrts. p. 173
(1985).

In behavioral studies in rats and monkeys trained to distinguish amphetamine from saline, MDMA mimicked amphetamine. With chronic administration, MDMA caused a degeneration of serotonin uptake sites, but no
change in affinity of the undamaged sites. These results were similar to,

but greater than, those seen with MDA.

Yamamoto, B.K. and Spanos, L.J. The Acute Effects of Methylenedioxy-methamphetamine on Dopamine Release in the Awake-behaving Rat. Eur. J. Pharmacol. 148 195-204 (1988).

The effects of MDMA on the caudate and nucleus accumbens dopamine release and metabolism were studied by in vivo voltammetry and HPLC with electrochemical detection. There was a dose-dependent dopamine release observed in both regions by both measures.

Yeh, S.Y. and Hsu, F-L. Neurotoxicity of Metabolites of MDA and MDMA (Ecstasy) in the Rat. Soc. Neurosci. Abstr., Vol. 13, Part 3, p. 906 (1987) No. 251.11.

MDA, MDMA, and a number of potential metabolites (4-OH- 3-OMe-amphetamine, alpha-methyldopamine, alpha-methylnor-epine-phrine) were studied in the rat, and the serotonin decreases measured. These metabolites have a lower neurotoxicity than the parent compound.

Yeh, S.Y., Battaglia, G., O'Hearn, E., Molliver, M.E., Kuhar, M.J. and De Souza, E.B. Effects of MDA and MDMA (Ecstasy) on Brain Monoaminer-gic Systems: In vivo studies. Soc. Neurosci. Abstr., Vol. 12, No. 336.5 (1986).

The chronic treatment of rats with MDMA or MDA (20 mg/Kg, twice daily, for 4 days) produced dramatic decreases in both serotonin and 5-HIAA in various brain locations. Other neurotransmitters and their metabolites were not affected.

(6) TOXICOLOGY

Brown, C.R., McKinney, H., Osterloh, J.D., Shulgin, A.T., Jacob III P. and Olson, K.R. Severe Adverse Reaction to 3,4-Methylenedioxymethamphet-amine (MDMA). Vet. Hum. Toxicol., 28 490 (1986).

A 32 year old female presumably ingested a "standard" dose, and became comatose, but survived. Serum level was reported to be 7 micrograms/mL.

Brown, C. and Osterloh, J. Multiple Severe Complications from Recrea-tional Ingestion of MDMA (Ecstasy). J. Amer. Med. Soc. 258 780-781 (1987).

A considerable body of clinical detail and selected laboratory finding is present in an apparent MDMA toxicity situation involving a 32 year old female. Serum levels of 7 micrograms/mL and urine levels of 410 and 816 micrograms/mL were reported (the latter upon admission and on the second day). An immunoenzyme assay for MDMA (using a system designed for amphetamine) reacted with MDMA at 25 micrograms/mL at the amphetamine cut-off point of 300 nanograms/mL. The observed complications were similar to those observed in amphetamine overdoses, and might possibly be due to an idiosyncratic reaction, an allergic reaction, or to malignant hyper-thermia.

Davis, W.M. and Borne, R.F. Pharmacologic Investigation of Compounds Related to 3,4-Methylenedioxyamphetamine (MDA). Substance and Alcohol Actions/Misuse, 5 105-110 (1984).

Acute toxicity studies on MDMA and several homologs, in mice, showed LD-50's of about 100 mg/Kg (i.p.) (for MDMA). In aggregate, the lethality was increased several-fold.

Davis, W.M., Hatoum, H.T. and Waters, I.W., Toxicity of MDA (3,4-Methylenedioxyamphetamine) Considered for Relevancy to Hazards of MDMA (Ecstasy) Abuse. Alcohol and Drug Abuse, 7 123-134 (1987).

The toxicological literature is reviewed, and it is suggested that the toxicological data obtained from MDA be extrapolated to MDMA. A comparison of these two drug is presented.

Dowling, G.P., McDonough III, E.T. and Bost, R.O. 'Eve' and 'Ecstasy' A Report of Five Deaths Associated with the Use of MDEA and MDMA. J. Amer. Med. Assoc. 257 1615-1617 (1987)

Five deaths occurred in the Dallas area which have involved either MDMA or MDE. One death was stated to be due to MDMA. Two of the others had had preexisting heart conditions, one had asthma, and one was electrocuted, apparently from having climbed and fallen from a power pole. In these latter cases, MDMA was not felt to have been the primary cause of death. It is suggested that a preexisting cardiac disease may predispose an individual to sudden death with MDMA. It was only with the asthma death that there was given a body level (blood) of MDMA, and it was 1.1 micrograms/mL.

Frith, C.H. 28-Day Oral Toxicity of Methylenedioxymeth- amphetamine Hydrochloride (MDMA) in Rats. Project Report, Toxicology Pathology Associates, Little Rock, Arkansas (1986)

A controlled toxicological study on some 100 rats with chronically administered MDMA (dosages up to 100 mg/Kg) showed several behavioral signs (hyperactivity, excitability, piloerection. exophthalmus, and salivation). Neither gross nor microscopic pathology was evident at necropsy.

Frith, C.H., 28-Day Oral Toxicity of Methylenedioxymeth- amphetamine Hydrochloride (MDMA) in Dogs. Project Report, Toxicology Pathology

Associates, Little Rock, Arkansas (1986)

A controlled toxicological study of some 24 dogs with chronically administered MDMA (dosages up to 15 mg/Kg) showed several behavioral signs
including circling, depression, dilated pupils, hyperactivity, rapid
breathing, and salivation. On necropsy, there were examples of reduced
testicular size, including microscopically noted atrophy. Prostatic
hyperplasia was present in two high dose males.

Frith, C.H., Chang, L.W., Lattin, D.L., Walls, R.C., Hamm, J. and Doblin, R.
Toxicity of Methylenedioxymethamphetamine (MDMA) in the Dog and
the Rat. Fundamental and Applied Tox. 9, 110-119 (1987).

Toxicity studies were performed on dogs and rats and signs are described.
No histopathological lesions within the CNS were observed in either
species, although unusual clinical observations were recorded.

Goad, P.T. Acute and Subacute Oral Toxicity Study of Methylenedioxymethamphetamine in Rats. Project Report, Intox Laboratories,
Redfield, Arkansas, (1985).

Subacute toxicity studies on rats in graded doses (25 mg/Kg/day in 25
mg increments to 300 mg) were conducted. In acute studies, the LD-50 is
given as 325 mg/Kg, some 6x the reported i.p. LD-50. No histological
evidence of brain damage was observed.

Hardman, H.F., Haavik, C.O. and Seevers, M.H. Relationship of the
Structure of Mescaline and Seven Analogs to Toxicity and Behavior in
Five Species of Laboratory Animals. Tox. and Appl. Pharmacology 25 #2
(June) pp. 299-309 (1973).

This report describes several studies supported by the Army Chemical
Center during the period 1953-1954, and declassified in 1969. MDMA was
one of eight compounds
(including also mescaline, DMPEA, MDPEA, MDA, DMA, TMA and
alpha-ethyl-MDPEA) studied in five animals (mouse, rat, guinea pig, dog,
and monkey).
The toxicology study showed MDMA to be one of the more toxic of the
drugs studied, in most animals second only to MDA. The average LD-50's
given were 97, 49 and 98 mg/Kg (for the mouse, rat and guinea pig, resp.
— following i.p. administration), and 16 and 26 mg/Kg (for the dog and
monkey, i.v. administration).
Behavioral studies in dog and monkey were made over the dosage ranges
of 5-50 and 10-75 mg/Kg respectively. These levels evoked a broad range
of motor activity, autonomic activity and CNS activity in both animals
(the dog more than the monkey) but the ranges studied included the lethal
dose levels. Interestingly the monkey showed behavior interpreted as
hallucinations for MDMA, whereas mescaline (an acknowledged hallucinogenic compound) produced no such behavior at doses more than 2x

higher (200 mg/Kg i.v.). Structure-activity relationships are discussed.

Hayner, G.N. and McKinney, H. MDMA The Dark Side of Ecstasy. J. Psychoactive Drugs 18 341-347 (1986).

The emergency treatment of two toxic episodes involving MDMA are described. One case, a 34 year old male, had a complex drug history involving mainly opiates, but the timing of the crisis suggested that MDMA injection was responsible. The other case, involving a 33 year old female, has been discussed in detail (see Brown et al., above). A listing of the side-effects that may be experienced in cases of MDMA toxicity is also presented.

Reynolds, P.C., Personal Communication, 1986.

A 35-years old male, who claimed to have taken MDMA, Valium, and LSD (and who died shortly after admission) had the following body levels (in micrograms/mL):

Blood	Urine	Bile	Gastric
MDMA	1.46	13.7	1.98	414 (total)
MDA	.03 (present)			

Neither diazepam nor nordiazepam were found.

Schmidt, C.J., Neurotoxicity of the Psychedelic Amphetamine, Methylene-dioxymethamphetamine. J. Pharm. Exptl. Therap. 240 1-7 (1987).

Evidence is presented that MDMA has a complex effect on rat serotoner-gic neurons, that results in a neurotoxic effect on the nerve terminals. A parallel is drawn to the neurotoxin parachloro-amphetamine.

Schmidt, C.J., Levin, J.A. and Loverberg, W., In Vitro and In Vivo Neuro-chemical Effects on Methylenedioxymethamphetamine on Striatal Monoaminergic Systems in the Rat Brain, Biochem. Pharmacol. 36 747-755 (1987)

This study compares the effects of MDMA and MDA on the neurotrans-mitter release in vitro and the (+) isomer is the more effective. The (+) isomer is also the more effective in vivo.

Shulgin, A.T. and Jacob III, P., 1-(3,4-Methylenedioxyphenyl)-3- aminobu-tane: A Potential Toxicological Problem. J. Toxicol. - Clin. Toxicol. 19, pp 109-110 (1982).

An alert is written for the toxicological community that through the ambiguity of the term "piperonylacetone" two different chemical precur-sors for both MDA and MDMA have been publicly advertised and made available. Efforts to synthesize MDMA might, through misrepresentation, yield a largely unexplored homolog.

Smilkstein, M.J., Smolinske, S.C., Kulig, K.W. and Rumack, B.H. MAO
Inhibitor/MDMA Interaction: Agony after Ecstasy. Vet. Hum. Toxicol. 28
490 (1986).

An abstract of a report of a 50 year old male who injected alleged MDMA
while on a fixed regimen of the monoamine oxidase inhibitor phenelzine.
He developed severe hypertension, diaphoresis, an altered mental status,
and marked hypertonicity. With supportive care he recovered fully in
some 6 hours. Caution is expressed in possible interactions between
MDMA and MAO inhibitors.

Smilkstein, M.J., Smolinske, S.C. and Rumack, B.H. A Case of MAO
Inhibitor/MDMA Interaction: Agony after Ecstasy. Clin. Toxicol. 25 149-
159 (1987).

This is the actual published paper that appeared as an abstract under
similar authorship and similar title above. There are considerable clinical
details concerning the emergency room intervention.

Verebey, K., Alrazi, J. and Jaffe, J.H. The Complications of "Ecstasy"
(MDMA). J. Am. Med. Assoc. 259 1649-1650 (1988). Osterloh, J. and
Brown, C., In Reply. ibid. 259 1650 (1988).

The body levels of MDMA and MDA following a single human trial of 50
mg are given. The peak plasma level seen (105.6 ng/Ml at 2 hrs.) decreased to 5.1 ng/Ml at 24 hrs. MDA occurred in plasma at lower levels,
and both compounds appeared in urine. This suggests that the toxic
incident reported by Brown and Osterloh may have followed a considerable overdose.

(7) CLINICAL STUDIES

Buffum, J. and Moser, C. MDMA and Human Sexual Function. J.
Psychoactive Drugs, 18 355-359 (1986).

A survey of some 300 MDMA users produced a response of 25%. An
analysis of the presented data is offered, organized as to types of activity
and performance. There was a significant increase in intimacy, and a
decrease (especially for males) in performance.

Downing, J. The Psychological and Physiological Effects of MDMA on
Normal Volunteers. J. Psychoactive Drugs 18 335-340 (1986).

This is certainly the most complete clinical study on the effects of MDMA
on the normal human subject. A total of 21 normal volunteers were
administered known amounts of MDMA, orally. The entire group had
analyses of blood chemistry, timed and frequent physiological measures,
including pulse and blood pressure (for all), and as well as neurological
and electrocardiographic tests (for some). The neurological and electro-

cardiogram evaluations were continued for 24 hours.

Physiologically, all subjects experienced an elevation in blood pressure and pulse rate, with a peaking on the average at about one hour. At the sixth hour, most subjects were at or below their pre-dose levels, and at 24 hours all were within their normal ranges. Eye dilation was seen in all subjects, more than half had jaw clench and an increased jaw reflex, which persisted in one subject at the 24 hour point. Some neurological reflexes were enhanced (deep tendon) or equivocal (plantar reflex), and there were signs of incoordination (finger-nose testing, gait) in some subjects, giving a strong warning against motor vehicle operation. One subject was nauseous, with vomiting, but there were no difficulties with either urination or defecation, and there were neither headaches nor insomnia. Appetite was suppressed in all subjects to varying degrees.

At the psychological level, all subjects reported a heightened sensual awareness, and three reported sexual arousal. It is concluded that MDMA produces remarkably consistent psychological effects that are transient, and is free of clinically apparent major toxicity.

Greer, G. MDMA: A New Psychotropic Compound and its Effects in Humans. Privately published, 333 Rosario Hill, Sante Fe, NM 87501. Copyright 1983. 15 pages.

The most complete study of the effects of MDMA published as of this date, describing the results of administration of MDMA to 29 human subjects (none with serious psychiatric problems) in a therapeutic setting. It is concluded that the best uses of MDMA are: facilitation of communication and intimacy between people involved in emotional relationships; as an adjunct to insight-oriented psychotherapy; and in the treatment of alcohol and drug abuse. He explains why MDMA does not lend itself to over- use, since its most desirable effects diminish with frequency of use.

Greer, G. Recommended Protocol for MDMA Sessions. Privately published. 333 Rosario Hill, Sante Fe, NM 87501. Copyright 1985. 6 pages.

This is a generalized protocol designed to cover the clinical use of MDMA. It reviews the issues of law, of safety, and of efficacy.

Greer, G. Using MDMA in Psychotherapy. Advances, 2 57-57 (1985).

A conference was held at Esalen March 10-15 1985, to discuss the potential of MDMA for therapy, and to evaluate its differences from earlier therapeutic tools such as LSD. A total of 13 subjects, with the supervision of several experienced psychiatrists, participated in a experiment designed to familiarize the potential clinician with the actions of MDMA. Most of the attendees had already known of the drug in a therapeutic context, and their collected comments are presented and discussed.

Greer, G. and Tolbert, R. Subjective Reports of the Effects of MDMA in a

Clinical Setting. J. Psychoactive Drugs 18 319-327 (1986).

This article summarizes and gives additional detail on the collection of 29 therapeutic trials discussed earlier. The format of drug administration, a review of both the benefits and the undesirable effects, and an outlining of the changes seen in the patients, is presented. There is a considerable body of retrospective evaluation.

Shulgin, A.T. and Nichols, D.E. Characterization of Three New Psychotomimetics, The Psychopharmacology of Hallucinogens, Eds. R.C. Stillman and R.E. Willette, Pergamon Press, New York. (1978).

The psychopharmacological properties of MDMA are presented, in company with two new compounds, para-DOT (2,5- dimethoxy-4-methylthioamphetamine) and alpha,O-DMS (5- methoxy-alpha-methyltryptamine). It is described as evoking an easily controlled altered state of consciousness with emotional and sensual overtones. It appears to be with little hallucinatory component. This is the first clinical report of the effects of MDMA in man.

Siegel, R.K. MDMA: Nonmedical Use and Intoxication. J. Psychoactive Drugs 18 349-354 (1986).

From a group of 415 acknowledged MDMA users, a sub- group of 44 were chosen for examinations and tests. They were interviewed, physically examined, and tested by several of a large battery of psychological evaluation procedures. From this, patterns of use and the nature of the intoxicating effects were deduced.
The author has concluded that the visual effects of MDMA intoxication were typical of the intoxications from the classical hallucinogens such as mescaline with imagery characteristic of drug-induced hallucinations, as well as those induced by isolation and stress. These are modified when attention is directed towards external events. There were, nonetheless, no abnormal profiles on the psychological tests. It is felt that the MDMA intoxication is neither uniformly controllable nor uniformly predictable.

Tatar, A. and Naranjo, C. MDMA in der Gruppenpsychotherapie. Symposion "Uber den derzeitigen Stand der Forschung auf dem Gebiet der psychoaktiven Substanzen." Nov. 29 - Dec. 12, 1985, in Hirschhorn/Neckar, Germany.

Two independent reports of clinical utility are presented. Both investigators report MDMA use in group settings. The groups consisted mainly of psychosomatic patients involving problems such as allergies, eczema, sexual dysfunction, troublesome urination, cardiac irregularities, and cancer. There were some positive changes reported, and in some cases there were no improvements. No details are presented.

Wolfson, P.E. Meetings at the Edge with Adam: A Man for All Seasons.

J. Psychoactive Drugs 18 329-333 (1986).

An extensive discussion is presented listing the potential virtues and hazards of MDMA use in the psychotherapeutic setting. The roles of drugs currently used, and those of MDMA-like action that might some day be available, are reviewed. A case report of the use of MDMA in a family problem situation is presented in considerable detail.

(8) ANALYSIS

Andrey, R.E. and Moffat, A.C. Gas-Liquid Chromatographic Retention Indices of 1318 Substances of Toxicological Interest on SE-30 or OV-1 Stationary Phase. J. Chromatog. 220 195-252 (1981).

The GC charactoristics of many abuse drugs are presented in a review format. MDMA is included without experimental detail.

Bailey, K., By, A.W., Legault, D. and Verner, D. Identification of the N-Methylated Analogs of the Hallucinogenic Amphetamines and Some Isomers. J.A.O.A.C., 58 pp 62-69 (1975).

MDMA and four analogous methamphetamine derivatives (corresponding to 2-, 3-, and 4-methoxyamphetamine (MA) and 3-methoxy-4,5-methylenedioxyamphetamine (MMDA)) were synthesized and spectroscopically characterized. The synthesis was from the corresponding phenylacetone through the Leuckart reaction with N-methylformamide. The reported m.p. (of the hydrochloride salt) is 147-8. The U.V., NMR, IR and mass spectral data are presented. Rf values (six systems) and GC retention times (four systems) are also given.

Churchill, K.T. Identification of 3,4-Methylenedioxymethamphetamine. Microgram 18 (9) 123-132 (1985).

An analytical profile, through spectrographic tools such as UV, TLC, GC, NMR, MS, is presented for a sample seized in Georgia. Comparisons with MDA are presented.

Eichmeier, L.S. and Caplis, M.E. The Forensic Chemist; An "Analytic Detective", Anal. Chem. 47 pp 841A-844A (1975).

An analytical anecdote is presented showing the logical procedure used to distinguish MDMA from closely related drugs such as MDA in a seized sample. MDMA was acknowledged to be similar to MDA but, whereas MDA is a controlled substance, MDMA was not then federally controlled.

Gough, T.A. and Baker, P.B. Identification of Major Drugs of Abuse Using Chromatography. J. Chromatog. Sci. 20 289-329 (1982).

An extensive review of the analytical identification of many abuse drugs is abstracted. MDMA is mentioned as one of these. There is no new experimental information presented.

Gupta, R.C. and Lundberg, G.D. Application of Gas Chromatography to Street Drug Analysis. Clin. Tox. 11 437-442 (1977).

A gas chromatography screening procedure is described, in which the retention times of over 100 drugs are compared to methapyriline or codeine. MDMA is among them.

Hansson, R.C. Clandestine Laboratories. Production of MDMA 3,4-methylene
dioxymethamphetamine. Analog. 9 (November, 10 pages) (1987).

A compilation of forensic information pertaining to MDMA is presented, including spectra (UV, MS, IR), synthetic approaches, and observations from clandestine laboratory operations (seen in Australia).

Hearn, W.L., Hime, G. and Andollo, W. Recognizing Ecstasy: Adam and Eve, the MDA Derivatives - Analytical Profiles. Abstracts of the CAT/SOFT Meetings, Oct. 29 - Nov. 1, 1986, Reno/Lake Tahoe, Nevada.

A study is reported comparing MDA, MDMA and MDE in the EMIT immunoanalytical assay system that is designed for amphetamine. Even though they are all of decreased reactivity, there is cross-reactivity and they may be picked up as positives. Using the bottom limit cut-off of 300 nanograms/mL for amphetamine there would be a response from as little as 10-15 micrograms/mL of MDMA. This is a value that might be encountered in the early stages of MDMA use.

Holsten, D.W. and Schieser, D.W. Controls over the Manufacture of MDMA. J. Psychoactive Drugs. 18 371-2 (1986).

A strong argument is made for attending to the quality of manufacture, and the basic concepts of ethical principles in the exploring of drugs that have not been evaluated against the usual pharmaceutical standards. Government interference in such studies becomes neccessary, to safe-guard the public.

Newmeyer, J.A. Some Considerations on the Prevalence of MDMA Use. J. Psychoactive Drugs 18 361-362 (1986).

An epidemiology survey of MDMA use (as of 1986) from the usual information sources (Drug Abuse Warning Network, DAWN; the Community Epidemiology Work Group, CEWG; police department reports, medical examiner or coroner's office reports) gives little indications that there is a medical problem associated with its use. Epidemiologically, it can not be considered at the present time a problem. It may well be that the material currently enjoys controlled, careful use by a number of cognoscenti (as did LSD in the early 1960's) and perhaps in future years a larger number of less sophisticated individuals will be drawn into its usage, and will find ways to evince adverse reactions, police involvement, and other unpleasant consequences.

Noggle Jr., F.T., DeRuiter, J. and Long, M.J., Spectrophotometric and Liquid Chromatographic Identification of 3,4-Methylenedioxyphenylisopropylamine and its N-Methyl and N-Ethyl Homologs, J. Assoc. Off. Anal. Chem., 69 pp 681-686 (1986).

A synthesis of MDEA (the N-ethyl homolog of MDA) is reported, and the infra-red spectra of the free bases, the hydrochloride salts, and the phenylisothiocyanate adducts are recorded, as is the HPLC retention behavior for both the bases and these derivatives.

Noggle Jr., F.T., DeRuiter, J., McMillian, C.L. and Clark, C.R. Liquid Chromatographic Analysis of some N-Alkyl-3,4-Methylenedioxyamphet-amines. J. Liq. Chromatog. 10 2497-2504 (1987).

The HPLC separation characteristics of MDA, MDMA, MDE and MDDM (N,N-dimethyl-MDA) are reported on a reversed phase column.

O'Brian, B.A., Bonicamp, J.M. and Jones, D.W., Differentiation of Amphetamine and its Major Hallucinogen Derivatives using Thinlayer Chromatography, J. Anal. Tox. 6, pp 143-147 (1982).

Two thin-layer chromatographic systems, and several procedures for detection, are described for MDMA and 18 analogs. The retention times and the visualization color changes are compared and described. Detection limits in urine were determined from artificially spiked samples. The reference sample of MDMA was synthesized from MDA by methylation with methyl iodide, and separation from the co- generated dimethyl and trimethylammonium homologs by liquid- liquid extraction and preparative TLC.

Renfroe, C.L. MDMA on the Street: Analysis Anonymous. J. Psychoactive Drugs 18 363-369 (1986).

In the twelve years (up to 1983) that PharmChem conducted its Analysis Anonymous service, they evaluated over 20,000 samples of street drugs. MDMA and MDA had been classified together (some 610 examples) and of these 72 had been alleged to be MDMA. In the years 1984-1985, a cooperating reference laboratory (S.P., Miami, Florida) reported an additional 29 alleged MDMA samples.
Of these 101 samples, over half proved to be, indeed, MDMA, and half of the remaining contained MDMA. This is considered a remarkably high validity rate. The origins, descriptions, and costs are discussed.

Ruangyuttikarn, W. and Moody, D.E. Comparison of Three Commercial Amphet-amine Immunoassays for Detection of Methamphetamine, Methylenedioxy-amphetamine, Methylenedioxymethamphetmaine, and Methylenedioxyethyl-amphetamine. J. Anal. Toxicol. 12 229-233 (1988).

Three commercial immunoassays for the detection of amphetamine in urine (Abuscreen, a radioimmune assay, RIA; EMIT, a homogeneous enzyme immunoassay procedure; and TDx, a fluorescent polarization immunoassay, FPIA) have been assayed for their responses to methamphetamine, MDA, MDMA, and MDE. Some cross-reactivity to amphetamine is seen with all compounds, but the response is extremely variable depending upon the assay employed.

Ruybal, R. Microcrystalline Test for MDMA. Microgram 19 (6) 79- 80 (1986).

MDMA gives a sensitive microcrystalline test with gold chloride. The crystal form is similar to that of methamphetamine.

Sedgwick, B., Lo, P. and Yee, M. Screening and Confirmation of 3,4-Methylenedioxymethamphetamine (MDMA) in Urine: Evaluation of 1000 Specimens. Abstracts of the CAT/SOFT Meetings, Oct. 29 - Nov. 1, 1986, Reno/Lake Tahoe, Nevada.

A sequence of 1000 "at risk" samples were screened for the presence of methamphetamine (MA) and/or MDMA (not distinguishable in the initial analysis). Of 133 presumptive positive tests, none proved to be positive for MDMA.

Shaw, M.A. and Peel, H.W. Thin-layer Chromatography of 3,4- methylenedioxyamphetamine, 3,4-Methylenedioxymethamphetamine and other Phenethylamine Derivatives. J. Chromatog. 104 pp 201-204 (1975).

A broad study is presented on the TLC analyses of many phenethylamines. The compound specifically named in the title, 3,4-methylenedioxymethamphetamine (MDMA), was a misprint that was subsequently corrected to the intended compound, MMDA. MDMA was not a part of this study.

Yamauchi, T. The Analysis of Stimulant-analogue Compounds (3,4-Methylenedioxymethamphetamine Hydrochloride). Kagaku Keisatsu Kenkyusho Hokoku, Hokagaku Hen. 39 23 (1986).

People from abroad have provided samples of drugs that had been heretofore unidentified in Japan. An analytical profile of one such drug, MDMA, is provided employing most modern spectroscopic tools.

(9) REVIEWS AND COMMENTARIES

(and a sampling of the magazine, newspaper, and radio commentary that was part of the popular scene at the time of illegalization).

Abramson, D.M. Ecstasy: The New Drug Underground. New Age

October, 1985. pp 35-40.

This article addresses the questions that are raised by the conflict of governmental banning of drugs that are of potential value in psychotherapy, and the therapists' determination to continue exploring their use.

Adamson, S. "Through the Gateway of the Heart: Accounts of Experiences with MDMA and other Empathogenic Substances." Four Trees Publications, San Francisco. Foreword by R. Metzner. 1985.

This book is a collection of some fifty personal accounts, largely involving MDMA. Some are from the notes of therapists, involving clinical usage, and others are personal accounts from self-exploration.

Adler, J., Getting High on 'Ecstasy', Newsweek, April 15, 1985, p. 96.

This is a short, apparently factual, overview of both the chemical and the "street" use of MDMA. It is generally sympathetic to its medical potential.

Anon: Several reports from the Brain/Mind Bulletin:

(1) MDMA: Compound raises medical and legal issues. Brain/Mind Bulletin, Vol. 10, #8, April 15, 1985.
The title article is presented, and nearly the entire issue is given over to a thorough coverage of the medical and scientific aspects of MDMA.

(2) Psychiatrists, drug-abuse specialists testify in L.A. at first MDMA hearing. Brain/Mind Bulletin, Vol. 10, #12 July 8, 1985.
A news report on the first round of hearings in Los Angeles, concerning the scheduling of MDMA. An overview of the testimony is presented.

(3) Judge proposes more lenient schedule for MDMA. Brain/Mind Bulletin, Vol. 11, #11 June 16, 1986.
Adminstrative Law Judge Francis Young recommended, at the conclusions of the MDMA hearings, that the DEA put the drug into Schedule III, partly to ease research with the compound, and partly due to the absence of demonstrated abuse of the drug.

(4) MDMA: Federal court decides that DEA used improper criteria. Brain/Mind Bulletin, Vol. 13, #2 November, 1987.
A report is given as to the First Court of Appeals in Boston, ruling that the DEA had not sufficiently considered the arguments concerning the current medical use of MDMA.

Anon: DEA Proposal to Ban New Psychedelic Protested. Substance Abuse Report, December, 1984. pp 4-5.

The several letters that were addressed to the DEA in response to its announcement in the Federal Register to consider the scheduling of MDMA are here abstracted and commented upon.

Anon: Ecstasy: 21st Century Entheogen. Private Tract, 28 pages.

This is an elaborate thesis that is directed totally to the promotion of the use of MDMA. There is a presumed question and answer section, that is designed for the cautiously curious.

Anon: MDMA. NIDA Capsules. Issued by the Press Office of the National Institute on Drug Abuse, Rockville, Maryland. July 1985.

A two-page precis describing the health problems encountered with MDMA use, its relationship to the neurotransmitters, and the moves being made at the Justice Department to combat "designer drugs" such as MDMA in the future.

Anon: Designer Drugs: A New Concern for the Drug Abuse Community. NIDA Notes, December, 1985, pp. 2-3.

A discussion of "designer drugs" is arranged in four groups: variations on fentanyl, on meperidine, on PCP, and on amphetamione and methamphetamine. MDMA fits this last group. The research directions of NIDA are discussed.

Barbour, J. Cracking Down: What You Must Know About Dangerous Drugs. The Associated Press. 1986.

This is a 63 page illustrated essay, aimed at stopping drug use and abuse by scaring the reader. Unfortunately, the information is not completely accurate. MDMA is spun together with other designer drugs as things that destroy the brain.

Barnes, D.M. New Data Intensifies the Agony over Ecstasy. Science 239 864-866 (1988).

A review and commentary is presented of the Winter Conference on Brain Research, 23-30 January, 1988, in which there was a section on MDMA. A distillation of the comments made, with the feeling that more clinical work is needed to define the value of MDMA, and that there would not likely be any further clinical work done. There are extensive quotations from some of the authors of recent animal studies on serotonin toxicity.

Barnett, R. DEA: RSVP re MDMA. Editorial from KCBS, July 29, 1985.

With the possibilty of therapeutic value seen in some psychiatric cases, KCBS felt that the action of the DEA (making MDMA illegal) short-circuited the hearings process, and was premature. A request is made to allow research on the effects and potentials of this drug to continue.

Baum, R.M. New Variety of Street Drugs Poses Growing Problem.

Chemical and Engineering News, September 9, 1985. pp. 7-16.

A completely professional article discussing the challenges presented to law enforcement officials, legislators and scientists, by the invention of analogues of illegal drugs by underground chemists. MDMA is held out as being quite apart from the fentanyl and meperidine examples, and is analysed at some length.

Beck, J. MDMA: The Popularization and Resulting Implications of a Recently Controlled Psychoactive Substance. Contemporary Drug Problems Spring, 1986. pp 23-63.

A historical analysis is made of the relationship between drug illegaliza-tion and social issues. MDMA is used as a specific example, and a considerable body of first-hand observations of its use is also presented.

Beck, J. and Morgan, P.A. Designer Drug Confusion: A Focus on MDMA. J. Drug Education 16 267-282 (1986).

This article discusses the competing definitions and issues surrounding the various designer drugs, but is primarily devoted to an examination of MDMA. A rationale is offered as to why interest in MDMA will continue to grow.

Bost, R.O., 3,4-Methylenedioxymethamphetamine (MDMA) and Other Amphet-amine Derivatives. J. Forensic Sci. 33 576-587 (1988).

A series of amphetamine derivaties are discussed as "Designer Drugs" with structures slightly modified from explicitly named illegal drugs. A number of emergency cases are presented, which are documented with MDA, MDMA and MDE involvement. A number of analytical procedures are demonstrated.

Buchanan, J. Ecstasy in the Emergency Department. Clinical Toxicology Update, 7 (#4, July-August) p 1-4 (1985).

A review of the history and the pharmacology of the psychoactive amphetamines is given. The overall recommendation for the emergency room is to expect an overdosed patient to present with signs similar to those with an amphetamine overdose, and to expect to treat primarily signs of anxiety and hypertension. The attending physician can expect the patient to be unaware of the actual toxin he has taken, and careful laboratory work will be needed to identify the chemical in body fluids and drug samples.

Callaway, E. The Biology of Information Processing. J. Psychoactive Drugs 18 315-318 (1986).

A review is presented of the difficulties that are classically part of the communication of information, and the roles of the many psychologists and physicians who have addressed the problem. The study of neuro-transmitters, and thus drugs that involve these brain chemicals, is part of the eventual understanding. The role of non-classic "unsleepy drugs" (stimulants) such as MDMA are speculated upon as potential tools in this study.

Climko, R.P., Roehrich, H., Sweeney, D.R. and Al-Razi, J. Ecstasy: A Review of MDMA and MDA. Int'l Journal of Psychiatry in Medicine. 16 359-372 (1986-87).

A review of the pharmacology and toxicity of MDA is presented, with some additional data for MDMA. A balanced presentation with 75 references.

Cohen, S. They Call It Ecstasy. Drug Abuse & Alcoholism Newsletter, Vista Hill Foundation. 14 # 6. September, 1985.

A basically negative overview of the prospects of MDMA in therapy. There is wistful note with the "we've been through all this before" feeling. LSD had hope, LSD failed, and this too shall fail.

Deluca, N. Closed Doors/Closed Minds. KCBS Editorial. July 10, 1986.

An opinion is expressed, that the easy answer to MDMA given by the federal government, illigalization by placement into Schedule I, was the wrong answer. It appears that MDMA warrants a closer look by thera-pists, and the DEA should not simply lock the drug away where it cannot be investigated.

Doblin, R. Murmurs in the Heart of the Beast: MDMA and the DEA, HHS, NIDA, NIMH, ADAMHA, FBI and the WHO. Privately printed. August 8, 1984.

This is a collection of many of the letters exchanged between between the DEA and the FDA, that led to the decision to place MDMA in the listings of scheduled drugs. Also included are the DAWN (medical emergency) reports, and letters written in response to the proposed scheduling.

Doblin, R. The Media Does MDMA. Privately printed, August 5, 1985 - July 2, 1987.

This is a collection of articles, newspaper accounts, writings from many sources, that touch upon MDMA. It is arranged in a collage.

Doblin, R., A Proposal for Orphan Pharmaceuticals, Inc. A Division of Neurobiological Technologies, Inc. August 4, 1987.

A review of the history of MDMA and the arguments for its legitimate commercial consideration are presented. The NTI Board of Directors did not accept this proposal.

Dowling, C.G. The Trouble with Ecstasy. Life Magazine, August, 1985. pp. 88-94.

A pictorial article timed to coincide with the first of the hearings concerning the eventual fate of MDMA, and with the effective placement of it under emergency legal control.

Ehrlich, B. Understanding Ecstasy: The MDM Story. Privately Printed Book Manuscript. About 70 pages. 1986.

This is a partial draft of a book, privately printed and circulated, covering the history and para-medical use of MDMA.

Ehrnstein, L.B., Reflections on Drug Enforcement and Drug Use. Psychedelic Monographs and Essays, 2 17-24 (1987).

This is an instructive and favorable review of the history and the possible usefulness of MDMA. There are suggestions offered as to how the inexperienced subject might approach MDMA for personal development.

Gallagher, W. The Looming Menace of Designer Drugs. Discover 7 #8 (August, 1986). p. 24.

A long and gloomy article on the growing problems of uncontrolled analogues of heroin. There is a heavy emphasis on the medical professional's use and involvement in drug abuse. A one page side-box gives a view of MDMA, with balance between therapeutic potential and the risks of using unevaluated and unapproved new drugs.

Gertz, K.R. "HugDrug" Alert: The Agony of Ecstasy. Harper's Bazaar, November 1985. p. 48.

A popular article is offered, with a balanced discussion of the case for, and the case against, the use of MDMA.

Glennon, R. A. Discriminative Stimulus Properties of Phenylisopropylamine Derivatives. Drug and Alcohol Dependence 17 119- 134 (1986).

A broad review of many substituted phenylisopropyl- amines and their responses in discriminative studies in animals trained to discriminate amphetamine (or, separately, DOM) from saline. MDMA produced no DOM-appropriate response (DOM is an hallucinogen) but did cross react with amphetamine (a stimulant).

Gold, M.S. Ecstasy, Etc. Alcoholism and Addiction Sept-Oct. 1985. p. 11.

Criticism of the popular use of untested drugs such as MDMA is presented. It is argued that all new "wonder euphorogenics" should be considered extremely dangerous until proven safe and effective for a specific condition by the FDA and the medical research community.

Grinspoon, L. and Bakalar, J.B. What is MDMA? Harvard Medical School
Mental Health Letter 2 #2 (August, 1985). p. 8.

A quite brief presentation of the cogent facts that define MDMA.

Grinspoon, L. and Bakalar, J.B. A Potential Psychotherapeutic Drug? The
Psychiatric Times, January, 1986. pp 4-5, 18.

A review of the development of the use of drugs in psychotherapy, and a
discussion of the role that a drug like MDMA might play in this medical
area.

Grinspoon, L. and Bakalar, J.B. Can Drugs be Used to Enhance the
Psychotherapeutic Process? Amer. J. Psychotherap. 40 393-404 (1986).

There is evidence that the psychotherapeutic process can be enhanced by
the use of drugs that invite self- disclosure and self-exploration. Such
drugs might help to fortify the therapeutic alliance and in other ways.
One drug that may prove promising for this purpose is the psychedelic
amphetamine MDMA.

Hagerty, C. "Designer Drug" Enforcement Act Seeks to Attack Problem at
Source. American Pharmacy NS25 #10 October, 1985 PP. 10-11.

An extensive argument is presented for the passage of the "Designer
Drug" Enforcement Act, to effectively attack the sources of new drugs.

Harris, L. S. The Stimulants and Hallucinogens under Consideration: A
Brief Overview of their Chemistry and Pharmacology. Drug and Alcohol
Dependence, 17 107-118 1986.

A literature review is made of a number of drugs that are under consideration for international control. MDMA is briefly mentioned, and
described as being in man more of a stimulant than a hallucinogen.

Hershkovits, D. Esctasy: The Truth About MDMA. High Times November, 1985. p. 33.

An interview was held with Richard Seymour, author of the book MDMA.
Many good and reasonable questions, directly and accurately answered.

Hollister, L.E. Clinical Aspects of Use of Phenylalkylamine and Indoleal-
kyl-amine Hallucinogens. Psychopharmacology Bulletin 22 977-979
(1986).

A generally negative evaluation of the use of hallucinogens (such as
MDA, MDMA, LSD) based largely on the potential of neurotoxicity and
the absence of clinical verification of value. Most of the value must be
gleaned from studies of twenty years ago, and the absence of recent
research is ascribed to unusually high toxicity or to the lack of interest.
The legal difficulties are not addressed.

Jones, R. Why the Thought Police Banned Ecstasy. Simply Living, 2 #10. p. 91-95.

A review of the United States controversy concerning MDMA as seen through Australian eyes. Implications of considerable use there in Australia.

Kirsch, M.M. "Designer Drugs" CompCare Publications, Minneapolis. 1986.

This book is organized into chapters that treat each of some half-dozen drugs that have been created or modified so as to circumvent explicit legal restrictions, or have recently emerged into popularity. One chapter, entitled "Ecstasy", spins together the popular lore concerning MDMA with quotations from various writers and lecturers and several anonymous users.

Klein, J., The New Drug They Call 'Ecstasy', New York (magazine), May 20, 1985, pp 38-43.

This is a popular article that brings together quotations that express the broad range of attitudes held by both the proponents and the opponents of the current clinical employment of MDMA. Some historical background is presented, as well as an articulate description of the effect the drug produces.

Leavy, J. Ecstasy: The Lure and the Peril. The Washington Post June 1, 1985. Zagoria, S. More "Peril" than "Lure." ibid. July 3, 1985,

A well researched and careful article reviewing all aspects of the MDMA palavar. The reply by Mr. Zagoria expressed the thought that Ms. Leavy's presentation was too enticing, with lure outweighing peril.

Leverant, R. MDMA Reconsidered. J. Psychoactive Drugs 18 373- 379 (1986).

A summations of thoughts and impressions gathered at the Oakland, California Conference on MDMA (May, 1986). The theme presented is the need of open-mindedness in the area of personal as well as clinical freedom of research, and MDMA was used as a focal point.

McConnell, H. MDMA. The Journal, The Addiction Research Foundation, Toronto. July 1, 1986 pp. 11-12.

A thorough review of the Oakland, California MDMA conference is presented, in considerable detail and with excellent balance.

Nasmyth, P. The Agony and the Ecstasy. The Face, October, 1986 p. 52.

A popularized article from England on the properties and the uses of
MDMA. It strongly suggests that the drug is already deeply instilled in
British culture.

Nichols, D.E., MDMA Represents a New Type of Pharmacologic Agent
and Cannot be Considered to be either a Hallucinogenic Agent or an
Amphetamine-type Stimulant.

This is an unpublished essay submitted both to the DEA and to the WHO
group, through the offices of Richard Cotton. It presents a point by point
analysis from both in vitro and in vivo studies of the pharmacological
properties of MDMA and its isomers, with MDA (a structurally related
hallucinogenic compound) and other amphetamines. He concludes that
its actions represent a new classification of pharmacology, and clinical
research with it in psychotherapy would argue against placing it in
Schedule I.

Nichols, D.E. Differences Between the Mechanism of Action of MDMA,
MBDB, and the Classic Hallucinogens. Identification of a New Therapeutic Class: Entactogens. J. Psychoactive Drugs 18 305-313 (1986).

This article presents a review of the extensive neurological and pharmacological evidence that supports the stand that MDMA and MBDB should
be classified neither as hallucinogens (psychedelic drugs) nor as simple
stimulants. An argument is made for a novel classification, entactogens.

O'Rourke, P.J. Tune In. Turn On. Go To The Office Late on Monday.
Rolling Stone, December 19, 1985 p. 109.

The MDMA popularity craze is presented in a humorous retrospective of
the drug attitudes of the 1960's.

Peroutka, S.J. Incidence of Recreational Use of 3,4-Methylenedioxymeth-
amphetamine (MDMA, "Ecstasy") on an Undergraduate Campus. New
England J. Med. 3171542-1543 (1987).

A random, and anonymous, poll of undergraduates at Stanford University
(California) showed that some 39% of all students were experienced with
MDMA (mean number of uses was 5.4, and dosage range was 60-250 mg).
To date, he finds no evidence to suggest that MDMA is neurotoxic in
humans.

Riedlinger, J.E. The Scheduling of MDMA: A Pharmacist's Perspective. J.
Psychoactive Drugs 17 167-171 (1985).

A critical viewpoint of the scheduling procedures employed with MDMA.
This paper is adapted from the original letter of protest sent to the DEA,
and from the written testimony presented at the hearings.

Rippchen, R. MDMA Die Neue Sympathiedroge. Der Gru"ne Zweig 103 Medieneexperimente D-6941 Lo"hrbach, West Germany 1986.

A book of some 47 pages, giving an immense body of information on MDMA (in German) including translations of articles by Greer. Also included is information on other drugs such as MDE and 2C-B.

Roberts, M. Drug Abuse. MDMA: "Madness, not Ecstasy" Crosstalk section, Psychology Today. June, 1986.

An update of an earlier article (Psychology Today, May, 1985) which emphasizes the neurological findings, and the concept of unregulated drug synthesis. Congressional action prohibiting the manufacture and distribution of similar drugs is urged.

Roberts, T.B., The MDMA Question. Section on Social Concerns. AHP Perspective. May, 1986. p. 12.

This is a soul-searching review asking the questions as to where we must acknowledge the line between the need of drug use in therapy, and the need of drug use in society. Provisions must be made, of course, for both.

Schulman, R. The Losing War Against "Designer Drugs." Business Week, June 24, 1985 pp. 101-104.

An overview of the MDMA controversy. A preview is presented of the pharmaceutical industry's response (OK to ban it, but not with the haste that might have a chilling effect on the development of new pharmaceuticals) and local law enforcement enthusiasm (Florida has granted the State Attorney General the power to place a drug on the Controlled Drug List in as little as 24 hours).

Seymour, R.B. "MDMA" Haight-Ashbury Publications, San Francisco. 1986

This is a volume devoted entirely to the single drug MDMA. Nine chapters discuss its origins, facts that apply to it, its bright side and dark side, in a carefully balanced presentation. It was made available for the Oakland, California symposium, MDMA: A Multidisciplinary Conference, May 17-18, 1986.

Seymour, R.B. Ecstasy on Trial. High Times, November, 1986. p. 33.

A retrospective review article of the controversies stirred up by the publicity that followed the government hearings and the illegalization of MDMA.

Seymour, R.B., Wesson, D.R. and Smith, D.E. Editor's Introduction. J.

Psychoactive Drugs. 18 287 (1986).

An introduction is made to an entire issue of the Journal, dedicated to the several papers presented at a two- day conference on the topic of MDMA. This was held May 17- 18, 1986, at the Health Education Center of the Merritt Peralta Medical Center, in Oakland California.

Shafer, J., MDMA: Psychedelic Drug Faces Regulation. Psychology Today, May, 1985. pp. 68-69.

This is a short overview presenting the clinical and legal views of a number of psychiatrists, administrators and researchers.

Shulgin, A.T. Twenty Years on an Ever-changing Quest, Psychedelic Reflections, Eds. L. Grinspoon and J.B. Bakalar, Human Science Press, New York (1983). pp. 205-212.

This is an essay on the philosophy of research associated with psychedelic drugs. MDMA is described briefly, with some of its history, pharmacology, and therapeutic potential.

Shulgin, A.T. What is MDMA? PharmChem Newsletter 14 #3 3-11 (1985).

A hypothetical interview is presented, distilling the questions fielded from many reporters, and the substance of the answers given to these questions.

Shulgin, A.T. The Background and Chemistry of MDMA. J. Psychoactive Drugs 18 291-304 (1986).

This review gathers together the physical properties of MDMA, and the published information as to toxicity and pharmacology, as of the date of the Oakland, CA conference (May, 1986).

Siegel, R.K. Chemical Ecstasies. Omni, August 1985. p. 29.

This short essay advises caution in the immediate acceptance of drugs that are enthusiastically promoted but which have not been thoroughly researched.

Smith, D.E. and Seymour, R.B. Abuse Folio: MDMA. High Times, May, 1986. p. 30.

This is one of a continuing series of drug information sheets, one being published in each issue of High Times. There is a neutral, factual presentation of the nature and use, and of the hazards and liabilities associated with the drug MDMA.

Smith, D.E., Wesson, D.R. and Buffum, J. MDMA: "Ecstasy" as an Adjunct to Psychotherapy and a Street Drug of Abuse. California Society for the Treatment of Alcoholism and Other Drug Dependencies News 12 (September) 1985 pp 1-3. A letter to the Editors in response: Holsten, D.W. and Schieser, D.W. Controls over the Manufacture of MDMA. The original authors' reply: ibid. 12 (December) 1985 pp 14-15.

A brief review of the therapeutic virtues and abuse risks that are associated with MDMA, and the chilling effect that illegalization of drugs has on medical resarch. They were reminded in rebuttal (Holsten and Schieser) that the exploratory use of new drugs outside of the controls that apply to the pharmaceutical industry carry real risks as to safety and quality of product.

Straus, H. From Crack to Ecstasy; Basement Chemists can Duplicate almost any Over-the-border Drug. American Health, June, 1987 pp. 50-54.

A brief review of the concept of special formulations or syntheses of drugs for the extra-medical market. MDMA is brought in as a minor example.

Toufexis, A. A Crackdown on Ecstasy. Time Magazine. June 10, 1985. P. 64.

A news report on the placing of MDMA into emergency Schedule I status. The complement to Newsweek's positive article.

Turkington, C. Brain Damage Found with Designer Drugs. Amer. Psychological Assn. Monitor March, 1986.

A negative review of the neurotransmitter research. This is probably the source of the oft-quoted "fact" that these drugs are the first demonstration of a neurotransmitter being modified to a neurotoxin.

Wolfson, P.E., Letter to Richard Cotton, Dewey, Ballantine, Bushby, Palmer & Wood, Washington, D.C.

A report is made of the effective use of MDMA in conjunction with psychotherapy, in the treatment of both depressed and schizophrenic patients. The apparent anti- manic and anti-paranoia action of MDMA allowed the opening of discourse and allowed intervention with more conventional therapy. It is suggested that there is a promising potential for its use in certain psychotic situations, and a telling argument is made against its legal classification in Schedules I or II.

Woolverton, W.L., A Review of the Effects of Repeated Administration of Selected Phenethylamines. Drug and Alcohol Dependence17 143-150 (1986)

A review from the literature of the chronic toxicological findings regarding a number of compounds that are being proposed for international control. One reference to MDMA is cited, the Fed. Proc. note (Virus, et al. 45 1066 (1986)) which has been published (see Commins, et al., 1987, section 6 above).

QUOTATIONS FROM REVIEWS IN WHICH MDMA HAS BEEN NOTED:

Burger, A. "Drugs and People" University Press of Virginia, Charlottesville, 1986. p. 65. This quotation, from the chapter on neurohormones, will be the sole example given of the irresponsible misinformation that can be published by experts in the field.

[in reference to designer drugs] "Others are synthetic compounds tried out by addicts in the hope that they might give them a new mental high. The most dangerous of these materials are 3-methylfentanyl and MDMA, a relative of methamphetamine. Both produce dangerous damage to the general health of the users and cause heroin-like addiction at unbelievably low doses."

Glennon, R.A., Rosecrans, J.A. and Young, R., Drug-induced Discrimination: A Description of the Paradigm and a Review of its Specific Application to the Study of Hallucinogenic Agents. Medical Research Reviews 3 289-340 (1983).

"Racemic - MDA produces (conditioned response) effects similar to those of DOM, however, administration of its N- methyl derivative, racemic MDMA, to the DOM-trained animals, resulted in disruption of behavior."

Nichols, D.E. and Glennon, R.A., Medicinal Chemistry and Structure-Activity Relationships of Hallucinogens, in Hallucinogens: Neurochemical, Behavioral, and Clinical Perspectives Ed. B.L. Jacobs, Raven Press, New York. (1984)

"N-Alkylation of the phenethylamines abolishes or greatly attenuates biological activity. Two noteworthy exceptions are the (N-methyl and N-ethyl) 3,4-methylenedioxy substituted compounds. These retain potency nearly comparable to the parent MDA, but present a different qualitative picture. Their duration of action is reduced to about 1-1/2 to 2 hours and they produce only minor disruption of normal sensory processing. They apparently amplify empathy and would seem to be ideal candidates as adjuncts to psychotherapy."

Shulgin, A.T., Psychotomimetic Drugs: Structure-Activity Relationships. Handbook of Psychopharmacology Volume 11; Stimulants, Eds. L.L.Iversen, S.D. Iversen and S.H. Snyder, Plenum Press, New York. p. 292. (1978)

"MDMA has a higher threshold level than does MDA but otherwise it is very similar in potency. Within the effective dose range (100-150 mg orally) the effects are first noted very quickly, usually within one-half hour following administration. With most subjects the plateau of effects is reported to occur within another one-half hour to one hour. The intoxication symptoms are largely dissipated in an additional two hours, except for a mild residual sympathomimetic stimulation, which can persist for several additional hours. There are few physical indicators of intoxication, and psychological sequelae are virtually nonexistent. Qualitatively, the drug appears to evoke an easily controlled altered state of consciousness with emotional and sensual overtones very reminiscent of low levels of MDA."

Shulgin, A.T., Hallucinogens. Burger's Medicinal Chemistry, 4th Edition, Part III, Ed. M.E. Wolff, Wiley and Son, New York. p 1120. (1981)

"This affective interaction (a state of sensory amplification and enhancement without appreciable sympathomimetic stimulation, an easy communication between subject and observer) is even more clearly evident in the N- methyl homolog of MDA (i.e., MDMA) which is substantially free of perceptual distortion at effective dosages (75-150 mg)."

Shulgin, A.T., Chemistry of Psychotomimetics, Psychotropic Agents Part III, Alcohol and Psychotomimetics; Psychotropic Effects of Central Acting Drugs, Eds. F. Hoffmeister and G. Stille, Springer-Verlag, Berlin. p 14. (1982)

"Several of these substituted amphetamine analogs have been studied as their N-methyl homologues (in analogy with the relationship between amphetamine and methamphetamine). Although most show a striking drop in potency, MDMA (the N- methyl homologue of MDA) retains full activity."

Stafford, P., Psychedelics Encyclopedia, Revised Edition, J.P. Tarcher, Inc., Los Angeles, CA p 289. (1983)

"Synthesis of MDMA, active in the doses of the 75-100 mg range and shorter and milder in its effects than MDA, was not reported in the scientific literature until 1960. It has since been established that MDMA was one of the "Experimental Agents" tested at Edgewood Chemical Warfare Service, where it was labeled EA-1475. (MDA was labeled EA-1299)."

Weil, A. and Rosen, W., Chocolate to Morphine; Understanding Mind-active Drugs, Houghton Mifflin Company, Boston, 1983. p 108

"A newer drug, MDM (methylenedioxymethylamphetamine, also known as MDMA, Adam, and "XTC"), gives the same general effect (as MDA) but lasts four to six hours instead of ten to twelve. Because of the shorter duration of action, it seems gentler on the body with less day-after fatigue."

(10) LEGAL HISTORY

(This section is organized chronologically)

1970

Sreenivasan, V.R. Problems in Identification of Methylenedioxy and
Methoxy Amphetamines. J. Crim. Law 63 304-312 (1972).

In a study of the spectral properties of several substituted amphetamine
analogs, the properties of an unknown sample seized from an apparent
drug abuser were recorded. The evidence indicated that this material was
MDMA. As this report was initially presented to a group of crime
laboratory chemists in August, 1970, this is probably the earliest documen-
tation of illicit usage of MDMA.

1972

Gaston, T.R. and Rasmussen, G.T. Identification of 3,4- Methylenedioxymethamphetamine. Microgram 5 pp. 60-63 (1972).

Several exhibits were encountered in the Chicago area, which were
identified as MDMA as the hydrochloride salt. Chromatographic and
spectrographic properties are presented.

1982

Anonymous. Request for Information, Microgram 15, p 126 (1982).

The Drug Control Section of the DEA (Drug Enforcement Administration)
has solicited information concerning the abuse potential of both MDMA
and MDE. The request covered the abuse potential, the illicit trafficking
and the clandestine syntheses, since 1977.

1984

Randolph, W.F., International Drug Scheduling; Convention on Psychotropic Substances; Stimulant and/or Hallucinogenic Drugs. Federal
Register 49 #140 July 19, 1984. Pp 29273-29274.
A request has been made from the Food and Drug Administration for
information and comments concerning the abuse potential, actual abuse,
medical usefulness and trafficking of 28 stimulants and/or hallucinogenic
drugs, including MDMA. International restrictions are being considered
by World Health Organization.

Mullen, F.M., Schedules of Controlled Substances Proposed Placement of
3,4-Methylenedioxymethamphetamine into Schedule I. Federal Register
49 #146 July 27, 1984. pp 30210-30211.

A request has been made for comments, objections, or requests for hearings concerning the proposal by the Drug Enforcement Administration (DEA) for the placement of MDMA into Schedule I of the Controlled Substances Act.

Cotton, R. Letter from Dewey, Ballantine, Bushby, Palmer & Wood, 1775 Pennsylvania Avenue, N.W., Washington, D.C. 20006 to F. M. Mullen, Jr., DEA. September 12, 1984.

This is a formal request for a hearing concerning the listing of MDMA as a Schedule I drug. The retaining parties are Professor Thomas B. Roberts, Ph.D., George Greer, M.D., Professor Lester Grinspoon, M.D. and Professor James Bakalar.

Mullen, F.M., Schedules of Controlled Substances. Proposed Placement of 3,4-Methylenedioxymethamphetamine into Schedule I. Hearing. Federal Register 49 #252 December 31, 1984. pp. 50732-50733.

This is notice of an initial hearing in the matter of the placement of MDMA into Schedule I of the Controlled Substances Act. This is to be held on February 1, 1985 and is intended to identify parties, issues and positions, and to determine procedures and set dates and locations for further proceedings.

1985

Young, F.L. Memorandum and Order. Docket No. 84-48. February 8, 1985.

A formal Memorandum and Order is addressed to the Drug Enforcement Administration, laying out the ground rules for the hearings to be held in the matter of the scheduling of MDMA.

Anon : Request for Information, Microgram, 18 25 (1985).

A brief review is presented of the requests for hearings regarding the scheduling of MDMA. A request is made for any information that might be found concerning illicit trafficking, clandestine synthesis, and medical emergencies or deaths associated with the use of MDMA. All such information is to be sent to the Drug Control Section of the DEA.

Young, F.L. Opinion and Recommended Decision on Preliminary Issue. Docket No. 84-48. June 1, 1985

The question of where to schedule a drug such as MDMA is considered. The Schedules have only one place for drugs without currently accepted medical use, Schedule I. But a second requirement that must be met is that the drug have a high abuse potential. There is no place for a drug without currently accepted medical use and less-than-high abuse potential.

The first opinion is that such a drug cannot be placed in any schedule. And if the administration does not accept that recommended decision, then placement should be into Schedule III, IV or V, depending upon the magnitude of the less-than-high abuse potential.

Lawn, J.C. Schedules of Controlled Sunstances; Temporary Placement of 3,4-Methylenedioxymethamphetamine (MDMA) into Schedule I. Federal Register 50 # 105, Friday, May 31, 1985. pp. 23118-23120.

The DEA invoked the Emergency Scheduling Act powers, to place MDMA into Schedule I on a temporary basis, effective July 1, 1985. This move is valid for a year, and can be extended for six months. This occurred just before the first hearing was to take place, to determine the appropriate schedule for MDMA.

[The chronology of the hearings was as follows:]

June 10, 1985   Los Angeles, California

July 10,11, 1985   Kansas City, Missouri

October 8,9,10,11, Nov. 1, 1985   Washington, D.C.

February 14, 1986 (submitting briefs, findings, conclusions, and oral arguments)   Washington, D.C.

1986

Anon: Verordnung des BAG u"ber die Beta"ubungsmittel und andere Stoffe und Pra"parate. March 17, 1986.

Effective April 22, 1986, MDMA has been entered into the Controlled Law structure of the Narcotics Laws of Switzerland.

Young, F.L. Opinion and Recommended Ruling, Findings of Fact, Conclusions of Law and Decision of Administrative Law Judge. Docket 84-48. May 22, 1986.

This 70 page decision was handed down as a product of the three hearings held as outlined above. A careful analysis is given of the phrase "currently accepted medical use" and of the phrase "accepted safety for use." The final recommendation was that MDMA be placed in Schedule III.

Stone, S.E. and Johnson, C.A. Government's Exceptions to the Opinion and Recommended Ruling, Findings of Fact, Conclusions of Law and Decision of the Administrative Law Judge. Docket No. 84- 48. June 13, 1986.

The attorneys for the DEA reply to the decision of Judge Young with a 37 page document, including statements that he had given little if any weight to the testimony and documents proferred by the DEA, and had systematically disregarded the evidence and arguments presented by the government. Their statement was a rejection of the suggestion of the Administrative Law judge, in that they maintained that MDMA is properly placed in Schedule I of the SCA because it has no currently accepted medical use, it lacks accepted safety for use under medical supervision, and it has a high potential for abuse.

Lawn, J.C. Schedules of Controlled Substances; Extension of Temporary Control of 3,4-Methylenedioxymethamphetamine (MDMA) in Schedule I. Federal Register 51 # 116 June 17, 1986. pp. 21911- 21912.

The provision that allows MDMA to be placed in Schedule I on an emergency basis (due to expire on July 1, 1986) has been extended for a period of 6 months or until some final action is taken, whichever comes first. The effective date is July 1, 1986.

Anon: Zweite Verordnung zur A"nderung beta"ubungsmittelrechticher Vor-schriften. July 23, 1986.

Effective July 28, 1986, MDMA was added to the equivalent of Schedule I status, in the German Drug Law. This was in the same act that added cathenone, DMA, and DOET.

Lawn, J.C. Order. Docket 84-48 August 11, 1986.

In reply to a motion by the respondents (Grinspoon, Greer et al.) to strike portions of the DEA exceptions that might allege bias on the part of the Administrative Law Judge, and to request an opportunity for oral presentation to the Administrator. The bias was apologized for, and struck. The opportunity for oral presentation was not allowed.

Kane, J. Memorandum and Opinion. Case No. 86-CR-153. In the United States District Court for the District of Colorado. Pees and McNeill, Defendants. October 1, 1986.

This is an early decision dismissing a prosecution charge for unlawful acts involving MDMA, on the basis that MDMA had been placed into Schedule I using the Emergency Scheduling Act, and the authority to invoke this Act was invested in the Attorney General, and the Attorney General had never subdelegated that authority to the DEA. This transfer had not occurred at the time of the charges being brought against the defendants, and the charges were dismissed.

Lawn, J.C. Schedules of Controlled Substances; Scheduling of 3,4-Methylenedioxymethamphetamine (MDMA) into Schedule I of the Controlled Substances Act. Federal Register 51 # 198. October 14, 1986. pp. 36552-36560.

This is a final placement of MDMA into Schedule I (except that subsequent litigation superceded this placement and resulted in a later final placement of MDMA into Schedule I). This begins with a complete review of the MDMA proceedings, including Administrative Law Judge Young's recommendation to place MDMA into Schedule III and a 92 point rebuttal of that recommendation. The main findings are that there is no currently accepted medical use for MDMA, that there is a high potential for abuse of MDMA, and that Congress has balanced the desirability of drug research against drug risks when it had written the CSA Schedules without mentioning facilitating research as a standard, and that therefore facilitation of drug research is not a valid ground for less restrictive classification of a drug. MDMA is placed in Schedule I effective November 13, 1986.

1987

Coffin, Torruella, and Pettin. United States Court of Appeals for the First Circuit. Lester Grinspoon, Petitioner, v. Drug Enforcement Administration, Respondent. September 18, 1987.

This is the opinion handed down in answer to the appeal made by Grinspoon (Petitioner) to the action of the DEA (Respondent) in placing MDMA in a permanent classification of a Schedule I drug. Most points were found for the DEA, but one specific claim of the petitioner, that MDMA has a currently accepted use in the United States, was accepted. The finding of the court was that the FDA approval was not the sole criterion for determining the acceptability of a drug for medical use. An order was issued to vacate MDMA from Schedule I.

1988

Lawn, J.C. Schedules of Controlled Substances; Deletion of 3,4- Methylenedioxymethamphetamine (MDMA) From Schedule I of the Controlled Substamces Act. Federal Register 53 2225 (1988) January 27, 1988.

Notice is posted in the Federal Register that MDMA has been vacated from Schedule One of the Controlled Substances Act and now falls under the purview of the Analogue Drug Act. This ruling was effective December 22, 1987, and will be effective until such time as the Administrator reconsidered the record in the scheduling procedures, and issues another final ruling.

Lawn, J.C. Schedules of Controlled Substances; Scheduling of 3,4-Methylenedioxymethamphetamine (MDMA) into Schedule I of the Controlled Substances Act; Remand. Federal Register 53 5156 (1988) February 22, 1988.

Notice is posted in the Federal Register that MDMA has been placed again into Schedule I. The DEA has accepted the Appellate Court's instruction to develop a standard for the term "accepted medical use," and they have done so. The conclusion is that MDMA is properly assigned to Schedule I, and ,as there have already been hearings, there is no need for any further delay. Effective date, March 23, 1988.

Meyers, M.A. In the United States District Court for the Southern District of Texas, Houston Division, The United Sates of America v. A.E. Quarles, CR. No. H-88-83. Memorandum in Support of Motion to Dismiss. March 25, 1988.

This memorandum (13 pages and attached literature) is an instructive vehicle addressing the applicability of the Analogue laws to MDMA, and the possible unconstitutional vagueness of the Act itself.

Hug, Boochever and Wiggins, Ninth Circuit Court of Appeals, California. United States, Plaintiff-Appellee v. W.W. Emerson, Defendant-Appellant.

An appeal was made, and was allowed, by three defendants, that the use of the Emergency Scheduling Act by the DEA for the placement of MDMA into Schedule I was improper, in that this power was invested specifically in the Attorney General, and that he had failed to subdelegate this authority to the DEA for its use.

Harbin, H. MDMA. Narcotics, Forfeiture, and Money-Laundering Update, U.S. Department of Justice, Criminal Division. Winter, 1988. pp. 14-19.

A brief legal history of MDMA is presented, detailing its changing status from emergency schedule, to permanent schedule, to non-schedule, to schedule again, and a case against its occasional status in-between as an analogue substance. In U.S. v. Spain (10th Circuit, 1987, 825 F.2d 1426), the MDMA conviction was undermined both by the absence of sub-delegation of emergency scheduling powers by the Attorney General to the DEA, and by the failure of the DEA to publish a formal scheduling order 30 days after the publication of its "notice-order", as required by statute. This latter failure was successful in overturning the conviction in the U.S. v. Caudel (5th Circuit, 1987, 828 F.2d 1111)
These reversals were based on the temporary scheduling status of MDMA. The vacating of the permanent scheduling Grinspoon v. DEA (1st Circuit 1987, 828 F.2d 881), coupled with these successful appeals of the temporary scheduling action, will certainly serve to allow further challenge to be made to any and all legal action that took place prior to the final and unchallenged placement of MDMA in Schedule I on March 23, 1988.

Psychoactive Books-by-Phone

Good books with great service : visa/mc - ups/cod - 10% off w/money order

THE CONTROLLED SUBSTANCES ACT
    Dr. Shulgin's reference on drugs, formulas, laws CONSUB 34.95 ___
PSYCHEDELIC CHEMISTRY
    Authoritative underground lab manual PCHEM 14.95___
ECSTASY: THE MDMA STORY
    History, chemistry, use, future, risks, bibliography ECSTAS 17.95_
MUSHROOM CULTIVATOR
    Best mushroom home cultivation guide MUSHC 24.95___
COCAINE HANDBOOK: AN ESSENTIAL REFERENCE
    Best book on illicit cocaine, 150 photos, charts, lab tips CHBK 24.95___
MARIJUANA BOTANY: CULTIVATION AND BREEDING OF CANNABIS
    Definitive guide to marijuana plant MBOT 14.95___
STEAL THIS URINE TEST
    Abbie Hoffman's guide on how to beat drug testing STEAL 5.95 ___
DESIGNER DRUGS
    Ecstasy, crack, china white, PCP and other drugs DD 7.95 ___
HISTORY OF PSYCHOACTIVE PLANTS
    Illustrated survey of sources, preparation and use HPP 14.95 ___
WAR ON DRUGS : HEROIN, COCAINE, CRIME AND PUBLIC POLICY
    Authoritative study of criminal drug culture WARDRGS 14.95 ___
THROUGH THE GATEWAY OF THE HEART
    Experiences with MDMA and related substances THART 14.50 ___

    select books and add up prices **SUBTOTAL$**_____
           Money Order Discount - 10% _____
           Shipping & handling charges _____
USA add $4/order, Canada add $5/order, Foreign add $5/book
California customers add sales tax 7% of subtotal
    __CHK or __MO for Books plus fees TOTALS $ _____
COD ($5fee) or visa/mc($2fee) call in for faster service
Make checks payable to Books-by-Phone (personal checks held to clear,
for best service & 10% discount send Money Order).
credit card MC __ Visa __ Exp date _____ - _____
card #: _____ / _____ / _____ / _____
Name_ _
Address _
City _ _ _ _ _ _ _ _ _ _ _ _ _ _ State _ _ _ _ _ ZIP _ _ _ _ _ _ _
I am over 21 (sign) _

Price & availability subject to change without notice. Drug education books are for sale to ADULTS ONLY for information in accord with 1st Amendment. Offer void where prohibited. No warranties made, use not advocated. Con-
sult your physician and attorney

BOOKS BY PHONE BOX 522 BERKELEY CA 94701
(800) 858-2665 USA (800) 992-2665 CA (415) 548-2124 INFO
Call Day or night for a FREE 16 page Catalog

INDEX